Encountering
NEW TESTAMENT Manuscripts

Encountering

NEW TESTAMENT Manuscripts

A Working Introduction to Textual Criticism

by JACK FINEGAN

William B. Eerdmans Publishing Company
Grand Rapids   Michigan

Library of Congress Cataloging in Publication Data

Finegan, Jack, 1908-
   Encountering New Testament manuscripts.

   Includes bibliographical references.
   1. Bible. N.T.—Criticism, Textual. 2. Bible.
N.T. Manuscripts. I. Title.
BS2325.F56 1974   225.6'1   74-1297
ISBN 0-8028-3445-0

Acknowledgments

Unless otherwise indicated, the English translation of the Greek text of the New Testament is that of the *New American Standard Bible, New Testament* (abbreviated NASB), insofar as that translation is based upon the Greek text under consideration at a given point. For permission to make these quotations acknowledgment is made to The Lockman Foundation, La Habra, California.

I am also glad to express appreciation to a student in my seminar on the Manuscripts and Text of the New Testament, Mr. Gerald F. Ahearn of the Jesuit School of Theology, Berkeley, for the preparation of the Table in the Appendix showing, with photographic exactness, the letters of the Greek alphabet as they were actually written by the scribes of several of the oldest of the New Testament papyri.

Acknowledgments for all photographs are made in the List of Illustrations.

Preface

While there are many other works on the textual criticism of the Greek New Testament—to not a few of which acknowledgment is made in the references in this book—it is hoped that the present book may have its place also, and that for two reasons in particular.

In the first place, the field is truly enormous and complex, and must appear forbidding and arcane to many, so this is an attempt to give as plain an account as possible of what is involved. In the second place, to read about the manuscripts and how they are compared, must necessarily fall somewhat short of the experience of actually seeing them and reading them directly, as I have made it my own effort to do all the way from London, Paris, and Rome, to Patmos and Mount Sinai, as well as here in the Museum of the Palestine Institute of Archeology of Pacific School of Religion. No book can actually provide that experience by itself, of course, but the present one endeavors to simulate it for the reader by setting forth portions of chief manuscripts in large photographs and showing how one reads therein.

Here, for example, is a fragment of papyrus only slightly more than four by two inches in size, written on both sides. By the style of its handwriting it is to be dated at about A.D. 125, and thus it is the oldest known surviving portion of any copy of any part of the New Testament. On each side of the fragment are only seven lines of writing, and in each line only a few words or parts of words are preserved. Yet the characters are carefully written, and there is enough that is legible that a portion of the Gospel according to John can be recognized. As far as the words are preserved, they fall in the eighteenth chapter of the Gospel, in verses 31-33 and 37-38. Other, later manuscripts contain more of the text, or all of it. From them it is possible to reconstruct a complete text around the preserved portions on this fragment. Since the preserved words fit in perfectly, a positive identification of the fragment is established.

In this case the agreement of this oldest fragment with such other manuscripts as there is reason to think are also among the best ones available, confirms that the available text is identical, down to every letter of every word, with what was being read almost nineteen hundred years ago.

In other cases there are of course differences among the manuscripts. Many of these appear to be the result of unintentional changes and outright mistakes. Some appear to be the result of intentional alterations. Therewith it becomes necessary to try to recognize the mistakes and discern the motives in intentional changes. Insofar as such understanding can be attained, there will be a basis for trying to decide which readings, where they differ, are the earlier and the more nearly original. Even where such a decision cannot be reached firmly—and there are many places where this is the case—much can be learned about how the writings called the New Testament were transmitted, and a general assessment of the dependability of that transmission can be made, a dependability that was in fact, on the whole, very great.

The present book endeavors, therefore, to describe plainly this undertaking and its materials and methods, and to provide guidance in actually reading some of the texts and drawing conclusions about them and the history of their transmission.

J.F.

Contents

List of Illustrations

List of Abbreviations

AJT   *The American Journal of Theology.*

Aland, *Kurzgefasste Liste*   Kurt Aland, *Kurzgefasste Liste der griechischen Handschriften des Neuen Testaments* (ANT 1). Berlin: Walter de Gruyter & Co., 1963.

Aland, *Synopsis*   Kurt Aland, ed., *Synopsis Quattuor Evangeliorum.* Stuttgart: Württembergische Bibelanstalt, 2d ed. 1964.

ANF   Alexander Roberts and James Donaldson, eds., rev. by A. Cleveland Coxe, *The Ante-Nicene Fathers, Translations of the Writings of the Fathers down to A.D. 325.* 10 vols. 1885-87.

ANT   *Arbeiten zur neutestamentlichen Textforschung,* issued by the Institut für neutestamentliche Textforschung der Westfälischen Wilhelms-Universität Münster/Westfalen. Berlin: Walter de Gruyter & Co., 1963 ff.

ASV   *American Standard Version.*

CHB   *The Cambridge History of the Bible, The West from the Reformation to the Present Day,* ed. S. L. Greenslade. Cambridge: The University Press, 1963.

Colwell   Ernest C. Colwell, *What Is the Best New Testament?* Chicago: The University of Chicago Press, 1952.

Colwell and Riddle   Ernest C. Colwell and Donald W. Riddle, *Studies in the Lectionary Text of the Greek New Testament,* I, *Prolegomena to the Study of the Lectionary Text of the Gospels.* Chicago: The University of Chicago Press, 1933.

EB   *The Encyclopaedia Britannica.* 14th ed. 1929, and later.

EGT   *The Expositor's Greek Testament,* ed. W. Robertson Nicoll. New York: George H. Doran Company, 5 vols., no date.

FANT   Jack Finegan, *The Archeology of the New Testament, The Life of Jesus and the Beginning of the Early Church.* Princeton: Princeton University Press, 1969.

FHBC   Jack Finegan, *Handbook of Biblical Chronology, Principles of Time Reckoning in the Ancient World and Problems of Chronology in the Bible.* Princeton: Princeton University Press, 1964.

FHRJ   Jack Finegan, *Hidden Records of the Life of Jesus, An introduction to the New Testament Apocrypha, and to some of the areas through which they were transmitted, namely, Jewish, Egyptian, and Gnostic Christianity, together with the earlier Gospel-type records in the Apocrypha, in Greek and Latin texts, translations, and explanations.* Philadelphia/Boston: Pilgrim Press, 1969.

FLAP   Jack Finegan, *Light from the Ancient Past, The Archeological Background of Judaism and Christianity.* Princeton: Princeton University Press, 2d ed. 1959.

GCS *Die griechischen christlichen Schriftsteller der ersten Jahrhunderte.*

Greenlee   J. Harold Greenlee, *Introduction to New Testament Textual Criticism.* Grand Rapids, Mich.: William B. Eerdmans Publishing Company, 1964.

Gregory, *Prolegomena*   Caspar R. Gregory, *Prolegomena*, Vol. III of Constantine Tischendorf, *Novum Testamentum Graece, editio octava critica maior.* Leipzig: J. C. Hinrichs, 1894.

Hatch, *Minuscule Manuscripts*   William H. P. Hatch, *Facsimiles and Descriptions of Minuscule Manuscripts of the New Testament.* Cambridge, Mass.: Harvard University Press, 1951.

HNT   *Handbuch zum Neuen Testament.*

HTR   *The Harvard Theological Review.*

Hug   *Hug's Introduction to the New Testament,* tr. by David Fosdick, Jr. (from Joh. Leonard Hug, *Einleitung in die Schriften des Neuen Testaments,* 3d ed. 1826). Andover: Gould and Newman, 1836.

ICC   *The International Critical Commentary.*

JBL   *Journal of Biblical Literature.*

JEA   *The Journal of Egyptian Archaeology.*

JTS   *The Journal of Theological Studies.*

Kenyon   Frederic Kenyon, *The Story of the Bible.* New York: E. P. Dutton & Co., Inc., 1937.

KJV   *King James Version.*

Lake   Kirsopp Lake, *The Text of the New Testament,* 6th ed. rev. by Silva New. London: Rivingtons, 1928.

LXX   The Septuagint.

Metzger   Bruce M. Metzger, *The Text of the New Testament, Its Transmission, Corruption, and Restoration.* New York and Oxford: Oxford University Press, 2d ed. 1968.

Moulton   Harold K. Moulton, *Papyrus, Parchment and Print, The Story of how the New Testament Text has reached us.* London: Lutterworth Press, 1967.

NASB   *New American Standard Bible, New Testament.*

NEB   *The New English Bible,* 2d ed. 1970.

Nestle, *Introduction*   Eberhard Nestle, *Introduction to the Textual Criticism of the Greek New Testament.* London: Williams and Norgate, 1901.

NPNFSS   Philip Schaff and Henry Wace, eds., *A Select Library of Nicene and Post-Nicene Fathers of the Christian Church,* Second Series. 14 vols. 1890-1900.

NT   New Testament.

NTS   *New Testament Studies.*

OP   *The Oxyrhynchus Papyri.*

OT   Old Testament.

RSV   *Revised Standard Version.*

SC   *Sources Chrétiennes.*

SD   *Studies and Documents,* founded by Kirsopp and Silva Lake, ed. by Jacob Geerlings.

SMTC   Ernest C. Colwell, *Studies in Methodology in Textual Criticism of the New Testament,* in B. M. Metzger, ed., *New Testament Tools and Studies,* IX. Leiden: E. J. Brill, 1969.

Souter   Alexander Souter, *The Text and Canon of the New Testament,* rev. by C. S. C. Williams. London: Gerald Duckworth & Co. Ltd., 1954.

Taylor   Vincent Taylor, *The Text of the New Testament.* London: Macmillan & Co. Ltd., 1961.

TCERK   *Twentieth Century Encyclopedia of Religious Knowledge, An Extension of the New Schaff-Herzog Encyclopedia of Religious Knowledge.* Grand Rapids, Mich.: Baker Book House, 2 vols. 1955.

TEV   *Good News for Modern Man, The New Testament in Today's English Version.* New York: American Bible Society, 1966.

Tregelles   Samuel P. Tregelles, *An Account of the Printed Text of the Greek New Testament.* London: Samuel Bagster and Sons, 1854.

Vincent   Marvin R. Vincent, *A History of the Textual Criticism of the New Testament.* New York: The Macmillan Company, 1899.

Vogels, *Handbuch*   Heinrich Vogels, *Handbuch der Textkritik des Neuen Testaments.* Bonn: Peter Hanstein Verlag, 2d ed. 1955.

Vogels, *Specimina*   Henr. Jos. Vogels, *Codicum Novi Testamenti Specimina.* Bonn: P. Hanstein, 1929.

von Soden   Hermann Freiherr von Soden, *Die Schriften des Neuen Testaments in Ihrer ältesten erreichbaren Textgestalt hergestellt auf Grund Ihrer Textgeschichte.* Göttingen: Vandenhoeck & Ruprecht, 2d ed. 1911-13.

ZNW   *Zeitschrift für die neutestamentliche Wissenschaft.*

Signs

[ ]   square brackets mark portions missing from a text and, upon occasion, supplied by the editor

( )   round brackets mark letters or words supplied to fill out an abbreviation in a text, or to express the sense in a translation

⟨ ⟩   angled brackets mark portions supplied in a text from some parallel or as required by the context

{ }   braces mark superfluous letters or words

. . .   dots indicate missing letters in a text, or omitted portion in a translation or quotation

Note: The use of one other sign is customary in the original publication of fragmentary and partly illegible manuscripts, namely, a dot placed under an uncertain letter in a transcription. For the more practical purposes of the present book, this dot has not been used. If enough of a given letter is preserved to make its recognition quite unmistakable, it is transcribed as if it were there in complete form. If so little of a letter is preserved that recognition of it is largely a guess, even though a quite justified guess, it is simply supplied within brackets along with other letters which may be missing altogether. An element of subjectivity in judgment is naturally involved in this procedure, but subjective judgment is not eliminated by the use of the dot either. A student who reads the transcriptions alongside the photographs should be able to understand readily in every case exactly what has been done.

For example, note Papyrus Rylands Greek 457 ($\mathfrak{P}^{52}$), as shown in the photograph in Fig. 3 and as transcribed in §§99,

100, and 105. On the *recto* (which is at the left side in the photograph) and in Line 6 (which is the next-to-the-bottom line) the transcription reads και ειπ. In fact the third letter is so dimly and partially preserved that, if it stood by itself, it might be judged quite uncertain and properly be marked with a dot indicating such uncertainty. Here, however, the obvious requirement of an Iota in this place, and the comparison of such traces of the letter as remain with the better preserved Iota in the next line immediately below it, justify making the transcription as if the Iota were in and of itself fully recognizable. Contrariwise in the next line immediately below (*recto* Line 7) there is the slightest trace of a letter at the extreme left margin, followed by a plainly recognizable ιω. By consulting a consecutively preserved text at this point it can be established that an Alpha is required immediately prior to the Iota and Omega. If the system with a dot under an uncertain letter were being employed, one might write ạιω as the transcription. But since the Alpha cannot actually be recognized as being that letter simply from the trace of a letter at the margin of the fragment, our transcription has simply supplied the letter within brackets and the dot has not been employed.

I. ANCIENT WRITING MATERIALS AND PRACTICES

A

On What Materials Books Were Written

1. Introduction

§1. In New Testament times two chief materials were used for writing. These were papyrus and parchment.

2. Papyrus

§2. In the Hebrew OT the word *gome'* (גמא) is etymologically connected with the idea of swallowing and hence of sucking up water, and is a general word for "rush" or "reed." It occurs in four passages in the OT and, in most or all of these occurrences, although it is rendered variously in various English translations, it probably refers specifically to the papyrus plant. In Ex 2:3 the "ark of bulrushes" (KJV), or "basket made of bulrushes" (RSV), for the baby Moses was probably a container of papyrus. In the Greek versions of Aquila and Symmachus the Hebrew word is here explicitly translated by the Greek word *papyrus* (πάπυρος). In Job 8:11 there is reference to the watery habitat of the papyrus plant, in the rhetorical question, "Can the rush grow up without mire?" (KJV), or "Can papyrus grow where there is no marsh?" (RSV). Here also the LXX translation uses the Greek word *papyrus.* In Is 18:2 Ethiopia is described as sending envoys by the Nile, "even in vessels of bulrushes upon the waters" (KJV), or "in vessels of papyrus upon the waters" (RSV). In this case the version of Theodotion uses the Greek word *papyrus,* but in the LXX the statement refers to ἐπιστολὰς βιβλίνας. The Greek word βίβλινος is an adjective referring to something made of βίβλος or βύβλος (cf. Theocritus XIV 15), and *biblos* or *byblos* (the spelling with the Upsilon instead of the Iota is probably the older spelling) is another name for *papyrus,* as will be seen shortly in references to be cited in Herodotus (§3) and Theophrastus (§4). The ἐπιστολὰς βιβλίνας in the LXX version of Is 18:2 are therefore probably "papyrus letters." Finally, in Is 35:7 the "rushes" (KJV, RSV) stand for an abundance of water, and are therefore probably also the papyrus.

§3. In his description of Egypt, Herodotus (c. 484-425 B.C.) mentions the *byblos* (βύβλος). It is a plant which, he says, is gathered from the marshes; the top is cut off and used for other purposes; the lower part is eaten (preferably having been roasted in a redhot oven) or sold (II 92). Also, Herodotus says later (II 100), the priests recite the names of the three hundred and thirty kings of Egypt from a *byblos* (ἐκ βύβλου). In this latter passage, it is plain that Herodotus is referring to a book, and it is equally plain that such a book was made from the *byblos* plant and was therefore called by the name of the plant. Since the marsh plant in question is quite evidently the papyrus, and since at this time the roll was the prevailing form of book (cf. §§13f.), the Greek of Herodotus may be translated to say that the priests recited the names of the kings "from a papyrus roll."

§4. In his systematic *Enquiry into Plants,* Theophrastus (c. 370-285 B.C.) describes (IV 8, 3-4) the same plant and calls it by its most familiar name, *papyrus* (πάπυρος). In his description this name is sometimes used for the plant in general, and again it is used with special reference to the stalk of the plant. This stalk he pictures as three-cornered and ten cubits (about fifteen feet) long. The plume above he considers useless, but the root, he says, was used instead of wood for a variety of articles. As for the stalk itself, i.e., the "papyrus" proper, it was useful for many purposes. For one thing, boats were made from it. This is confirmed, of course, by the frequent representation of papyrus boats on the monuments of ancient Egypt (FLAP Fig. 43), while boats of the same kind are still in use on Lake Tana in Ethiopia, and similar ones on Lake Titicaca in South America. "And from the *biblos* (ἐκ τῆς βίβλου)," Theophrastus continues, "they weave sails, mats, a kind of raiment, coverlets, ropes, and many other things." Here we have the same word, *biblos,* which Herodotus used (§3), with the spelling with the Iota which, in later times, became more customary than the spelling with the Upsilon. From the usage here and also in other classical writers, the word could refer particularly to the rind or to the pith of the plant, i.e., to the portions that were most useful for the manufacture of various things. But, at least to foreigners, Theophrastus goes on, the most familiar of all the uses of papyrus was its use for the *biblia* (τὰ βιβλία). The word *biblia* is the plural of *biblion,* and *biblion* or *byblion* (βιβλίον or βυβλίον) is a diminutive and very frequently used form of *biblos* or *byblos.* Here Theophrastus is plainly referring to the books which were made from the papyrus plant, and again his Greek, like that of Herodotus (§3), may be translated as a reference to "papyrus rolls." In fashion somewhat similar to the Greek βίβλος and βιβλίον, we find in Latin the word *liber* (related to Greek λέπω, "to peel") as the designation of the inner bark or rind of a tree or especially of the papyrus plant, and therefore as the general word meaning book.

§5. As to how the papyrus plant was made into writing material, the most detailed description is given by Pliny (A.D. 23-79) in his *Natural History* (XIII 21-27). For the plant, Pliny uses

§3

Ancient Writing Materials and Practices

20

the Latin word *papyrus,* directly equivalent to the Greek πάπυρος. For the writing material made out of the plant, he uses the Latin word *charta.* This is the direct equivalent of the Greek χάρτης, of which the diminutive is χαρτάριον or χαρτίον. This word describes either a sheet or sometimes a whole roll of papyrus, and the diminutive designates a small piece of the same material, but in any case the reference is to papyrus as prepared for writing. It is, accordingly, proper to translate χάρτης (e.g., in II Jn 12 KJV, RSV, NASB) and *charta* (e.g., in Pliny) by the English word "paper," although the English word (cf. German *Papier* and French *papier*) obviously derives etymologically from Latin *papyrus* and Greek πάπυρος.

§6. "The process of making paper (*charta*) from papyrus," writes Pliny (XIII 23, 74), "is to split it with a needle into very thin strips made as broad as possible, the best quality being in the center of the plant, and so on in the order of its splitting up." These fibers were then "woven," says Pliny (XIII 23, 77), on a board which was moistened with muddy Nile water, the latter supplying the effect of glue (cf. F. N. Hepper and T. Reynolds in JEA 53 [1967], pp. 156f.). An upright layer of fibers was smeared onto the board, then a layer of cross-strips, thus making a latticework. The two layers were then pressed together, and dried in the sun. The resultant paper was cut into sheets as much as twelve to eighteen inches in width in the better examples; the sheets were pasted together to make a roll, never more than twenty sheets to a roll (XIII 23, 77; 24, 78ff.). Grades of paper (XIII 23, 74-76) were determined by the quality of the fibers used, and by the fineness, stoutness, whiteness, and smoothness of the product. Augustus paper and Claudius paper, named after the emperors, were the best. Fannian paper, made in the workshop of Fannius at Rome, was ten inches wide; amphitheater paper, manufactured in the amphitheater of Alexandria, was one inch less. Saitic paper, named from the Egyptian town (Saïs in the Delta) where it was made, was narrower and less good; finally "emporitic" paper was not good enough for writing, but served for wrappers for merchandise, and took its name from the Greek word for merchant (ἔμπορος).

§7. Corresponding with the preceding description (§6), the make-up of a piece of papyrus may be plainly seen in an immediately available example, namely, Oxyrhynchus Papyrus 1677 (Bernard P. Grenfell and Arthur S. Hunt, *The Oxyrhynchus Papyri,* XIV [London: The Egypt Exploration Society, 1920], pp. 136-137), which is now Pacific School of Religion Papyrus 3, and is shown in photographs made by infrared light in Figs. 1-2. This is a sheet of papyrus which is about 5.0 by 5.7 inches in size. On the front (*recto*) side the fibers may be seen running horizontally, on the back (*verso*) running vertically. In the upper left-hand corner of the *verso,* diagonally crossed strips of papyrus may be seen, by which the piece was strengthened at that point. On the *recto* is the text of a letter which was written by a certain Agathus to a certain Aphrodite. It begins: Χαῖρε, Ἀφροδείτη, Ἄγαθός σε ἀσπάζομαι, "Greetings, Aphrodite, I Agathus salute you." The letter was carried by a certain Doxa (whose name is added above the fourth line and appears again in the last line), who was also to hand over a sealed order, immediate acknowledgment of which was requested. Information and instructions in these regards are found in the body of the letter, which also contains good wishes to Aphrodite and salutations to a number of other persons. A portion of the letter, but probably only a small portion, is lost at the bottom where the papyrus is broken off. Toward the right side on the *verso* is the partially preserved address for the letter. It is written at right angles to the text on the *recto,* and thus it follows horizontally the direction of the fibers on the *verso.* The address is now partly illegible, but probably reads: [Ἀφροδείτη] π(αρὰ) Ἀγάθου, "[To Aphrodite] f(rom) Agathus." The papyrus is attributed by Grenfell and Hunt (OP XIV, p. 136) to the third century of the Christian era.

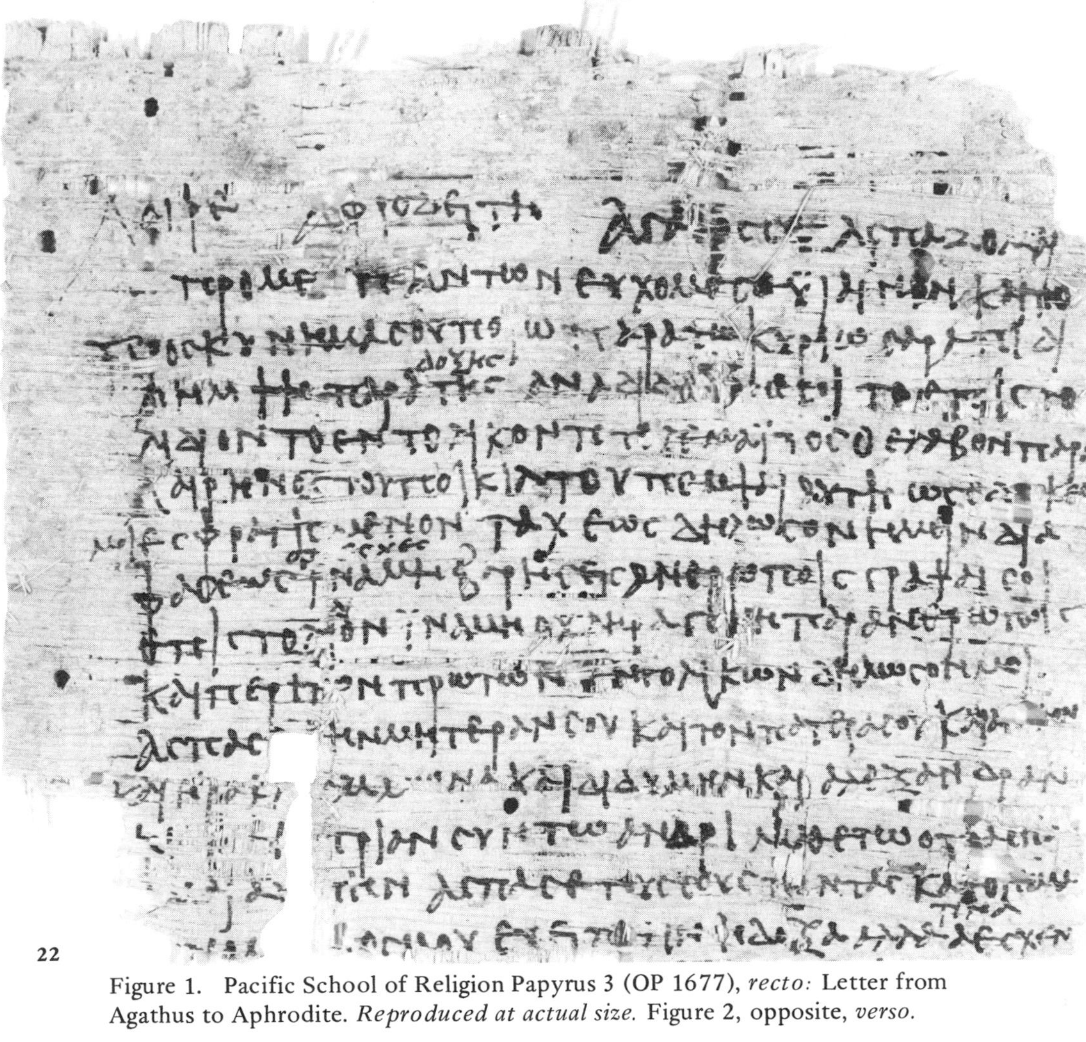

Figure 1. Pacific School of Religion Papyrus 3 (OP 1677), *recto:* Letter from Agathus to Aphrodite. *Reproduced at actual size.* Figure 2, opposite, *verso.*

3. Parchment

§8. Parchment was the other chief writing material in New Testament times. Whereas papyrus is a writing material made from a plant, parchment is a writing material made from animal skins. In the Hebrew OT the regular word for animal skin, usually referring to the hide of a dead animal, is *'ôr* (עור), and this is regularly translated in the LXX by δέρμα, the usual Greek word for skin or hide, and obviously a root of English "dermatology," etc. Several other Hebrew words in the OT are translated in the LXX by δέρρις, also a Greek word for skin. While both δέρμα and δέρρις refer properly to unworked hide, it is evident in many of the passages where the LXX uses these terms that it is prepared hide, or tanned leather, which is referred to. Thus in Ex 25:5, which concerns materials for the tabernacle, the rams' skins (designated by the Hebrew word given above) are "dyed red" (the Hebrew term is a participle of the regular word "to be red," and the LXX correspondingly translates ἠρυθροδανωμένα), and the probability is that the skins were made red in the process of tanning. Hence, while the KJV here translates literally, "rams' skins dyed red," the RSV renders, "tanned rams' skins." In Greek there is also another word which means properly a prepared hide or a piece of tanned leather. This is the noun διφθέρα, and the corresponding adjective is διφθέρινος. Thus in Ex 39:34, which also has to do with the covering of the tabernacle, the Hebrew text again refers to "rams' skins dyed red" (KJV), but the LXX (39:21) introduces the word just mentioned, and reads: τὰς διφθέρας δέρματα κριῶν ἠρυθροδανωμένα, which we may translate as, "the pieces of leather, even rams' skins dyed red." As to the procedure of tanning, by which animal skin is made into the tougher and less permeable material called leather, it involves impregnation with some form of tannin such as oak bark, and is a process that was known from ancient times.

§9. Even in the form of leather, animal skins provided a material on which to write. The Letter of Aristeas, composed probably in the second century B.C. to tell of the translation of the Hebrew Pentateuch into Greek under Ptolemy II Philadelphus (285-246 B.C.) in Egypt, says (4, ed. Moses Hadas, *Aristeas to Philocrates* [1951], pp. 94f.; cf. Henry G. Meecham, *The Letter of Aristeas* [1935], pp. 173f.) that the divine Law exists among the Jews in Palestine, written on leather skins in Hebrew characters (διὰ τὸ γεγράφθαι παρ' αὐτοῖς ἐν διφθέραις ἑβραικοῖς γράμμασιν). The same Letter also (176, Hadas, pp. 168f.) describes "the precious leather skins, in which the Law was inscribed in writing of gold in Jewish characters" (ταῖς διαφόροις διφθέραις, ἐν αἷς ἡ νομοθεσία γεγραμμένη χρυσογραφία τοῖς Ἰουδαικοῖς γράμμασι), which were brought to Egypt for the making of the translation; and Josephus (*Ant.* XII 2, 11 §89) uses much the same language in his paraphrase of the same account. In the latter passage, both in The Letter of Aristeas and in Josephus, the Egyptian king is said to have questioned the elders who brought the leather skins, "concerning the books" (περὶ τῶν βιβλίων), so it is evident that the word βιβλίον, which we have already found used for papyrus rolls (§4), was employed also for books made of leather. In Herodotus (V 58), also, the βύβλος and the διφθέρα are interchangeable terms, when he reports: "Thus also the Ionians have from ancient times called papyrus sheets skins (καὶ τὰς βύβλους διφθέρας καλέουσι ἀπὸ τοῦ παλαιοῦ οἱ Ἴωνες), because formerly for lack of papyrus (βύβλων) they used the skins (διφθέρῃσι) of sheet and goats; and even to this day there are many foreigners who write on such skins (πολλοὶ τῶν βαρβάρων ἐς τοιαύτας διφθέρας γράφουσι)." The Jews, however, by no means considered it barbarian to write on leather skins, but evidently preferred this material, for in the case of the Dead Sea Scrolls, for example, some were written on papyrus but most were on leather (J. T. Milik, *Ten Years of Discovery in the Wilderness of Judaea* [1959], p. 21).

§10. In contrast with the treatment of animal skin used in

making leather, there is a different process used to make parchment, a form of animal skin that is an even better writing material than leather. In general the making of parchment involves some such steps as soaking the skin in limewater, scraping off the hair on the one side and the flesh on the other, stretching and drying the skin in a frame, smoothing it with pumice, and dressing it with chalk. According to Pliny (*Nat. Hist.* XIII 21, 70), who cites as the source of his information in this connection the Roman scholar Marcus Varro (c. 116-c. 27 B.C.), the invention of parchment took place at Pergamum. The account, in Pliny, as to what happened, has to do with the rivalry of King Ptolemy of Egypt and King Eumenes of Pergamum over their respective libraries. These kings were probably King Ptolemy V Epiphanes (203-181 B.C.) and King Eumenes II (197-159), the latter being the builder of the famous Altar of Zeus at Pergamum (FLAP p. 345). Because of the rivalry and obviously, the story implies, in order to handicap the development of the library of King Eumenes, King Ptolemy suppressed the export of paper. Here, for the word translated "paper," Pliny uses the term *charta,* which, as noted above (§5), was the regular term for writing material made out of papyrus. At this juncture, obviously in order to make up for the shortage of papyrus, as the story given by Varro and passed on by Pliny further implies, parchment was invented at Pergamum (*idem Varro membranas Pergami tradit repertas*). While this story may have a romantic character and may not require to be taken literally, it may at the same time very well reflect an actual preeminence of the city of Pergamum in the manufacture and distribution of parchment.

§ 11. For parchment the Greek language sometimes continued to use the word διφθέρα, which was originally and properly the term for tanned leather (§ 8). In Latin, however, the word *membrana,* which meant the skin that covers parts (*membra*) of the body, and is the root of the English "membrane," became the term for parchment and was so used, for example, by Pliny in the quotation just given (§ 10). This word was taken over into Greek as μεμβράνα. Both of the Greek words just mentioned are used together in a fourth- or fifth-century letter from Oxyrhynchus (OP No. 2156, Lines 9-10), which speaks of the sending of τὴν διφθέραν [τ]ῶν μεμβρανῶν ἐν τετραδίοις, i.e., the leather skin of parchments in quaternions, the latter probably being each a sheet of parchment folded to make two leaves and four pages, as a part of a section for a book (cf. § 18). In addition the Greek language used for parchment the word περγαμηνή. Περγαμηνός is plainly an adjective referring to Pergamum, and ἡ Περγαμηνή is the district of Pergamum, for example, in Strabo (XII 8, 2). So the use of περγαμηνή as the term meaning parchment is in accordance with the idea of the introduction or the prevalence of parchment at Pergamum, as indicated by Varro and Pliny (§ 10). Thus, for example, the sixth-century Byzantine historian, Joannes Laurentius Lydus ("the Lydian"), writes (Περὶ μηνῶν, or *De Mensibus,* I 28 [ed. R. Wünsch, 1898, p. 14]), using the neuter plural: Ῥωμαῖοι τὰ μεμβράνα Περγαμηνὰ καλοῦσιν, i.e., literally, the Romans call the "membranes" "Pergamenes." Correspondingly in Latin *Pergamenus* was the adjective referring to Pergamum, and *pergamena* became a term for parchment and, eventually, the root of the word "parchment" in English.

B

In What Form Books Were Made

1. Introduction

§12. As there were two chief materials used for writing in New Testament times, so there were also two chief forms in which books were made. These were the roll and the codex.

2. The Roll

§13. It is obvious that both papyrus and parchment could be made into books in the form of a roll. As for the use of papyrus in this form, we have already noted (§6) the statement of Pliny (XIII 23, 77) that up to twenty sheets of papyrus were pasted together to make a roll, and have observed that in Herodotus (II 100) the word βύβλος probably refers to a book that was a papyrus roll (§3), even as in Theophrastus (*Enquiry into Plants* IV 8, 4) the word βιβλία probably describes books that are papyrus rolls (§4). Furthermore, papyrus rolls are abundantly pictured in art and represented in extant examples, from ancient Egypt onward (FLAP Figs. 136-139). As for the use of leather and parchment in the same form, it has already been observed (§9) that the larger number of the Dead Sea Scrolls were on leather, and these documents, it may now be added, were predominantly in the form of rolls, of which ten or so have been preserved complete (Milik, *Ten Years of Discovery in the Wilderness of Judaea,* p. 20).

§14. In Hebrew the general word for "book" is *sefer* (ספר). The use of this word in Is 34:4, where it is predicted that "the heavens shall be rolled together as a *sefer,*" shows that the word had the ordinary meaning of a book in the form of a roll, hence both KJV and RSV here translate *sefer* as "scroll," although in many other places (e.g., Ex 17:14) they both render the same word simply as "book." Another Hebrew word, however, has the specific meaning of a "roll," namely, *megillah* (מגלה), which comes from the root *galal* (גלל), meaning "to roll." The two words *megillah* and *sefer* are used together to mean a "roll book" or "book roll" in Ps 40:7 (Hebrew 40:8), where the LXX (Ps 39:8) renders ἐν κεφαλίδι βιβλίου (with the same Greek where the passage is quoted in Heb 10:7), and RSV translates, "in the roll of the book"; in Jer 36:2, 4, where the LXX

(Jer 43:2, 4) renders χαρτίον βιβλίου, "a paper (cf. §5) of a book," and RSV translates, "a scroll"; and in Ezk 2:9, where LXX renders κεφαλὶς βιβλίου, and RSV translates, "a written scroll." The Greek word κεφαλίς, by which the LXX renders *megillah* in two of the three preceding passages, is the diminutive of κεφαλή, "head," and thus can mean the capital of a column, or the knob on the end of a stick, and a roll, by implication from the end of a stick on which a manuscript is rolled. Although used with *sefer* and βιβλίον respectively in the preceding passages, *megillah* and κεφαλίς can each perfectly well stand alone to mean "roll" or "scroll." With respect to Ezekiel's scroll, they appear thus immediately in Ezk 3:1, in the Hebrew and in the LXX respectively. As for βίβλος and βιβλίον, it has already been established (§§2-4, 9) that these are the usual Greek words for book, and that the latter in particular often has the specific meaning of a book in the form of a roll. Thus, for example, in Lk 4:17 "the book (βιβλίον) of the prophet Isaiah" was undoubtedly a leather roll; while in II Tim 4:13 "the books, especially the parchments" (τὰ βιβλία, μάλιστα τὰς μεμβράνας), could have been papyrus and parchment rolls (FLAP p. 392). Likewise, the rolling up of a βιβλίον provides a vivid figure of speech when, in Rev 6:14, the sky is described as split apart "like a scroll (βιβλίον) when it is rolled up." In Latin, in turn, the word *volumen* (from the verb *volvere*, "to roll") means a thing that is rolled up, hence a roll book. This provides the root meaning of English "volume," which is used in the KJV translation of Heb 10:7 (Ps 40:7), "in the volume of the book," where the Latin translation, however, only uses the general word for book and renders, *in capite libri.*

3. The Codex

§15. The roll form of a book was, of course, in many ways inconvenient. A more convenient form was devised with the invention of the codex, in which leaves are fastened together as in a modern book. The Latin word *caudex* or *codex* means, in the first instance, the trunk of a tree and, then, a block of wood split up into tablets or leaves. The wooden tablets (perhaps coated with wax to write on) were bound together to make a book; the same was done with leaves or sheets of papyrus or parchment. So a codex is a leaf book.

§16. Wooden tablets used as writing material are extant in examples from Pompeii, with dates corresponding to A.D. 53 and 55, and already in the latter part of the first century there are references in Roman writers to what are almost certainly codices of parchment. Thus in about A.D. 85 Martial composed a number of verses to accompany presents such as the Romans gave to their friends at the Saturnalia. These poems (found in Book XIV of his Epigrams) contain references to pocket editions in the form of parchment (*membrana*) books of Homer, Virgil, Cicero, and Livy. Concerning such an edition of Virgil (*Vergilius in membranis*), Martial remarks on how much such a small parchment book would hold (XIV 186).

Similarly he recommends a sort of pocket-edition parchment of Cicero (*Cicero in membranis*) as a handy traveling companion (XIV 188). With the emphasis on the compact character of these books, it is probable that we are dealing with codices (cf. Jack Finegan in HTR 49 [1956], pp. 86f.).

§17. As to the relative frequency of use of the roll and of the codex, in an enumeration of 476 second-century non-Christian literary papyrus manuscripts from Egypt, 465 or more than 97 percent are in the form of the roll; but eight Christian biblical papyri known from the same century are all in the form of the codex. Likewise in the entire period extending to shortly after the end of the fourth century, out of 111 biblical manuscripts or fragments from Egypt, 99 are codices (for references see HTR 49 [1956], pp. 86f.). That the codex increased in use in comparison with the use of the roll is natural in view of the many obvious advantages of the leaf book, not the least of which is that it is more feasible to write on both sides of a leaf, and hence such a book is cheaper. But the statistics just given indicate a particular and very early preference for the codex form on the part of Christians. This also is natural in view of the advantages of the codex with respect to matters of particular interest to the Christians. For example, the single Gospel according to Luke would probably have filled an average papyrus roll of approximately thirty feet in length, and Paul's ten collected church letters (including Philemon) would probably have occupied two ordinary rolls (FLAP p. 393), but all Four Gospels or all of the Letters of Paul could readily be brought together in a single codex book. Likewise it is much more difficult to turn quickly to a specific passage in a roll, and much easier to do so in a codex. As to use of materials, it is also obvious that parchment had the advantage of durability, particularly in climates less dry than the climate of Egypt, and thus it gradually superseded papyrus. Thus, finally, Bible manuscripts came to be predominantly, in form and material, codices of parchment. But the word βιβλία, which in the first instance meant papyrus rolls, continued to attach to the entire collection. In Latin the same plural, *biblia*, was eventually taken as singular, and so the name Bible emerged.

C

Some Technical Details

1. Quire and Folio

§18. To make a roll it is evident that a long strip of papyrus or of parchment is wrapped around on itself or on a rod. To make a codex, a sheet of papyrus or parchment is folded in the middle to make two leaves or folios (from Latin *folium,* "leaf"), or a number of sheets are folded together to make a larger number of leaves (cf. §11). Such an arrangement is called a quire, from Latin quattuor, "four," because four sheets were often folded together to make eight leaves. Several quires may be fastened together to make the entire codex, or many sheets may be piled on top of each other and all folded over together to constitute the codex out of a single quire. The latter is the case, for example, with $\mathfrak{P}^{46}$ (cf. below §90), where 52 sheets of papyrus were folded together to make 104 folios.

2. Recto and Verso

§19. *Recto* means the right or front side of a leaf, in the case of papyrus the side where the fibers run horizontally; *verso* means the reverse or left side of a leaf, i.e., the back side, and in the case of papyrus this is the side where the fibers run vertically (cf. above §7). In making a codex, the *recto* and the *verso* of the sheets may be placed alternately uppermost, so that wherever the book is opened a *recto* page faces a *recto,* and a *verso* faces a *verso.* In a parchment manuscript a similar arrangement brought a hair side of the material (which was darker) to face a hair side, and a flesh side (which was lighter) to face a flesh side wherever the book was opened.

3. Column and Ruling

§20. On a roll, the writing was usually arranged in a series of columns, each perhaps two or three inches in width. In a codex there might be from one to several columns of writing on a page. In order to write in straight lines, the scribe would follow the horizontal fibers on the *recto* side of papyrus. On parchment straight lines were established with pinpricks, and guidelines were ruled on the material, including also markings for the margins of the columns.

4. Opisthograph and Palimpsest

§21. In the case of a roll it was usually only the inner surface that carried the writing, except perhaps for address, title, or other small item, on the back. Sometimes, however, both sides were used, and the result was "a book written inside and on the back" (βιβλίον γεγραμμένον ἔσωθεν [or ἔμπροσθεν] καὶ ὄπισθεν [or ἔξωθεν]), as the one mentioned in Rev 5:1. Such a roll is called an opisthograph. Sometimes, also, a manuscript, usually a parchment, was erased of its original writing, and another text was written over it. Such a manuscript is called a palimpsest, or "scraped again" manuscript, from Greek πάλιν, "again," and ψάω, "to rub away." Of 250 NT uncial manuscripts (§53), 52 are palimpsests.

5. Pen and Ink

§22. Writing "with pen and ink" (διὰ μέλανος καὶ καλάμου) is mentioned in III Jn 13, "with paper and ink" (διὰ χάρτου καὶ μέλανος) in II Jn 12, and "with ink" (μέλανι) in II Cor 3:3. The κάλαμος is in the first instance a reed, and then a reed pen, made by drying the reed, sharpening it to a point, and splitting the point into two parts. From μέλας, meaning "black," the neuter τὸ μέλαν is the word for ink. This was made from carbon in the form of soot, which was mixed with gum and water. With red ocher or red iron oxide a red ink was made. The latter color was often used for titles, headings, and initial letters or lines, and on this account from the Latin *ruber*, which means "red," we derive the word rubric.

6. Uncial and Minuscule

§23. In general, there were two forms of ancient handwriting in Greek, one a nonliterary script which was a cursive or running hand used for everyday writing, and the other a literary script which was a more formal and careful kind of hand. In the literary handwriting, capital letters were first used, as they were used in inscriptions (see A. G. Woodhead, *The Study of Greek Inscriptions*. Cambridge: The University Press, 1959), and these gradually developed into what are known as uncial characters. In the uncial form, the letters are generally more rounded, and this is particularly the case with Sigma (Σ), Epsilon (E), and Omega (Ω), which are written C, Є, and ω. The name of the uncial letters is derived from the Latin word *uncia*, which means the twelfth part of anything, and thus the twelfth part of a foot, an inch. In what way uncial letters represented the twelfth part of something is not fully clear, but perhaps at some point or other there were twelve of them in an ordinary line of writing. In fact this is frequently the number of characters in a line of Codex Sinaiticus (fourth century, see §148); in Codex Vaticanus, however, written at about the same time, there are more letters in a line (16-18, see §141). Altogether, writing of the uncial style is known from at least the third century B.C. to the tenth century of the

Christian era. Manuscripts written in the uncial style may themselves be known as uncials. For either a capital or an uncial letter the term majuscule (from Latin *majusculus,* "somewhat greater," diminutive of *major*) is also used, and it is likewise common to speak of manuscripts written in the large letters as majuscules. In time, however, the cursive hand of the nonliterary script was itself developed into a form which, while still capable of being written rapidly, was regular and elegant enough to be used for literary purposes. This form of letter is called minuscule (from Latin *minusculus,* "rather small"), and manuscripts written in these letters are often themselves called minuscules. In this script the letters are not only smaller than the capitals or the uncials, but many of them are connected without raising the pen. The minuscule script was probably introduced at the beginning of the ninth century, and the small letters soon superseded the uncial characters, and continued in use as long as books were copied by hand. Thus the older NT Greek manuscripts are majuscules or uncials, and the later manuscripts are minuscules. Numerically speaking, the great mass of them all are minuscules (cf. §53).

7. Punctuation and Abbreviation

§24. In the earliest NT manuscripts, letters are written more or less continuously, and there is little or no spacing between words or sentences. There is also little or no punctuation. In 𝔓⁵² (for the abbreviations by which NT manuscripts are referred to, see below §§48ff.), a fragment from the first half of the second century and presently the oldest known portion of NT text, some of the words may be slightly separated and, in the first line, there are two dots (dieresis) over an initial vowel (Iota), presumably to indicate that it is to be pronounced in a separate syllable from the vowels (Omicron and Upsilon) immediately following (cf. §98). In the course of time, gradually increasing use of other marks is found, particularly the use of a point, which is often placed not in the low position of a present-day period, but rather in a middle or high position between words or at the end of a sentence.

§25. In almost the earliest NT manuscripts, the sacred names (*nomina sacra*) and certain other words occurring in the text are abbreviated. In 𝔓⁵² no such name occurs, but in 𝔓⁶⁴, a text of the latter part of the second century (§90), the words Lord (in the vocative, κύριε) and Jesus ('Ιησοῦς) are abbreviated (*recto,* Column 1, Line 2, and Column 2, Line 1; Mt 26:22, 31) (Colin Roberts in HTR 46 [1953], pp. 233-237). Although quite difficult to make out because of the fragmentary condition of the papyrus, the first of these words was most probably reduced in the abbreviation to the first and last letters (KЄ), and the second word was contracted to the first two letters (IH). Also, although now not to be seen at all because of the damage to the papyrus, there was undoubtedly in each case a line drawn above the letters to mark the abbreviation. In addition to contracting a word to its first and last letters, or its first two letters, as in these examples, other variations in abbreviations include reduction to the first two and the last letters, the first and the last two letters, the first, a middle, and the last letter, and the first two and the last two letters or consonants. In each case a line is drawn above the letters. Examples of these several fashions, including other words so abbreviated, are: ἄνθρωπος (Man), A̅N̅C̅, A̅N̅O̅C̅; θεός (God), Θ̅C̅; Ἰησοῦς (Jesus), I̅C̅, I̅H̅C̅; υἱός (Son), Y̅C̅; πατήρ (Father), Π̅Ρ̅, Π̅Η̅Ρ̅; πνεῦμα (Spirit), Π̅Ν̅Α̅; σταυρός (Cross), C̅T̅C̅, C̅T̅Ρ̅C̅; Χριστός (Christ), X̅C̅, X̅Ρ̅C̅. Particularly interesting is the occurrence already around A.D. 200 in 𝔓⁶⁶ (Papyrus Bodmer II, see below §§107ff.) and 𝔓⁷⁵ (Papyrus Bodmer XIV-XV, see below §§120ff.), and also in other later manuscripts, of an abbreviation of σταυρός and also of σταυρόω, "crucify," in which the Tau and the Rho are written together in a cross monogram, so that, e.g., the noun in the genitive singular (σταυροῦ) (Jn 19:19 in 𝔓⁶⁶) is written σ̅ρ̅οῦ, and the verb in the third person singular first aorist subjunctive passive (σταυρωθῇ) (Jn 19:16 in 𝔓⁶⁶) is abbreviated σ̅ρ̅θη (FANT pp. 253f.; Kurt Aland, "Bemerkungen zum Alter und zur Entstehung des Christogrammes anhand von Beobachtungen bei 𝔓⁶⁶ und 𝔓⁷⁵," in *Studien zur Überlieferung des Neuen Testaments und Seines Textes* [ANT 2, 1967], pp. 173-179).

8. Sections, Canons, and Lections

§26. In 𝔓⁶⁴ (see above §25) another interesting feature of the text is that in Line 1 in Column 2 on the *recto* the initial letter of the first word (αὐτοῖς, "to them") projects into the left margin. At this point the Greek text which we know as Mt 26:31 reads: Τότε λέγει αὐτοῖς ὁ Ἰησοῦς, πάντες ὑμεῖς σκανδαλισθήσεσθε . . . , "Then Jesus said to them, 'You will all fall away. . . .' " This appears in Lines 1 and 2 in Column 2 of the *recto* of 𝔓⁶⁴ as follows, the abbreviation of the name of Jesus being allowed to stand, and the missing parts of the other words being supplied in brackets:

ΑΥΤΟΙC Ο IH ΠΑΝ[ΤΕC]
CΚΑΝΔΑΛΙCΘΗ[CΕCΘΕ]

Presumably the preceding words of the sentence, ΤΟΤΕ ΛΕΓΕΙ, appeared in the last part of the line above these two lines, where the papyrus is now completely broken away. The projection of the initial letter of ΑΥΤΟΙC into the margin calls attention, therefore, to the first complete line of a section of text which actually begins with the first word (ΤΟΤΕ) of the sentence, standing in the latter part of the preceding line. The same kind of a marking of the beginning of a section appears also at this point in Codex Bezae (§§160ff.) and Codex Alexandrinus (§§172ff.) (the latter reads καί instead of τότε), while in Codex Vaticanus (§§139ff.) a space is left before τότε, likewise for the purpose of calling attention to the beginning of a section. Thus a system of section divisions of the text of NT books is at least as old as the second century.

§27. In Codex Vaticanus (fourth century) at the point just indicated, where there is a space before τότε, there is also a number in the left margin ($\overline{\rho\mu\theta}$ = 149) (for Greek numerals see FHBC p. 5). Numbers such as this begin at the beginning of Mt ($\overline{a}$ = 1) and extend to the end ($\overline{\rho o}$ = 170), thus dividing the entire Gospel into 170 sections. Similar divisions exist in Codex Vaticanus in Mark ($\overline{\xi\beta}$ = 62 sections), Luke ($\overline{\rho\nu\beta}$ = 152 sections), and John ($\overline{\pi}$ = 80 sections), and also in other books of the NT.

§28. Sections, such as just described, are known as κεφάλαια. Like κεφαλίς (see above §14), κεφάλαιον is derived from κεφαλή, "head," and thus means something that belongs to a head, therefore a section or a chapter. Likewise from Latin *caput,* "head," diminutive *capitulum,* is derived English "chapter." In Codex Alexandrinus (fifth century), which has a different system of κεφάλαια (68 in Mt, 48 in Mk, 83 in Lk, 18 in Jn) than Codex Vaticanus, each section is also provided with a τίτλος (Latin *titulus*), i.e., a title or superscription giving a concise summary of the contents of the section; and all of these titles are collected at the beginning of the book to provide a brief table of contents. Thus in Mk (the beginning of Mt is lost in Codex Alexandrinus), the opening part of the Gospel (1:1-22) is evidently treated as a preface (as was often done); the first marked section (α) begins at 1:23 and is entitled, Περὶ τοῦ δαιμονιζομένου, Concerning the man possessed by a demon; the second section (β) begins at 1:29 and is entitled, Περὶ τῆς πενθερᾶς Πέτρου, Concerning the mother-in-law of Peter; and so on. For a list of κεφάλαια and their τίτλοι see von Soden I 1, pp. 405ff. As compared with the sections described above, the chapter division which appears in present-day Bibles was instituted by Stephen Langton (he studied and taught in the University of Paris, was later Archbishop of Canterbury, and died in 1228) at the beginning of the thirteenth century, and adopted by the Dominican Cardinal Hugo de Sancto Caro, or Hugo of St. Cher (died in 1263), in 1238, in his biblical concordance called *Sacrorum bibliorum concordantiae* (Vogels, *Handbuch,* p. 24); while the division into verses derives from an edition of the NT in Greek and Latin by Robert Estienne in 1550 (see below §63).

§29. With respect to the Four Gospels, Eusebius devised another system of sections, smaller and more numerous (namely, 355 sections in Mt, 233 in Mk, 342 in Lk, and 232 in Jn) than in the systems noted above (§28), and accompanied these with a set of ten tables, which he called canons (κανόνες) (for this word in various meanings see FHRJ p. 3). As he explained in a letter to a certain Carpianus, the sections were numbered consecutively in each Gospel, and each section number was accompanied also by a canon number. In turn the canons contained lists of the parallel sections (indicated by their respective numbers) in the several Gospels. As Eusebius explained to Carpianus, the first canon contained numbers in which all Four Gospels said things very similar (ἐν οἷς τὰ παραπλήσια εἰρήκασιν οἱ τέσσαρες); the second in which the three, Mt, Mk, Lk, did likewise;

the third in which the three, Mt, Lk, Jn, did so; and so on, until most of the possible combinations of Gospels were provided for. So useful was this entire system for the comparative study of the Four Gospels (prior to the time of modern synopses or parallel editions), that the materials of it were copied in a great many Byzantine manuscripts. Taken from these manuscripts, the Eusebian section numbers and canons are printed regularly in Nestle's *Novum Testamentum Graece* (now Nestle-Aland, published by the Württembergische Bibelanstalt, Stuttgart, and the American Bible Society, New York, see below §79); the sections are listed consecutively in von Soden I 1, pp. 388-402; and the Letter of Eusebius to Carpianus is translated by Harold H. Oliver in *Novum Testamentum* 3 (1959), pp. 138-145. In practice one looks, for example, at the section Jn 2:14-16 and finds the section number κa = 21, together with a reference to canon a = 1. Referring to the first canon, in which passages that are parallel to each other in all Four Gospels are indicated, one finds on a horizontal line with the number 21 in the column for Jn the following references with respect to the other three Gospels, Mt 211, Mk 121, Lk 238. Turning to these Gospels, the section numbered 211 in Mt consists of Mt 21:12-13, number 121 in Mk consists of Mk 11:15 (beginning with, "And he entered the temple. . . .") -17, and number 238 in Lk consists of Lk 19:45-46. At each of these three Gospel passages, also, there is a reference to the first canon, therefore the process just described could have been initiated equally well at the point of any one of the four passages in question. Altogether, the four passages in which the Four Gospels narrate the Cleansing of the Temple have been quickly and accurately identified.

§30. In the course of time there was also made a selection of passages in the Gospels, Acts, and Letters of the NT to be read in the services of the church on Saturdays and Sundays, on feast days, and on other weekdays. These lections are marked in the margins or between the lines of some of the later uncial manuscripts, and in many of the minuscules, with the abbreviations $a\rho\chi$ (for $\dot{a}\rho\chi\dot{\eta}$) and $\tau\epsilon\lambda$ (for $\tau\dot{\epsilon}\lambda o\varsigma$) to show the "beginning" and the "end" of what was to be read. Also a note written in the margin in red ink may give the day to which the reading pertains. In addition, actual manuscripts were prepared in which the several readings were arranged in the order in which they would come up to be read. Such a lectionary manuscript is called an Evangelion ($E\dot{v}a\gamma\gamma\dot{\epsilon}\lambda\iota o\nu$) when it contains readings from the Gospels, an Apostolos ('$A\pi\dot{o}\sigma\tau o\lambda o\varsigma$) when it has lections from the Acts and Letters, and an Apostoloevangelion ('$A\pi o\sigma\tau o\lambda o\epsilon\nu a\gamma\gamma\dot{\epsilon}\lambda\iota o\nu$) when it has readings from Gospels, Acts, and Letters. Also a lectionary that provides lessons for the church year, beginning with Easter, is called a Synaxarion ($\Sigma\nu\nu a\xi\dot{a}\rho\iota o\nu$), while one containing lessons for the various saints' days and festivals, beginning with the start of the civil year on the first of September, is called a Menologion ($M\eta\nu o\lambda\dot{o}\gamma\iota o\nu$). In the Gospels the daily reading is usually introduced by an established phrase known as an *incipit*, literally a "here begins." Some half dozen of these recur most frequently, namely:

(1) τῷ καιρῷ ἐκείνῳ, "On a certain occasion";

(2) εἶπεν ὁ κύριος τοῖς ἑαυτοῦ μαθηταῖς, "The Lord said to his disciples";

(3) εἶπεν ὁ κύριος πρὸς τοὺς ἐληλυθότας πρὸς αὐτὸν Ἰουδαίους, "The Lord said to the Jews who had come to him";

(4) εἶπεν ὁ κύριος πρὸς τοὺς πεπιστευκότας αὐτῷ Ἰουδαίους, "The Lord said to the Jews who had believed in him";

(5) εἶπεν ὁ κύριος, "The Lord said";

(6) εἶπεν ὁ κύριος τὴν παραβολὴν ταύτην, "The Lord spoke this parable."

The time to which the reading belongs is usually indicated in the margin or above the opening of the lection. Thus, for example, the readings from Easter to Pentecost are taken from the Gospel according to John, and Jn 1:1-17 is indicated as the lection τῇ ἁγίᾳ καὶ μεγάλῃ κυριακῇ τοῦ Πάσχα, "on the holy and great Lord's day (i.e., Sunday) of the Passover (i.e., Easter)," Jn 1:18-28 τῇ β̄ τῆς διακινησίμου, "on the second day (i.e., Monday) of the six days of Easter week," Jn 3:16-21 τῇ γ̄ τῆς β̄ ἑβδομάδος, "on the third day (i.e., Tuesday) of the second week," Jn 21:14-25 τῷ σαββάτῳ τῆς Πεντηκοστῆς, "on the Sabbath (i.e., Saturday) of the week preceding Pentecost Sunday," and so on. Lectionary manuscripts, such as have now been described, number around 2000 (§53), ranging from fragments to complete copies. In date, there are fragments from the sixth century, and complete manuscripts from the eighth century and onwards. A considerable number are uncials, but the majority are minuscules. On this subject see Colwell and Riddle.

9. Prologues and Colophons

§31. The prologues which will be discussed now are brief introductory statements prefixed, in various manuscripts, to NT books. The first group consists of the so-called Marcionite Prologues to the Letters of Paul. As we learn largely from Tertullian, who wrote *Against Marcion* about A.D. 207, Marcion was born in Sinope in Pontus, came to Rome in about A.D. 140 and, some four years later, organized there a separate Christian community of his own. He rejected the OT, whose creator God was of an utterly different character, he believed, from the good God of Jesus, and advocated an anti-Judaistic and strongly Pauline form of Christianity. In place of the OT he formed a canon of acceptable writings consisting of a Gospel and an Apostle, to which he also added a work of his own called *Antitheses.* From Tertullian's detailed discussion of Marcion, in which he appears to work consecutively through Marcion's canon, we gather that the Gospel of Marcion was probably an abridged version of the Gospel according to Luke, and that the Apostle consisted of ten Pauline Letters, also somewhat altered. The Pauline Letters were the church letters plus the Letter to Philemon. Among the church letters, Ephesians was called Laodiceans by Marcion (*Against Marcion* V 17). The order of the letters was: Galatians, (I and II) Corinthians, Romans, (I and II) Thessalonians, Laodiceans (Ephesians), Colossians, Philippians, and Philemon.

§32. The Prologues connected with the name of Marcion were known to Pelagius (c. A.D. 400) and used in the prologue of his *Expositions of the Pauline Letters;* and they are preserved in numerous Latin manuscripts of the Bible, of which the oldest is Codex Fuldensis of the sixth century. Although existent in Latin, the language shows that the Prologues were originally composed in Greek. The Prologues to the church letters (Galatians, Corinthians, Romans, Thessalonians, Laodiceans [Ephesians], Colossians, Philippians) follow a regular pattern. Those who received the letters are identified as to nationality, thus, for example, the Galatians are identified as Greeks. The churches are then assessed as to their position in respect to the true faith, and Paul, called simply the apostle, is described as either admonishing them to return to it if they have fallen away from it (Galatians, Corinthians, Romans, Colossians), or praising them if they have adhered to it (Thessalonians, Ephesians [Laodiceans], Philippians). Finally the place from which the letter was written is stated, for example, Galatians from Ephesus, and sometimes the person is also mentioned by or through whom the letter came, for example, Philippians was written from prison in Rome by or through (*per*) Epaphroditus. The Latin *per* corresponds to the Greek διά which occurs in I Pet 5:12 ("Through [RSV by] Silvanus . . . I have written to you. . . .") with the probable meaning that Silvanus was the amanuensis or even the draftsman of the letter; but it is also found, for example, in a note in many manuscripts at the end of the Letter to the Romans, ἐγράφη ἀπὸ Κορίνθου διὰ Φοίβης τῆς διακόνου; and here, since the scribe of the letter (Tertius) is already explicitly mentioned in 16:22, it must mean that the letter was written from Corinth and carried by Phoebe the deaconess. The latter meaning presumably applies in most of the Prologues. The Prologues for the personal Pauline Letters (I and II Timothy, Titus, Philemon) are briefer, yet similar in form and content.

§33. In the prologues the false prophets draw men back into the law and circumcision (*in legem et circumcisionem,* Galatians), or into the law and the prophets (*in legem et prophetas,* Romans), while the (true) apostle wins them back to the word of truth (*verbum veritatis,* Galatians) and to the true evangelical faith (*ad veram evangelicam fidem,* Romans), which is plainly "the truth of the gospel" (ἡ ἀλήθεια τοῦ εὐαγγελίου), as in Gal 2:5, 14. Galatians was, of course, Marcion's favorite Pauline Letter, which he placed at the head of the series in his own canon of those Letters, and it is plain that the stand of the Prologues is in harmony with the position of Marcion. Also the inner relations of the Prologues to the church Letters and to Philemon probably make the best sense when the Prologues are arranged in the same order as the Letters in Marcion's canon. For these reasons the Marcionite character of the Prologues may be considered established. At the same time it is true that Marcion did not include the Pastoral Letters in his canon, yet these Prologues include ones for I and II Timothy and Titus which seem to go well with the others. Therefore it is probable that the Prologues come from the followers of Marcion rather than from Marcion himself, a conclusion substantiated by Tertullian's failure to mention the Prologues although he otherwise appears to deal so exhaustively with the writings of Marcion. Nevertheless the Prologues must have originated at an early date, probably in the second half of the second century or not later than the beginning of the third. For the recognition of the Marcionite character of the Prologues by Dom de Bruyne (*Revue Bénédictine,* 1907, pp. 1ff.) and by Peter Corssen independently, see the latter in ZNW 10 (1909), pp. 37-44, 97-102. For the text of the Prologues, arranged in the order of Marcion's canon, see Adolf von Harnack, *Marcion: Das Evangelium vom fremden Gott* (Leipzig: J. C. Hinrichs, 1921), pp. 136*-141*; and in ZNW 25 (1926), pp. 160-163; cf. Souter pp. 188-191; E. C. Blackman, *Marcion and His Influence* (London: S.P.C.K., 1948), pp. 52-54.

§34. The second group of prologues to be mentioned here are the so-called anti-Marcionite Prologues to the Gospels. These are found in at least thirty-eight manuscripts, and provide introductory statements at the beginning of the Gospels according to Mark, Luke, and John. Presumably there was also at one time a Prologue for the Gospel according to Matthew. The text of each Prologue is in Latin, and the Prologue to the Gospel according to Luke is also preserved in Greek, the language in which all were probably written originally. The text of the Prologue to the Gospel according to John includes a reference to the exposure of the heretical views of Marcion by Papias, and to an excommunication of Marcion by John (presumably meaning the Apostle). While direct communication between the Apostle John and Marcion may seem doubtful (although Marcion might have come through Asia Minor, where Papias and perhaps also John lived, on his way to Rome), the inclusion of this reference gives ground for the common designation of these Prologues as anti-Marcionite. Like the Marcionite Prologues, these too may be as early as the second half of the second century. See Blackman, *Marcion and His Influence,* pp. 54-57, with references to de Bruyne in *Revue Bénédictine,* 1928, pp. 193-214, and von Harnack in *Sitzungsberichte der preussischen Akademie,* 1928, pp. 322-341. The Latin and Greek texts of the Prologues, as edited by Harnack, are given in Aland, *Synopsis,* pp. 532-533.

§35. In distinction from the prologue, such as those just mentioned, which provides informative material at the head of a book in an ancient manuscript, the colophon is an inscription at the end. The word in Greek, κολοφών, means a top, finishing, or end; and the related verb, κολοφωνέω, means to put the crown on. In such a note at the end, there is often given the name of the scribe who copied the manuscript, or other information about the making of it, or the scribe makes some comment about his labor or appends a prayer or a warning against altering the work. In the last sense, Rev 22:18-19 amounts to a colophon, while Eusebius (*Ch. Hist.* V 20, 2) says that at the end of a treatise by Irenaeus, *On the Ogdoad,* which is no longer extant, there was a note which ran as follows: "I adjure you who shall copy out this book, by our Lord Jesus Christ and by his glorious advent when he comes to judge the living and the dead, that you compare what you copy, and correct it carefully by this transcript from which you copy, and that you likewise copy this adjuration and put it in the transcript."

10. Stichometry and Euthaliana

§36. Insofar as the somewhat fragmentary papyrus preserves it, there is at the end of each of the Letters of Paul in $\mathfrak{P}^{46}$ (§90), a codex of around A.D. 200, an abbreviation written like this, $\sigma\tau\iota^{\chi}$, followed by another Greek letter or letters which are numerals. The abbreviation stands for the Greek word $\sigma\tau\iota\chi$oς, plural $\sigma\tau\iota\chi$oι. This word means a row or line, as a row of trees, or a line of soldiers, and hence is also used for a line of writing, or a verse. From it is derived the word stichometry, for the science of the measurement of books. Researches in stichometry by Charles Graux (in *Revue de Philologie* 2 [1878], pp. 97-143), J. Rendel Harris (*Stichometry*, 1893; and in *The New Schaff-Herzog Encyclopedia of Religious Knowledge* XI, pp. 91-94), and others, have shown that the stichos probably corresponded originally to a line of hexameter verse such as was used by Homer and Virgil, and amounted usually to sixteen (or sometimes fifteen) syllables, or approximately 34 to 38 letters. Accordingly a manuscript was measured by the number of stichoi it contained, and scribes were probably paid and the market price of the manuscript determined in relation to this figure. In $\mathfrak{P}^{46}$ the stichoi notations appear to have been added very soon after the original copying of the manuscript, say in the early third century. In Codex Sinaiticus ($\aleph$ or S), of the fourth century, there are stichometric notations at the end of most of the Letters of Paul, but nowhere else in the entire Bible in this manuscript. These are probably from a scribe other than those who copied the NT, but contemporary with them and working in conjunction with them.

§37. As a single example of the subject under consideration, the stichometry of the Letter to the Ephesians may be discussed. The number of Greek letters in Ephesians was calculated by Graux (cf. above §36) as 11,932. Dividing this figure by an assumed average of 36 letters in a stichos, the number of stichoi in Ephesians is 331. Reading the Westcott and Hort (§74) text of Ephesians in stichoi of 16 syllables, Rendel Harris (cf. above §36) arrived at 325 stichoi, but when he allowed for the possibility of abbreviations (cf. above §25) in the text by subtracting one syllable at every occurrence of $\theta\epsilon$óς and $\chi\rho\iota\sigma$τς and two syllables for Ἰ$\eta\sigma$ο$\tilde{\upsilon}\varsigma$ and $\kappa\acute{\upsilon}\rho\iota$ο$\varsigma$, the result was 314 stichoi. In $\mathfrak{P}^{46}$, the oldest manuscript available with stichometric notations attached (§36), the attempt to actually count the number of Greek letters in the text is complicated by the fact that in the partially fragmentary condition of the papyrus several lines of writing are missing from most of the pages. The probable reading of the lost lines has been restored by Frederic G. Kenyon (*The Chester*

Beatty Biblical Papyri, Fasc. III Supp., Pauline Epistles, Text [1936], Plates [1937]) as long as no more than two lines are missing, and may be restored beyond that from other editions of the Greek text of the NT. Using Kenyon and Westcott and Hort in this way, the counted and estimated number of letters in Ephesians is 11,482. The text of $\mathfrak{P}^{46}$ utilizes many abbreviations of sacred names and words. When the letters left out because of the abbreviations are supplied again, the total count for Ephesians in $\mathfrak{P}^{46}$ is 11,911. This is remarkably close to the figure of 11,932 calculated by Graux and, divided by an assumed 36 letters in a stichos, gives almost the same result obtained above, namely, 330.86 stichoi. But taking the text as it stands, with the abbreviations, and dividing 11,482 by 36 the result is 318.94 stichoi. Now, looking at the stichometric notation at the end of Ephesians in $\mathfrak{P}^{46}$ we find the number given by the Greek letters Tau, Iota, and Vau, which make 316. Thus the number arrived at by our own calculation (319) is remarkably close to the number (316) actually assigned in the manuscript for the stichoi in Ephesians. Compared with this, the number of stichoi for Ephesians in Codex Sinaiticus (ℵ or S) is given as CTIXⲰN ΓΙΒ = 312. For stichometry see also Jack Finegan in HTR 49 (1956), pp. 95-103.

§38. In distinction from counting the extent of a written text in terms of the number of stichoi therein, another practice was to actually copy the text in lines corresponding to the sense. If the line comprised a single phrase, it was called a κόμμα or comma (plural, commata), the Greek word meaning "that which is cut off." If the line comprised a single clause, it was called a κῶλον or colon (plural, cola), this Greek word meaning a limb, or member of the body. In terms of syllables, a comma was defined as a combination of words not in excess of eight syllables, a colon as a combination of at least nine but not more than sixteen (Metzger p. 29 n. 5). Since a stichos was normally a unit of sixteen syllables, the comma and usually also the colon were units of smaller size. The arrangement of a manuscript in such sense-lines was undoubtedly intended to be a help to the reader, particularly to one reading aloud; and the length of the units probably had some relationship also to the length of time a reader could continue before he renewed his breath again. The arrangement and measurement of a manuscript in terms of sense-lines or space-lines is called colometry.

§39. Examples of colometrically arranged manuscripts may be seen in three very interesting codices, all probably of the sixth century in date, namely, Codex Bezae, Codex Claromontanus, and Codex Coislianus. Codex Bezae (D, cf. below §§160ff.), now at Cambridge, is a bilingual manuscript of the Four Gospels (in the order Mt, Jn, Lk, Mk) and Acts, with the Greek text on the left-hand page and the Latin on the right, each page written in thirty-three colometric lines (for sample pages of Greek and Latin, see Vogels, *Specimina,* Pls. 18-19). The Latin text is not simply a translation of the Greek, but each text has influenced the other, and sometimes the scribe has used Latin characters in writing Greek words. For example, in Jn 5:38, instead of ἀπέστειλεν ("sent," aorist indicative), this manuscript has ἀπέσταλκε ("has sent," perfect indicative), and the scribe has written the word not with a Greek Lambda but with a Latin L, namely, ΑΠΕϹΤΑLΚΕ.

§40. Codex Claromontanus (Dᴾ), in Paris, contains the thirteen Pauline Letters, then the so-called Canon Claromontanus, which will be described momentarily, and after that, probably added later, the Letter to the Hebrews. Again, the manuscript is bilingual, with the Greek on the left and the Latin on the right, and the pages are written colometrically, with twenty-one lines on the page (for sample pages of Greek and Latin, see Vogels, *Specimina,* Pls. 20-21). In this case the Latin is relatively independent of the Greek, and has been shown to be for the most part identical with the Latin text used by Lucifer of Cagliari in Sardinia in the fourth century (Souter p. 26). The so-called Canon Claromontanus, which stands in this manuscript immediately after the Letter to Philemon, is an incomplete list of the books of the OT and the NT, together with the number of lines in each. Written here in Latin, the list may go back to a Greek original of around A.D. 300. In its NT portion the list is reproduced in Souter pp. 194f. Reference in the Canon to the number of lines in a book is with the Latin word *versus,* which, like στίχος, also means row, line, or verse. Here, however, the reference must be, not to stichoi, but to cola or commata, i.e., to the sense-lines or place-lines in which the manuscript is actually written. As compared with the stichometry of 𝔓⁴⁶, where the Letter to the Ephesians, for example, was credited with 316 stichoi (see above §37), the relevant notation here reads: *Ad Efesios ver. CCCLXXV,* i.e., the Letter to the Ephesians is written in 375 sense-lines, and this figure is in agreement with the smaller average length of a colon or comma in comparison with a stichos.

§41. Codex Coislianus (Hᴾ), also called Codex Euthalianus, is a Greek manuscript of the Pauline Letters which once belonged to the Monastery of the Great Laura on Mount Athos. While some leaves remain there, others are scattered among libraries in Kiev, Leningrad, Moscow, Paris, and Turin. Preserved in the extant leaves are portions of I and II Corinthians, Galatians, Colossians, I Thessalonians, Hebrews, I and II Timothy, and Titus. The Greek text is written colometrically, with a single column and with sixteen lines on a page (for a sample page from the Bibliothèque Nationale, Paris, see Vogels, *Specimina,* Pl. 8). At the end of the manuscript at the end of the Letter to Titus is a colophon which is still preserved on one of the leaves in the Bibliothèque Nationale. Like the rest of the manuscript, the colophon was doubtless not first composed when this copy was made, but was transcribed along with everything else from the exemplar from which the present scribe worked. The colophon (which is reproduced by J. Armitage Robinson, *Texts and Studies,* III *Euthaliana,* p. 3) begins with a line of writing which has been almost completely obliterated, and then continues as follows:

ἔγραψα καὶ ἐξεθέμην κα
τὰ δύναμιν στειχηρόν

τόδε τὸ τεῦχος Παύλου
τοῦ ἀποστόλου

Speaking in the first person, the author of these words says that he wrote and set forth the book of the Apostle Paul, as far as he was able, στειχηρόν. This word, also spelled στιχηρόν and στιχηδόν, is related to στίχος, and means in rows, or lines. Here it plainly means that this person prepared an edition of the Pauline Letters in the form of sense-lines, which is the form in which the present manuscript exists. A little farther along in the colophon, the writer also says:

ἀντεβλήθη δὲ ἡ βίβλος
πρὸς τὸ ἐν καισαρία ἀντί
γραφο^ν τῆς βιβλιοθήκης
τοῦ ἁγίου Παμφίλου χειρὶ
γεγραμμένον

So the manuscript (not necessarily Codex H^P itself, but the original copy from which H^P derives) was compared with, i.e., was corrected by comparison with, a copy in the library of Caesarea written by the hand of Pamphilus, the famous friend of Eusebius.

§42. The colophon just described is also preserved in another manuscript, namely, a twelfth-century minuscule in the National Library in Naples (Library No. II. A. 7; Gregory No. 88; Wettstein and Tischendorf No. 93; von Soden No. *a*200; see von Soden I 1, pp. 57, 92, 677). Here the name Εὐάγριος, Evagrius, stands in the nominative as the subject of ἔγραψα, "wrote," and it seems probable that the same name was once in the first line of the colophon in H^P (§41), now obliterated (Robinson, *Euthaliana,* p. 71). The likely person to recognize here is Evagrius Ponticus (A.D. 345-399). He was born in Pontus, was a deacon and eloquent preacher in Constantinople, was associated with the lady Melania, friend of Rufinus, in Jerusalem, and thereafter lived as an ascetic in the Nitrian and Scetic deserts in Egypt (Sozomen, *Ch. Hist.* VI 30, 6-11). While in Jerusalem he could easily have compared his manuscript with the exemplar of Pamphilus in Caesarea. The books of Evagrius were translated into Latin by Rufinus, the pupil of Jerome, but Jerome later disagreed with Rufinus and attacked Evagrius for his acceptance of the doctrines of Origen. Later, in the Origenistic controversies of the sixth and seventh centuries, Evagrius was condemned as a heretic, and this could account for his name being erased in the obliterated line of text in the manuscript H^P. If the identification just worked out is correct, then credit may be given to Evagrius in the fourth century for the preparation of a codex of the Letters of Paul which was arranged στιχηρόν, i.e., in sense-lines.

§43. Along with section divisions and lists thereof (§§26ff.), prologues and colophons (§§31ff.), stichometric notations (§§36f.), and colometric arrangements (§§38ff.), NT manuscripts have yet other miscellaneous added material. In many cases much of this material is associated with the name of Euthalius (Εὐθάλιος). In many manuscripts of the Letters of Paul, and of the Book of Acts and the Catholic Letters, there is a prologue which contains this name and the designation διάκονος, "deacon," or ἐπίσκοπος Σούλκης, "bishop of Sulci" (a progression in office which would be natural). The Prologue of Euthalius to his edition of the Letters of Paul is found, for example, in a tenth-century minuscule in the Vatican Library (Library No. Gr. 1971; Gregory No. 1845; Tischendorf No. 431; von Soden No. a64), which contains both the Acts and Catholic Letters and the Pauline Letters; in an eleventh-century minuscule in the Biblioteca Reginensis of the Vatican Library (Library No. Reg. Gr. 179; Gregory No. 181; Tischendorf No. 46; von Soden No. a101), which contains the Acts and Catholic Letters and the Pauline Letters; in a twelfth-century minuscule in the Library of the Escorial in Spain (Library No. T III 17; Gregory No. 2004; Tischendorf No. 470; von Soden No. a56 [this number also includes Gregory No. 1835, since von Soden believes that 1835 and 2004 belong together]), which contains the Pauline Letters and the Book of Revelation; in a minuscule written by a monk named Andreas in A.D. 1111, in the British Museum (Library No. Addition 28816; Gregory No. 203; Tischendorf No. 477; von Soden No. a203), which contains, in fragmentary condition, the Acts and Catholic Letters, the Letters of Paul, and the Book of Revelation; and in many other manuscripts (von Soden I 1, pp. 650-656). As found in these manuscripts, the Prologue of Euthalius the Deacon (πρόλογος Εὐθαλίου διακόνου, so in 2004 = a56), or the Prologue of Euthalius the Bishop of Sulci (Εὐθαλίου ἐπισκόπου Σούλκης πρόλογος, so in 181 = a101 and 203 = a203; in 1845 = a64 any superscription is lacking) to the Letters of Paul begins with a dedication to a "most honored Father" (πάτερ τιμιώτατε), who is not further identified, and then continues with three main sections. The first section provides a sketch of the Life of Paul (closing with mention of the day on which his memorial festival was observed at Rome, ἡ πρὸ τριῶν καλανδῶν Ἰουλίων = June 29); the second section gives short summaries of the fourteen Pauline Letters (Hebrews is introduced after II Thessalonians; in connection with the Letter to Philemon, it is stated that Onesimus underwent martyrdom at Rome under Tertullus by the breaking of his legs); and the third section contains a chronology of the Life of Paul derived, as it is explicitly stated, from the *Chronicle* of Eusebius (ἐκ τῶν χρονικῶν κανόνων Εὐσεβίου τοῦ Παμφίλου). At the end of the second section, in which he has summarized the Pauline Letters, Euthalius states that in front of each letter he will provide a setting forth (ἔκθεσις) of its sections (τῶν κεφαλαίων) as they were arranged by an honored predecessor, a summary (ἀνακεφαλαίωσις) of lections (τῶν ἀναγνώσεων), and a summary of testimonies, i.e., of quotations from the Holy Scriptures (τῶν θείων μαρτυριῶν).

§44. The Prologue of Euthalius to his edition of the Book of Acts and the Catholic Letters is found in the Vatican and British Museum manuscripts (Gregory Nos. 1845, 181, 203) already mentioned (§43), and in many others. For the Book of Acts (von Soden I 1, pp. 667-669) most of the manuscripts begin with the simple title,

Prologue of the Acts (πρόλογος τῶν πράξεων). As in his work on the Letters of Paul, so here also in respect to the Acts and the Catholic Letters, the main emphasis of Euthalius is on setting forth the text in short sentences as a help to intelligent reading aloud (στιχηδὸν ἀναγνούς τε καὶ γράψας . . . . στιχηδὸν συνθεὶς τούτων τὸ ὗφος κατὰ τὴν ἐμαυτοῦ συμμετρίαν πρὸς εὔσημον ἀνάγνωσιν). Also there is given a very brief summary of the contents of the Book of Acts. For the Catholic Letters (von Soden I 1, p. 673), which form the second part of the edition of the Book of Acts, there is no further individual superscription. Three features of the work are pointed out, however, namely, the arrangement of the text in sentences, the summaries of the chapters, and the table of Scripture quotations, called testimonies (Ἐγὼ δέ τοι στιχηδὸν τὰς καθολικὰς καθεξῆς ἐπιστολὰς ἀναγνώσομαι, τὴν τῶν κεφαλαίων ἔκθεσιν ἄμα καὶ θείων μαρτυριῶν μετρίως ἐνθένδε ποιούμενος). Both in the Prologue of the Acts and the Prologue of the Catholic Epistles there is mention of a certain Athanasius, described in the first instance as a most dear brother (ἀδελφὲ Ἀθανάσιε προσφιλέστατε), and in the second as a most honored brother (ἀδελφὲ Ἀθανάσιε τιμιώτατε). Like the most honored Father, to whom the edition of the Letters of Paul was dedicated (see above §43), this Athanasius is the one to whom the edition of the Acts and Catholic Letters is dedicated.

§45. In addition to the Prologues of Euthalius, the manuscripts already mentioned (§43) and many others, e.g., an eleventh-century minuscule in the Monastery of the Laura on Mount Athos (Library No. Γ´ 63; Gregory No. 1770; von Soden No. a1067), which is a fragmentary codex of the Letters of Paul from I Corinthians to Titus, and an eleventh-century minuscule in the Monastery of St. Catherine at Mount Sinai (Library No. 274; Gregory No. 1244; von Soden No. a75), which contains the Acts and Catholic Letters and the Letters of Paul, provide in accompaniment to the text various materials such as are mentioned in the Prologues and other materials as well. While it is not probable that all of this comes from Euthalius, since it exceeds what he said he intended to provide, and while part of what Euthalius did provide came, as he himself said, from scholars prior to himself, it is nevertheless common to refer to the entire mass of materials, however extensive or limited, as the Euthalian apparatus. In addition to the tables of lections, tables of quotations, and summaries of chapters, which have already been mentioned (§§43-44), this apparatus includes upon occasion a hypothesis (ὑπόθεσις) or brief introduction to a book, a program (πρόγραμμα) or explanation of the numeration of following sections, and a martyrion or brief statement of the martyrdom of the Apostle Paul (Μαρτύριον Παύλου τοῦ ἀποστόλου). Incidentally, this last gives the same date of June 29, which the Prologue of Euthalius to the Letters of Paul gives as the date of the Roman festival of Paul, as if it were the date of the martyrdom of the apostle (here the date is also written as μηνὸς Ἰουνίου εἰκοστῇ ἐννάτῃ ἡμέρα) (for the significance of the date see FLAP pp. 473f.).

§46. As to the date of Euthalius, since the Prologue to the

Letters of Paul gives a chronology of the Life of Paul explicitly stated (see above §43) to be derived from the *Chronicle* of Eusebius (published c. A.D. 303), his date must be after that. If the "brother Athanasius" mentioned in the Prologue to the Acts and Catholic Letters (§44) could be identified with the famous bishop of Alexandria (died in 372), another date would be available for positive reference (Robinson, *Euthaliana*, p. 101), but the identification is not consistent with the next item of evidence, which requires a later date for Euthalius. In an eleventh-century parchment codex in the Monastery of the Laura on Mount Athos (Library No. 149) there is a "Confession of Euthalius, bishop of Sulci, concerning the orthodox faith" (Εὐθαλίου ἐπισκόπου Σούλκης ὁμολογία περὶ τῆς ὀρθοδόξου πίστεως). In this, after setting forth his own trinitarian and christological affirmations, Euthalius also states his rejection of the confession of a certain John the Exceptor which was directed against Maximus of blessed memory (a leader of orthodoxy who died A.D. 662), and compares the same with the so-called Letter of Ibas to Maris and with the writings of Theodoret against Cyril, both of which were condemned by the Second Council of Constantinople in 553. From these references, therefore, it appears that Euthalius must be put in the second half of the seventh century (von Soden I 1, p. 643). As for Sulci, where he was bishop, this was probably the place of that name on the island of Plumbaria, off the southwestern coast of Sardinia. At that time and place, then, Euthalius may have published a revised edition of materials of the sort described above, some of which came from the work of preceding scholars such as Evagrius (§42), to which he perhaps added new matter of his own, so that in time the whole apparatus came to be known by his name (William H. P. Hatch in TCERK p. 401).

11. Paleography

§47. Since paleography is, by definition, the scientific study of ancient writings, it includes, in the broad sense, all that has been discussed already and all that is in this book. In a narrower sense, it has to do particularly with determining the date of ancient texts by their style of handwriting. In general, as already explained (§23), the older NT manuscripts are written in uncial characters, which were in use from before the Christian era down into the tenth century, and the later manuscripts are written in minuscule characters, which were probably introduced at the beginning of the ninth century and soon came to be used almost exclusively. Within these broad divisions it is to some extent possible to trace in yet greater detail the evolution that took place in styles of handwriting. While everybody's handwriting differs, yet, especially before the time of printing, the handwriting of a particular period tended to have many common characteristics. Also on some or many documents there are dates, and some documents are found in archeological contexts, the date of which can be determined with some precision. Therefore it is possible to establish an at least approximate sequence of styles of handwriting, and to locate newly found manuscripts within such a sequence as already established. For samples of Greek handwriting in ancient manuscripts arranged in the order of their probable respective dates, one may see, for the literary hand in general, C. H. Roberts, *Greek Literary Hands 350 B.C.-A.D. 400* (Oxford: Clarendon Press, 1956); for the uncials, William H. P. Hatch, *The Principal Uncial Manuscripts of the New Testament* (Chicago: University of Chicago Press, 1939); and for the minuscules, Hatch, *Facsimiles and Descriptions of Minuscule Manuscripts of the New Testament* (Cambridge: Harvard University Press, 1951); cf. Bruce M. Metzger, "Paleography," in *Encyclopedia Americana* (1966), 21, pp. 163-166. For a Table of the Letters of the Greek Alphabet as Written in Several of the Oldest New Testament Papyri, see the Appendix of the present book.

II. HISTORY OF TEXTUAL CRITICISM

A

The Listing of Manuscripts

1. Introduction

§48. In general, as we have seen, the manuscripts of the NT run from papyri to parchments, and from uncials to minuscules. In most cases these manuscripts are in the possession of libraries, museums, monasteries, etc., where each has its own designation in accordance with the practice of the individual institution. But altogether there are so many manuscripts, and they are so widely scattered and variously designated, that some kind of universally acceptable designation of each, and comprehensive listing of all, are needed.

2. Wettstein and Tischendorf

§49. The basic system for designating and listing NT manuscripts by letters and numbers, which is still today the most widely used system, was standardized by Johann Jakob Wettstein (1693-1754). Wettstein taught at Basel and at Amsterdam, and at Amsterdam in 1751-1752 issued (ex Officina Dommeriana) a two-volume critical edition of the Greek NT, to which he had devoted forty years of labor. Following an idea originated by Brian Walton in 1657 (§66), and employed by Richard Bentley around 1720 (§68), he listed the available uncials by capital Latin letters, A for Codex Alexandrinus, B for Codex Vaticanus, and so on, and the available minuscules by Arabic numerals, 1, 2, 3, and so on. He also grouped the manuscripts according as they contained the Four Gospels, the Letters of Paul, the Acts and Catholic Letters, and the book of Revelation. At that time his list of manuscripts for the Gospels, for example, ran in capital letters for uncials from A to O, and in Arabic numerals for minuscules from 1 to 112 (see his Vol. I, pp. 220-221). In addition to variant readings from these manuscripts, he also collected in this edition many quotations from rabbinical authors and from Greek and Latin classical and patristic writers, to compare in form and content with NT passages and words. His great work was entitled, Ἡ ΚΑΙΝῊ ΔΙΑΘΗΚΗ, *Novum Testamentum Graecum editionis receptae cum lectionibus variantibus Codicum MSS., Editionum aliarum, Versionum et Patrum, nec non commentario pleniore ex scriptoribus* veteribus Hebraeis, Graecis et Latinis historiam et vim verborum illustrante, opera et studio Joannis Jacobi Wetstenii, Tomus I, Continens Quatuor Evangelia (1751), Tomus II, Continens Epistolas Pauli, Acta Apostolorum, Epistolas Canonicas et Apocalypsin (1752).

§50. The system of Wettstein was continued, with additions, by Constantine Tischendorf (1815-1874). Tischendorf was Professor of New Testament at Leipzig, traveled widely in Europe and the Middle East to study and discover ancient Bible manuscripts, and issued a series of critical editions of the Greek NT. His major eighth edition was published at Leipzig in two volumes in 1869-1872 (J. C. Hinrichs), under the title, *Novum Testamentum Graece, ad antiquissimos testes denuo recensuit, apparatum criticum omni studio perfectum apposuit commentationem isagogicam praetexuit Constantinus Tischendorf, editio octava critica maior* (I, 1869; II, 1872), with an *editio critica minor ex VIII. maiore desumpta* in 1877. In 1844 he had discovered (cf. FLAP pp. 435f.) in the Monastery of St. Catherine at Mount Sinai the great Codex Sinaiticus (as he called it) which, it is generally acknowledged, is of the middle of the fourth century in date and almost as old as Codex Vaticanus. Tischendorf himself gave preference to this manuscript, and put it at the head of his list of uncials. As a designation that would logically come ahead of the A-B-C sequence already established, he assigned to it the Hebrew letter Aleph (א). Also by this time the known uncials were so numerous as to exceed the limits of the Latin alphabet, and so, after the Latin letter Z, Tischendorf went on with the Greek capital letters which were unmistakably different from Latin capitals, namely, Gamma, Delta, Theta, etc. (see his Vol. I, of the 8th ed., pp. IX, XIII-XIV).

3. Gregory and His Successors

§51. Caspar René Gregory (1846-1917) was born in Philadelphia, and went to Leipzig to study under Tischendorf, but reached there only to find that the latter was deceased. Taking up and going on with Tischendorf's work, Gregory himself became Professor of New Testament in the University of Leipzig. At Leipzig in 1900-1909 he published his own *Textkritik des Neuen Testamentes,* in three consecutively paged volumes (J. C. Hinrichs, I, 1900; II, 1902; III, 1909). In this work, in the first volume (pp. 18ff.), Gregory continued to list the uncials which had been longest known by the then familiar Hebrew Aleph for Codex Sinaiticus, followed by Latin and Greek capital letters for the others. He also noted (p. 122) that some wished to avoid the introduction of a Hebrew character in the series and proposed instead to use the capital letter S to stand for Sinaiticus. Otherwise the letter S was used as the designation of Greek manuscript No. 354 in the Vatican Library, a copy of the Gospels dated A.D. 949, and relatively of much less importance, so the adoption of S for Sinaiticus would not cause undue confusion. This suggestion was adopted by Hans Lietzmann in his *Einführung in die Textgeschichte der Paulusbriefe* (in *An die Römer*, HNT 8, Tübingen, J. C. B. Mohr [Paul Siebeck], 3d ed. 1928, p. 6), and is now used, for example, in *Gospel Parallels, A Synopsis of the First Three Gospels,* ed. Burton H. Throckmorton, Jr. (New York: Thomas Nelson & Sons, 2d ed. 1957, p. viii) but is not used, for example, in *Synopsis Quattuor Evangeliorum,* ed. Kurt Aland (Stuttgart: Württembergische Bibelanstalt, 2d ed. 1964), where (p. XV) ℵ designates Codex Sinaiticus, and (p. XVII) S remains the sign alone for the Vatican Gr. 354 manuscript.

§52. Already by the time of Gregory, however, the Hebrew, Latin, and Greek characters were no longer sufficient to cover all the available uncial manuscripts, while among these the texts on papyrus had become numerous enough, in distinction from those on parchment, to call for separate treatment. Therefore, in his third volume, Gregory undertook, although with trepidation (p. 60 n. 1), to make an entire new listing (pp. 1017f.). According to his new arrangement, the list of Greek NT manuscripts comprises three parts. First come the uncials, designated still, as far as the characters reach, by the Hebrew Aleph and the Latin and Greek capitals. But each of these is also given a number in a series capable of indefinite extension, to include the uncials already exceeding the letter designations, and to include manuscripts yet to be discovered and catalogued. These numbers begin with Zero and are printed in boldface type. Thus Codex Sinaiticus is shown as ℵ and also as **01**, Codex Alexandrinus as A and **02**, Codex Vaticanus as B and **03**, and so on. In Gregory's list these numbers ran at that time to **0165**. After the uncials come the papyri. These are designated by the letter P printed in Old German or other distinctive type, with a superior number, thus, $\mathfrak{P}^1$, $\mathfrak{P}^2$, $\mathfrak{P}^3$, and so on. In Gregory's list there were fourteen papyri. In third place, after the uncials and papyri, come the minuscules. These are still designated, as before, by Arabic numerals, 1, 2, 3, and so on. In Gregory's list these ran to **2304**. In describing these manuscripts, Gregory also used abbreviations to indicate their contents, e (*Evangelien*) for Gospels, a (*Apostelgeschichte*) for Acts, c (*Katholische Briefe*) for the Catholic Letters, p (*Paulinische Briefe*) for the Pauline Letters, and r (*revelatio*) for Revelation. Beyond the manuscripts with consecutive NT text are the lectionaries (§30). Preceded by the small letter *l* (for lectionary), these are also numbered, *l* 1, *l* 2, and so on. Beyond these are the versions, i.e., the manuscripts with the text of the NT translated not only into Latin as in D, D^p, etc. (cf. §§39-40), but also into other languages, Syriac, Bohairic, Sahidic, Ethiopic, Armenian (abbreviated respectively syr, bo, sa, eth, arm, etc.), and so on. Altogether, Gregory's catalogue must have included over 4000 manuscripts. In addition he listed alphabetically, from Acacius (c. A.D. 340) to Zonar (c. A.D. 1110), the church writers whose quotations of NT passages make them also valuable witnesses to the text, the more so because their time and place are often known with precision, which is not always the case with the manuscripts.

§53. Essentially the system of Gregory is that which prevailed and is still followed, except that now the papyri are ordinarily listed first, followed by the parchment uncials, the minuscules, the lectionaries, the versions, and the church fathers, in that order. After Gregory, the responsibility for the continuation of his list was assumed by Ernst von Dobschütz (1870-1934), Professor of New Testament in Halle, then by Walter Eltester, and finally by Kurt Aland. The additional installments of the list have been published in the *Zeitschrift für die neutestamentliche Wissenschaft* (abbreviated ZNW), of which Eltester is editor (for references see FLAP p. 416 n. 5, 6), and a compilation of the whole, except for versions and church fathers, has been issued by Aland, as director of the Institut für neutestamentliche Textforschung an der Westfälischen Wilhelms-Universität Münster/Westfalen, under the title *Kurzgefasste Liste der griechischen Handschriften des Neuen Testaments* (ANT 1, 1963). In the *Kurzgefasste Liste* are catalogued (with concise indication of content [e for Gospels, a for Acts and Catholic Letters, and r for Revelation], date, material, pages, columns, lines, format, and place) papyri from $\mathfrak{P}^1$ to $\mathfrak{P}^{76}$, parchment majuscules or uncials from **01** to **0250**, minuscules from 1 to 2646, and lectionaries from *l* 1 to *l* 1997, a total of no fewer than 4969 items. In addition the *Kurzgefasste Liste* provides a concordance of the signs or numbers used by Tischendorf, Gregory, and von Soden (see below § § 55ff.), and an index of the libraries in which the manuscripts are found and of the individual library numbers by which they are there designated (for a concordance of signs see also Benedikt Kraft, *Die Zeichen für die wichtigeren Handschriften des griechischen Neuen Testaments* [Freiburg: Verlag Herder, 3d ed. 1955]).

§ 54. The keeping of the list of the manuscripts is, of course, an endless task. In supplement to the *Kurzgefasste Liste* of 1963, Aland reported in 1967 (in "Das Neue Testament auf Papyrus," in *Studien zur Überlieferung des Neuen Testaments und Seines Textes*, ANT 2, pp. 91-136) that the official list of the papyri now numbers 78. The items newly published, and thus available for inclusion in the list are: $\mathfrak{P}^{77}$ (= OP 2683), a codex fragment of Mt 23:30-39, written in the later second century, and thus one of the oldest NT texts; and $\mathfrak{P}^{78}$ (= OP 2684), a double leaf from a small codex, perhaps an amulet, with Jude 4-5, 7-8, written in the third or earlier fourth century. In addition to these, provisional assignment of numbers was also announced (ANT 2, p. 91 n. 2) for three more papyri, which were awaiting publication, namely, $\mathfrak{P}^{79}$, a papyrus in the Berliner Staatlichen Museen, and $\mathfrak{P}^{80}$ and $\mathfrak{P}^{81}$, papyri found at Khirbet Mird (cf. FLAP p. 280). Again in 1969, Kurt Aland reported (in *Materialien zur neutestamentlichen Handschriftkunde*, ANT 3) that altogether another 300 newly known Greek NT manuscripts are now to be added to the complete catalogue.

4. von Soden

§ 55. In the meantime an entire other system of listing the manuscripts of the NT was elaborated, but has not gained general acceptance, although its signs appear in the concordances (cf. §53). This was the work of Hermann Freiherr von Soden (1852-1914), Professor of New Testament at the University of Berlin. In 1911-1913 he published at Göttingen (Vandenhoeck and Ruprecht) his *Die Schriften des Neuen Testaments in Ihrer ältesten erreichbaren Textgestalt hergestellt auf Grund Ihrer Textgeschichte* (Part I, *Untersuchungen,* in three divisions, pages numbered consecutively, 1911; Part II, *Text mit Apparat,* 1913). Here the known Greek manuscripts (not including the lectionaries) are divided into three groups according to their contents, and are labeled with a small Greek letter to indicate the same. The letter Delta (δ) stands for διαθήκη, "testament," and marks a manuscript that contains the whole NT (with or without the book of Revelation). The letter Epsilon (ε) stands for εὐαγγέλιον, "gospel," and marks a manuscript containing the Four Gospels. The letter Alpha (α) stands for ἀπόστολος, "apostle," and indicates a manuscript containing the book of Acts and the Letters (with or without the book of Revelation). Following the letter comes a number, the several digits of which provide information concerning the date and details of the contents of the manuscript. In this system, Codex Vaticanus (which is Gr. 1209 in the Vatican Library, B in the lists of Wettstein and Tischendorf, and 03 in the numbers of Gregory) becomes δ1; Codex Sinaiticus (London, British Museum, Addition 43725; א or S; 01) is δ2; Codex Ephraemi (Paris, Bibliothèque Nationale, Gr. 9; C; 04) is δ3; Codex Alexandrinus (London, British Museum, Royal MS. 1 D VIII; A; 02) is δ4; and so on.

§55

The Listing of Manuscripts

B

The Scientific Study of the Text

1. The Problem of Textual Variants

§ 56. Not only are there many manuscripts, and fragments there-of, of the NT, but the various manuscripts have many differences among themselves. Presumably if we could ever recover the original manuscript of a NT book it would be very close to what its author intended. Even here, however, the text might not be completely correct. If the author wrote it himself, he could have made mistakes; if he dictated it to a scribe, the latter could have made mistakes. Even prior to the actual writing on papyrus or parchment, error can enter. A scribe can hear incorrectly. Particularly in Greek, the difference between a long vowel and a short vowel can make a difference in the meaning of a word, and the difference between the two when spoken can be difficult to catch. A notable example of the possibility of confusion in this respect exists in Rom 5:1. If Paul said, εἰρήνην ἔχομεν (using the short vowel, Omicron, in the verb to express the present indicative), he declared that "we have peace" with God; but if he said, εἰρήνην ἔχωμεν (using the long vowel, Omega, in the verb to express the present subjunctive), then he exhorted, "let us have peace" with God. Tertius himself, who wrote for Paul (Rom 16:22), conceivably could have been uncertain as to which Paul had said. The same kind of problem could certainly arise not only when the original author was dictating to his amanuensis, but also when copies of manuscripts were made by dictation to scribes. Nor is the same kind of possibility of error absent when copying is done by looking at an exemplar and attempting to reproduce it. Here various Greek letters look somewhat alike (e.g., Sigma [C] and Epsilon [Є] in the uncials), and may be confused; words may have the same ending, and the eye skip from one to the other, omitting what is in between; a word may be copied once when it stands twice in the exemplar, or vice versa; and so on, with all the many possibilities for accidental alteration of the text which are only too well known to the modern typist as well.

§ 57. Alongside unintentional changes, there could be intentional changes made when manuscripts were copied. Scribes may change the spelling of names or introduce corrections in grammar. They may recall and give a quotation or its source differently, be familiar with a parallel passage and introduce an assimilation to it, or be influenced by a known translation of the document in another language. They may introduce an explanation, obviate an apparent difficulty or contradiction, or copy into the text what was originally only a marginal notation. It is theoretically possible, though not as often verifiable, that they might make a change for a dogmatic reason.

§ 58. In illustration of the deficiencies of scribes, the critical comment of Jerome to Lucinius concerning certain copyists may be recalled. Lucinius was a wealthy Spaniard, generous in benefactions and zealous in study of the Scriptures. He intended to visit Jerome in Bethlehem and, in A.D. 397, sent six copyists (Jerome, *Letter* LXXV 4) on ahead to transcribe the writings of Jerome. In the next year, as the scribes returned home, Jerome sent with them a letter (Jerome, *Letter* LXXI), which reached Lucinius only shortly before his death. The death of Lucinius forestalled his projected visit to Bethlehem, and led to a second letter of condolence from Jerome (*Letter* LXXV) to the widow, Theodora. In the letter Jerome sent with the scribes, he reported to Lucinius on their work; and it is to be hoped that the missive was safely sealed so that the copyists could not read what he said about them. Jerome wrote (*Letter* LXXI 5, NPNFSS p. 153):

> As for my poor works which, from no merits of theirs but simply from your own kindness, you say that you desire to have, I have given them to your servants to transcribe. I have seen the paper-copies made by them, and I have repeatedly ordered them to correct them by a diligent comparison with the originals. . . . If then you find errors or omissions which interfere with the sense, these you must impute not to me but to your own servants; they are due to the ignorance or carelessness of the copyists, who write down not what they find but what they take to be the meaning, and do but expose their own mistakes when they try to correct those of others.

Nevertheless, in spite of the very real possibilities for corruption of the text in the course of its transmission, and the actual existence of many differences among the various manuscripts of the NT, the work of the copyists of the NT was, on the whole, done with great care and fidelity. It has, in fact, been seriously estimated that there are substantial variations in hardly more than a thousandth part of the entire text (an estimate by Fenton J. A. Hort [§ 74], quoted with approval by Caspar René Gregory, *Canon and Text of the New Testament* [New York: Charles Scribner's Sons, 1907], p. 528).

2. The Establishment of the Textus Receptus

§ 59. Given many different NT manuscripts with many differences among them, even though they are not large differences, it is obviously desirable to try to discern among the various readings that which is most probably the closest possible to what was written originally and what was intended by the original authors. To do this, one naturally looks for the earliest available manuscripts (although an early manuscript that was poorly copied, or copied from a poor exemplar, might not be as good as a late manuscript that was carefully copied and from a good exemplar), and one institutes comparisons among the various manuscripts, the latter process being known as collation. How modern study in the area of textual criticism has developed to do these things is a long and complex story, in which a few main points may now be indicated.

§60. The first printed Greek NT was a part of an elaborate five-volume edition of the Bible in Hebrew, Aramaic, Greek, and Latin. This was issued under Cardinal Francisco Ximenez de Cisneros (1436-1517) of Spain, at the university at Alcalá de Henares (near Madrid), which was the old Roman Complutum, hence the work was known as the Complutensian Polyglot. The fifth or NT volume was printed first, with a date of January 10, 1514; the whole was finished in 1517, and was in circulation some years after that, perhaps first about 1522. What manuscripts were used as the basis for the Greek NT is not known, but it is stated in the work that they were *antiquissima et emendatissima,* and that they were supplied by Pope Leo X (1513-1521) from the Apostolic Library at Rome; since he became Pope only the year before the volume was printed it is possible the manuscripts were sent by his predecessor, Pope Julius II (1503-1513) (Vincent pp. 49f.; Hug p. 181). So, although we do not know what the manuscripts were, we recognize the proper concern that they should be the oldest and most free from fault possible.

§61. The second printed Greek NT, and probably the first to be in actual circulation, was prepared by the Dutch scholar Desiderius Erasmus (1466?-1536), and published in Basel, Switzerland, on March 1, 1516 (Souter p. 87). Like the editors of the Complutensian Polyglot, Erasmus also affirmed that he had used the oldest and most correct manuscripts (*vetustissimis simul et emendatissimis,* Nestle, *Introduction,* p. 3 n. 2). Actually what he used were only a half dozen minuscules, chiefly in the University Library at Basel. Of these the earliest was a relatively good manuscript of the twelfth century (Basel, University Library, A.N. IV 2; Gregory No. 1 eap; Tischendorf No. 1; von Soden No. $\delta 254$), which contains the entire NT except for the book of Revelation; but this he thought of little value, since it had many readings different from those in the other manuscripts available to him (Tregelles, p. 28 n.; Vogels, *Handbuch,* p. 65). What he finally put in the hands of the printer, with a few corrections which he introduced from a few other manuscripts, were several less good codices, all probably of the twelfth century, namely, one manuscript for the Gospels (Basel, University Library, A.N. IV, 1; Gregory No. 2 e; Tischendorf No. 2; von Soden No. $\epsilon 1214$); one for the Acts and Catholic Letters (Basel, University Library, A.N. IV, 4; Gregory No. 2 ap; Tischendorf No. 2; von Soden No. a 253); and one for the book of Revelation, which he borrowed from the German humanist Johann Reuchlin (1455-1522), and which was rediscovered by Franz Delitzsch in 1861 in the Öttingen-Wallerstein Library in Schloss Harburg/Donauwörth in Mayhingen, Germany (Library No. I, 1, 40, 1; Gregory No. 1 r; Tischendorf No. 1; von Soden No. Aν^{20}). The last manuscript lacked Rev 22:16-21, so for these verses Erasmus made a retranslation from the Latin text back into Greek, and thus supplied what was missing (Nestle, *Introduction,* p. 4; Vogels, *Handbuch,* p. 65).

§62. In all, the Greek NT of Erasmus went through five editions. In the course thereof, many corrections and changes were made, many of the changes being due to the influence of the Complutensian Polyglot (§60). Of all the items involved, the one that occasioned the most interest and the most controversy was the passage that appears in the KJV as I Jn 5:7-8, the so-called *comma Johanneum,* concerning the three witnesses in heaven. The first certain quotation of the passage is by the Spanish heretic Priscillian (died A.D. 385), who gives it in Latin (*Liber Apologeticus,* ed. Schepps, Vienna Corpus XVIII, 1889, quoted by A. E. Brooke, *Johannine Epistles,* ICC, 1912, p. 158): *Sicut Ioannes ait: Tria sunt quae testimonium dicunt in terra: aqua caro et sanguis; et haec tria in unum sunt. et tria sunt quae testimonium dicunt in caelo: pater, verbum et spiritus; et haec tria unum sunt in Christo Iesu.* After that, from the fifth century and onward, the passage was gradually included in manuscripts of the Latin Vulgate, and from the Latin it passed eventually into some Greek manuscripts. While it was included in the text of the Complutensian Polyglot, Erasmus did not find it in his Greek manuscripts and did not put it in his first editions. He did promise, however, that if a Greek manuscript were produced which contained the words, he would insert them. Such a manuscript was found in what he called Codex Britannicus, which is now known as Codex Montfortianus (Vogels, *Handbuch,* p. 66). It is a copy of the entire NT, written on paper, and now in Trinity College, Dublin (Library No. A 4. 21; Gregory No. 61; Tischendorf No. 34; von Soden δ603). So, although he still did not believe that the passage was original, Erasmus included it in his third edition (1522). The words, as found in the manuscript, were: ὅτι τρεῖς εἰσιν οἱ μαρτυροῦντες ἐν τῷ οὐρανῷ, πατήρ, λόγος, καὶ πνεῦμα· καὶ οὗτοι οἱ τρεῖς ἕν εἰσιν. καὶ τρεῖς εἰσιν μαρτυροῦντες ἐν τῇ γῇ πνεῦμα, ὕδωρ, καὶ αἷμα. To this Erasmus added ἅγιον after πνεῦμα, inserted οἱ before the second μαρτυροῦντες, and καὶ before ὕδωρ, and let stand at the end καὶ οἱ τρεῖς εἰς τὸ ἕν εἰσιν (Tregelles pp. 22, 26 n.). The derivation of the passage from Latin is shown by the lack of the articles (ὁ πατήρ, ὁ λόγος, τὸ πνεῦμα, τὸ ὕδωρ, τὸ αἷμα), and Erasmus did not put these in. They were supplied, however, in the Complutensian Polyglot and in other manuscripts, and so arose substantially the reading that is found in the KJV (cf. below §88): "For there are three that bear record in heaven, the Father, the Word, and the Holy Ghost: and these three are one. And there are three that bear witness in earth, the spirit, and the water, and the blood: and these three agree in one."

§63. In turn, the Greek texts of the Complutensian Polyglot (§60) and of Erasmus (§§61-62) became the basis of a Greek NT published in Paris in 1546 and following by Robert Estienne, known in Latin as Robertus Stephanus and in English as Robert Stephen (also Stephens) (Tregelles pp. 30-33). In the third or folio edition of this work, published in 1550, the text of Erasmus, probably in his fifth edition (1535), was followed almost exclusively; but other readings were placed in the margin from collations of a number of manuscripts made by the editor's son, Henri (Henricus, Henry). In yet a fourth edition, published in Geneva in 1551, two Latin versions, the Vulgate and the version of Erasmus, were placed on either side of the Greek text. Also in this edition, for the first time, the text was divided into numbered verses which are substantially those of modern usage ever since (cf. above §28). For verse differences in various editions, see Ezra Abbot in Gregory, *Prolegomena,* pp. 167-182.

§64. In the next step, the text of Stephen was largely followed in a series of editions of the Greek NT which were published (the first in 1565) by Théodore de Bèze, or Theodore Beza (1519-1605), known in church history as professor, and friend and successor of Calvin (died in 1564), at Geneva. For many years Beza had in his possession two relatively old and important manuscripts, now known as D (Codex Bezae, or Codex Cantabrigiensis) (see below §§160ff.) and D^p (Codex Claromontanus) (described above, §39). The former of the two manuscripts was found, he said, in the monastery of St. Irenaeus at Lyons, and he gave it in 1581 to the University of Cambridge (University Library Ms. Nn. 2.41; Gregory No. 05; von Soden No. δ5); the latter was found, he said, in a monastery at Clermont in Beauvais (85 miles from Lyons), and it came eventually to the Bibliothèque Nationale in Paris (Library No. Gr. 107; Gregory No. 06; von Soden No. α1026). He did not, however, make much use of the two manuscripts, for they had many different readings from the other manuscripts with which he was most familiar. Nevertheless, Beza did exercise some critical judgment with respect to some passages that were absent, or variously rendered, in some manuscripts. With respect to Jn 8:1-12, for example, he wrote (Tregelles p. 34): "As far as I am concerned, I do not conceal that I justly regard as suspected what the ancients with such consent either rejected or did not know of. Also such a variety in the reading causes me to doubt the fidelity of the whole of that narration."

§65. Once again, a text substantially made up from the texts of Stephen (§63) and of Beza (§64) was published by two brothers, Bonaventure and Abraham Elzevir, in Leiden in 1624 (Tregelles pp. 34f.; Vincent pp. 60f.; Nestle, *Introduction,* p. 13). This work went through a number of editions, and was very popular because of its neat printing and small and convenient size. In the preface to the second edition (1633) it was boldly declared that even the most minute mistakes (*vel minutissimae mendae*) had been corrected, and the reader was told: "Therefore thou hast the text now received by all, in which we give nothing altered or corrupted" (*Textum ergo habes nunc ab omnibus receptum, in quo nihil immutatum aut corruptum damus*). From these words came the name, Textus Receptus (abbreviated TR), to mean the commonly accepted text of the Greek NT. More precisely, in England this usually meant the third edition of Stephen (1550), and for this reason the Textus Receptus is also sometimes abbreviated by the Greek letter ς (final Sigma) to stand for the initial of Stephanus; while on the Continent the reference was usually to the second edition of the Elzevirs (1633). At all events, the differences between the two editions were not numerous. From this survey of its history it is evident that the Textus Receptus, in spite of the impressive name it attained, rested actually upon relatively few, relatively late, and relatively poor manuscripts, namely, upon those known to Ximenes, Erasmus, Stephen, and Beza, of which in fact the best (D and D^p [§64]; and Codex 1 [§61]) were the least used. Nevertheless the Textus Receptus was indeed "received," and accepted as the standard for the next two hundred years. In the form in which it was available at the time, it was the NT basis of the King James or Authorized Version in 1611, which was "newly translated out of the originall tongues," as well as of the earlier sixteenth-century English translations (Tyndale 1525, Coverdale 1535, Matthew 1537, Geneva Bible 1560, Bishops' Bible 1568) which, by their specific instructions (Alice Parmelee, *A Guidebook to the Bible* [New York: Harper & Brothers, 1948], pp. 285f.), the new translators "diligently compared and revised." For the agreement of KJV with TR in sixty-four distinctive passages in the Gospel according to John, see Colwell pp. 86f., 100-104.

3. The Development of a Critical Approach

§66. As more, older, and better manuscripts became known than those that were known to Ximenes, Erasmus, Stephen, and Beza (§65), it became possible to recognize that the Textus Receptus was not the best text of the NT, and to endeavor, on the basis of the age and character of the then available manuscripts, to come closer to the original text. For some time the work that was done consisted largely in simply bringing together the variant readings found in the various manuscripts. Ordinarily the Textus Receptus was still printed as if it were the standard text, and the variants were shown in comparison with it, a method that is still, in fact, a useful method in the collation (§59) of manuscripts (Greenlee pp. 135ff.). Thus Brian Walton (1600-1661), later Bishop of Chester, issued the London Polyglot (Syriac, Ethiopic, Arabic, Persian, Greek, and Latin) in 1657, and in the fifth volume, containing the NT, printed the Greek text of Stephen's third edition (1550), with the readings of Codex Alexandrinus in the lower margin. The latter manuscript (cf. below §§173f.), which had been given to King Charles I in 1628 by Cyril Lucar, patriarch of Constantinople and previously patriarch of Alexandria (FLAP p. 438), was here for the first time designated by the capital letter A (= London, British Museum, Royal 1 D VIII; Gregory No. 02; von Soden No. δ4), thus originating the practice of indicating the uncials by such capitals (cf. above §49). In a sixth volume of critical apparatus, Walton gave readings from a number of other manuscripts, including Codex Bezae (D), Codex Claromontanus (D^p), and the famous but not old Codex Montfortianus (Gregory No. 61; cf. above §62) (Gregory, *Prolegomena,* pp. 220f.; Vincent pp. 64f.).

§67. Likewise the Greek NT of John Mill (1645-1707), a fellow of Queen's College, Oxford, published in 1707 after thirty years of work and only two weeks before Mill's own death, printed the text of Stephen's third edition of 1550 (of which it became, in England, essentially the standard edition), together with a very large collection of variant readings from Greek manuscripts (including Codices Alexandrinus [A], Bezae [D], Claromontanus [D^p], Laudianus [E^a, a sixth-century bilingual manuscript of Acts, Latin on the left-hand page, Greek on the right-hand page, given by William Laud, Archbishop of Canterbury and Chancellor of Oxford, to Oxford in 1636, Bodleian Library, Laud. 35; Gregory No. 08; von Soden No. a1001]), and also from versions (including Codex Huntington 17, a Bohairic copy of the Gospels from the year 1174, in the Bodleian Library at Oxford) and from church fathers, Mill being the first to work systematically with sources in the last two categories. He was also the first to state the number of various readings that he found in the NT text, a figure he put at 30,000 (Tregelles pp. 35, 41-45; Gregory, *Prolegomena,* pp. 224-228; Vincent pp. 67f.; Vogels, *Handbuch,* pp. 2, 41, 128).

§68.   By this time there were those who held that, if there were this many variants, the text of the NT was altogether uncertain, and others who were more inclined than ever to simply defend the Textus Receptus and to resist any critical tampering with it. Both positions were ably controverted, and significant new proposals were made, by Richard Bentley (1662-1742), Master of Trinity College, Cambridge. In reply to *A Discourse of Freethinking* published in London in 1713 by the English deist Anthony Collins (1676-1729), which attacked the authority of the Scriptures because of the existence of so many textual variants, Bentley assumed the role of an imaginary professor in Leipzig, and wrote under the name of Phileleutherus Lipsiensis (Tregelles pp. 49-57). It was a great benefit, he argued, that there were so many manuscripts of the NT, some obtained from Egypt, some from Asia, and others found in the West. The distances of the places and the numbers of the books show that they could not have been fabricated by collusion. That there are differences in different copies lies in the nature of things. Compared with 30,000 variants in the NT text (§67), he was sure there were 20,000 different readings in the manuscripts of a single Latin author, namely, Terence, of whose works he had himself made a critical edition. "If half the number of manuscripts were collated for Terence with that niceness and minuteness which has been used in twice as many for the New Testament," he said, "the number of the variations would amount to above 50,000." Precisely, "where the copies of any author are numerous, though the various readings always increase in proportion, there the text, by an accurate collation of them made by skillful and judicious hands, is ever the more correct, and comes nearer to the true words of the author." As to the currently accepted texts, "I find," he wrote, "that by taking two thousand errors out of the Pope's Vulgate [by which he meant the Clementine-Sixtine edition issued in 1592 by Clement VIII, cf. FHRJ p. 32], and as many out of the Protestant Pope Stephen's [by which he meant the 1550 text of Stephanus, cf. §63], I can set out an edition of each in columns, without using any book under nine hundred years old, that shall so exactly agree word for word, and, what at first amazed me, order for order, that no two tallies nor two indentures, can agree better." It is evident that he thought the Textus Receptus should be replaced by a critically edited text, based directly upon the oldest manuscripts and the best readings. In 1720 he issued *Proposals for Printing* such a text in both Greek and Latin, and accompanied this with the last chapter of the book of Revelation as a specimen of what he intended. Like Brian Walton (§66), Bentley also designated the major manuscripts by letters, A, B, C, etc. (Tregelles p. 64). He even obtained for his intended edition a collation of Codex Vaticanus (Tregelles p. 65). But, in spite of his significant proposals and extended labors, Bentley did not actually complete a new edition of the NT text such as he envisioned. The Textus Receptus had been in the position of authority for a century (§65), and it would remain dominant for yet another hundred years (§72).

§69. In the meantime, more precise attention was given to the questions of how to assess the many variant readings, and how to evaluate the many manuscripts from which they were gathered. With respect to these questions Johann Albrecht Bengel (1687-1752) made important suggestions. Bengel was a student at Tübingen, a teacher at Denkendorf, and eventually Superintendent of the Evangelical Lutheran Church of Württemberg (Tregelles pp. 69-71; Vincent pp. 87-90; Nestle, *Introduction,* pp. 16-17). In 1725 he published at Denkendorf a *Prodromus Novi Testamenti Graeci recte cauteque adornandi,* or Forerunner to a proposed Greek NT; and in 1734 he published the Greek NT itself at Tübingen. With respect to the assessment of variant readings, he set forth the canon, *proclivi scriptioni praestat ardua,* "the difficult is to be preferred to the easy reading," a rule for choice still recognized as usually sound, and now often stated in the shorter form, *lectio difficilior placet.* With respect to the evaluation of the manuscripts, he recognized that they were not just to be counted but classified, and he distinguished for the first time two large groups or families of manuscripts. These were the Asiatic manuscripts, which came mostly from Constantinople, were more numerous, and inferior; and the African manuscripts, which were fewer, but older and more valuable. The African manuscripts were themselves put in two subdivisions, one represented by Codex Alexandrinus (A), the other by the Old Latin version. Although Bengel's theory of families was attacked by his contemporary, J. J. Wettstein (Vincent pp. 90f.; for Wettstein, cf. above §49), it was due to have much influence in the future.

§70. The theory of groups of manuscripts was next carried further by Johann Salomo Semler (1725-1791), Professor of Theology at Halle, and by Johann Jakob Griesbach (1745-1812), Semler's pupil at Halle and later himself Professor of New Testament at Jena. Semler (Vincent pp. 92-93) used the term "recension" (Latin *recensio*), which properly means a revising of a text by an editor, in a loose sense as equivalent to a "family" of manuscripts, and classified the manuscripts in three recensions, Alexandrian (used by Egyptian writers), Oriental (used at Antioch and Constantinople), and Western (found in the Latin versions); but he did not himself publish a Greek NT. Griesbach (Vincent pp. 99-104) also distinguished three groups of manuscripts, namely, Western (early, but full of errors of copyists), Alexandrian (an attempt to revise the Western text), and Constantinopolitan or Byzantine (including the great majority of manuscripts). He also stated no less than fifteen critical canons, including these: (1) no reading can be considered preferable unless supported by at least some ancient witnesses; (2) all criticism must depend upon study of recensions or classes of documents, not just of individual manuscripts; (3) the shorter reading is to be preferred to the longer; and, as Bengel had already suggested (§69), (4) the more difficult reading is to be preferred to the easier. On the basis of these theories, Griesbach published several editions of a Greek NT between 1774 and 1806, in which the text was at least at many places different from the Textus Receptus.

§71. Although he did not himself publish a Greek NT, Johann Leonhard Hug (1765-1846), a Roman Catholic Professor of New Testament at Freiburg, suggested in his *Einleitung in die Schriften des Neuen Testaments* (Stuttgart and Tübingen, 2 vols., 1808) a new system of recensions (§70) (Vincent pp. 105f.; Tregelles pp. 90f.). According to his reconstruction of the situation, the text of the NT underwent alterations of all sorts up until about the middle of the third century. The unrevised text which existed at that time is to be seen in Codex Bezae (D) and other related sources. It may be called the κοινὴ ἔκδοσις, *vulgata editio*, or "common edition." Then several scholars of the ancient church, in different places, undertook to correct and revise this text. One revision was made by Origen in Palestine and was accepted by Jerome; one was made by Hesychius, an Egyptian bishop, and was adopted as the text of the NT in Egypt; and one was made by Lucian, a presbyter of Antioch, and was accepted in Asia, although Jerome condemned both of the latter two (cf. FHRJ p. 19). These recensions, concluded Hug, are at the basis of the older manuscripts that have come down to us. Of the older manuscripts, he was able to see Codex Vaticanus (of which Bentley had obtained a collation [§68] when it was in Paris from 1809 to 1815 (cf. FLAP p. 433, and see below §140) and, in a work entitled *De antiquitate codicis Vaticani commentatio* (1810), he correctly assessed its age (middle of the fourth century) and recognized its importance (Gregory, *Prolegomena*, p. 362).

§72. Finally, instead of printing the Textus Receptus any longer, either entirely or mainly, the decisive step was taken of printing a text that was based directly upon what were judged to be the oldest and best available manuscripts and upon the readings that, by critical canons, were deemed the most nearly original. Such a critical text had been in effect proposed by the classical scholar, Richard Bentley, a century before (§68), and was now actually set forth, with acknowledgment to Bentley, by another classical scholar, namely, Karl Lachmann (1793-1851), Professor of Classical Philology in Berlin

(Vincent pp. 110-114). In a Greek NT first published at Berlin in 1831 (larger edition, Vol. I 1842, Vol. II 1850), Lachmann based the text on the few early uncials available to him, and disregarded the late minuscules and the Textus Receptus altogether. Therewith he expressed only the modest hope of being able to present the oldest attainable text, i.e., the text that was in use in the fourth century when the oldest uncials were copied.

4. Modern Critical Editions

§73.   The work of Constantine Tischendorf (1815-1874), Professor of New Testament at Leipzig, has already been referred to (§50), with particular reference to his discovery of Codex Sinaiticus (ℵ) and his publication of critical editions of the Greek NT, climaxing with the eighth major critical edition in 1869-1872. Altogether his labors (Vincent pp. 117-129) as discoverer, collator, editor, and writer (Gregory, *Prolegomena,* pp. 7-22) were enormous. It was his purpose to become acquainted with all the known uncial manuscripts by personal examination, and he is credited with also discovering for the first time 18 uncials and 6 minuscules, and with editing for the first time 25 uncials and making new editions of 11 others (Kenyon p. 72). The manuscripts he edited included not only his own Codex Sinaiticus (1862), but also Codex Vaticanus. Of the latter there had been a collation made for Bentley (§68), a study of its antiquity by Hug (§71), and two poor editions by Cardinal Angelo Mai in 1857 and 1859; but Tischendorf for the first time, and under difficulties, brought out in 1867 a superior edition. Thus the one man for the first time made available to the scholarly world the two most valuable copies of the Bible in existence. In his own critical editions of the Greek NT, Tischendorf published the best text to which his investigations led, and accompanied it with a full textual apparatus. As to ancient recensions, he believed that revisions were made by Hesychius and Lucian, but that a revision by Origen was only an imagination of Hug (cf. §71). The importance of any manuscript, he held, was to be assessed from its age and the character of its text, rather than from the class or group to which it belonged. His canons of criticism (Tregelles pp. 119-121) may be summarized in these statements: (1) the text is to be sought from the most ancient evidence, meaning especially the oldest Greek manuscripts; (2) a reading peculiar to a single document is to be considered suspect; (3) an obvious scribal error is to be rejected even though well supported in the manuscripts; (4) in parallel passages the tendency of copyists would be to make the readings agree, and therefore, in such passages, testimonies are to be preferred which are not in precise accordance; (5) that reading is to be preferred which could have given occasion to the others, or which appears to comprise the elements of the others; and (6) that reading is to be preferred which accords with NT Greek or with the style of the individual writer. In all, he was persuaded of the great importance of Codex Sinaiticus, and the readings of this manuscript tend to predominate in his final text, so that, as compared with his preceding seventh edition (*editio septima critica maior*), his eighth edition (*editio octava critica maior*), issued in 1869-1872 after the publication in 1862 of Codex Sinaiticus, contained, it has been estimated, some 3500 changes in the text. Particularly important was the massive critical apparatus Tischendorf brought together, to present compactly a very large number of variant readings from the manuscripts, the versions, and the church fathers.

§ 74. The next modern critical edition of the Greek NT to attain very wide recognition was that of Brooke Foss Westcott (1825-1901) and Fenton John Anthony Hort (1828-1892), both Professors of Divinity at Cambridge (Vincent pp. 145-155; Kenyon pp. 82-84). This was entitled *The New Testament in the Original Greek,* and was published at Cambridge and London in two volumes in 1881, after nearly thirty years of labor. The first volume contained the Greek text, the second the statement of the principles followed by the editors. While the second volume also contained notes on certain readings, Westcott and Hort did not supply a critical apparatus but used the vast collections of such materials already available, notably in Tischendorf. Unlike Tischendorf, however, they placed heavy emphasis upon the attempt to recognize text types in groups of manuscripts, and in this they followed such predecessors as Griesbach (§ 70). This procedure they called the genealogical method, and wrote of it as follows (Introduction and Appendix [= Vol. II], p. 57): "The proper method of Genealogy consists . . . in the more or less complete recovery of the texts of successive ancestors by analysis and comparison of the varying texts of their respective descendants, each ancestral text so recovered being in its turn used, in conjunction with other similar texts, for the recovery of the text of a yet earlier common ancestor."

§ 75. The text types recognized by Westcott and Hort were four in number: (1) The oldest they called the Neutral text, i.e., the one most free from later corruption and mixture. It was to be found above all in Codex Vaticanus (B), and also to a large extent in Codex Sinaiticus (א). Where B and א agree we have the strongest evidence for the earliest accessible form of the text, and are not far from the original itself. (2) The Alexandrian text is also early, and represents careful work at such a literary center as Alexandria. It is found in Codex Ephraemi (C), in the Coptic versions, especially the Bohairic, and in the Alexandrian church fathers, Clement and Origen and others. (3) The Western type of text is found in manuscripts that belong in the West geographically, namely, Codex Bezae (D) and Codex Claromontanus (D^p), which are bilingual (Greek and Latin), and Old Latin versions, but also in manuscripts belonging in the East geographically, notably the Old Syriac (Curetonian) version. This text is characterized by much paraphrase and interpolation. If in some cases the Neutral text includes some material not in the normally all-inclusive Western text, that material may be suspected of being an interpolation in the Neutral text, and it may be called (perhaps confusingly) a Western noninterpolation. (4) The Syrian text probably originated in a revision made in the neighborhood of Antioch of Syria about the end of the fourth century, and is found in Codex Alexandrinus (A) in the Gospels and in later uncials, in the later Syriac (Peshitta), in most of the minuscules, and in Chrysostom (Bishop of Antioch in Syria until 398) and in many of the later church fathers (by contrast, it cannot be traced in the ante-Nicene fathers). Finally, in its latest form, this is the Textus Receptus. On the whole it is a text that tries to combine and harmonize the readings of the other text types. "The qualities which the authors of the Syrian text seem to have most desired to impress on it are lucidity and completeness. They were evidently anxious to remove all stumbling-blocks out of the way of the ordinary reader, so far as this could be done without recourse to violent measures. They were apparently equally desirous that he should have the benefit of instructive matter contained in all the existing texts, provided it did not confuse the context or introduce seeming contradictions. New omissions accordingly are rare, and where they occur are usually found to contribute to apparent simplicity. New interpolations on the other hand are abundant, most of them being due to harmonistic or other assimilation, fortunately capricious and incomplete. Both in matter and in diction the Syrian text is conspicuously a full text. It delights in pronouns, conjunctions, and expletives and supplied links of all kinds, as well as in more considerable additions. As distinguished from the bold vigor of the 'Western' scribes, and the refined scholarship of the Alexandrians, the spirit of its own corrections is at once sensible and feeble. Entirely blameless on either literary or religious grounds as regards vulgarised or unworthy diction, yet showing no marks of either critical or spiritual insight, it presents the New Testament in a form smooth and attractive, but appreciably impoverished in sense and force, more fitted for cursory perusal or recitation than for repeated and diligent study" (*Introduction and Appendix,* pp. 134f.).

§ 76. From this analysis, it is evident that the critical text of Westcott and Hort will largely agree with Codex Vaticanus, and this is in fact the case. From it they depart only in a few special instances, notably in "Western noninterpolations" (§75), and in obvious scribal errors. Now it so happened that at the same time Westcott and Hort were working on their Greek text they were also serving as members of the committee appointed by the Convocation of Canterbury in 1870 to make a revised edition of the previously Authorized or King James Version of the English Bible. With respect to the Greek text to be translated, the revision committee said: "A revision of the Greek text was the necessary foundation of our work, but it did not fall within our province to construct a continuous and complete Greek text. In many cases the English rendering was considered to represent correctly either of two competing readings in the Greek, and then the question of the text was usually not raised." In fact, the revisers may be said to have, for all practical purposes, followed the text of Westcott and Hort closely, although not completely. An analysis of their text shows that where Codex Vaticanus

(B) stood alone they did not usually follow it; where Codex Vaticanus and Codex Sinaiticus (ℵ) stood together but were otherwise alone they followed the two in over half of the cases in question; where the same two manuscripts and some other early uncial were in agreement, they usually accepted this combined authority; and where B and ℵ were in agreement with two or more of the other early uncials this combination was almost always accepted as decisive. As compared with the Textus Receptus upon which the King James Version of 1611 was based (§65), therefore, the Greek text underlying the English Revised Version was a very much better critical text, and it has been estimated that it varies from the 1611 text in at least 5788 readings. At the same time, as Frederic Kenyon remarks (Kenyon pp. 84, 86), the editors were "not governed by the instinctive sense of style which was the heritage of King James's translators," and the version "never can be the magnificent monument of English which the Authorised Version is." The English Revised Version of the NT was published in 1881, simultaneously with the publication of the Westcott and Hort Greek text; in a slightly modified form, embodying the varying preferences of the American members of the revision committee, the same translation was published in the United States in 1901, where it has generally been known as the American Standard Version (ASV).

§77. Bernhard Weiss (1827-1918), Professor of New Testament Exegesis at Kiel and (beginning in 1877) at Berlin, published a Greek NT in three volumes at Leipzig in 1894-1900, with a second small edition in 1902-1905 (C. R. Gregory in AJT 1 [1897], pp. 28-36; K. Lake in AJT 7 [1903], pp. 249f.). As a scholar long concerned with NT exegesis, he said that he had been constantly troubled in his work by the uncertainty of the text; even with regard to Tischendorf he remarked that the collations needed to be verified anew. His own method, however, was not to undertake a large new work of collation, but rather to utilize the variations collected by others and in each important case to try to determine which reading had the greater intrinsic likelihood of being the correct reading. The kinds of errors he noted were grouped under the headings of (1) harmonization among the Gospels, (2) interchange of words, (3) omissions and additions, (4) alterations of order, and (5) orthographical variations. As a result of this kind of investigation, it was his conclusion that no manuscript is free from error, but that of them all Codex Vaticanus (B) is the best. In one set of statistics he judged that Codex Alexandrinus (A) was only once alone in having the right reading, Codex Sinaiticus (ℵ) was three times alone, and Codex Vaticanus was eighty-five times alone in having the right reading. In the final result, therefore, the text printed by Weiss depended heavily upon Codex Vaticanus.

§78. With a number of critical editions of the Greek NT in hand, it became of interest to compare the results of the several editors, and even to prepare a text that would exhibit such consensus as was found in them. This was done in England by Richard Francis Weymouth (1822-1902), a Baptist layman and headmaster of a school for boys in London, also the author of the translation called *The New Testament in Modern Speech,* published posthumously in 1903. His Greek text was called *The Resultant Greek Testament,* and was published in London in the first edition in 1886, in a "cheap edition" in 1892, and in a third edition in 1905 after his own death. In this he took primary account of ten editions, namely, those of (1) Lachmann, the larger edition of 1842-1850 (cf. above §72); (2) Samuel Prideaux Tregelles (1813-1875), a text following critical principles similar to those of Lachmann, published in London in 1857-1872; (3) Tischendorf, the major eighth edition, 1869-1872 (§73); (4) Henry Alford (1810-1871), the latest editions, 1871-1877; (5) the Bâle edition, edited in 1880 for the Bible Society of Bâle by Dr. Stockmeyer and Professor Riggenbach, and much under the influence of Tischendorf; (6) Westcott and Hort, 1881 (§§74-76); (7) the readings, as far as they could be ascertained, of the committee for the English Revised Version of 1881 (§76); (8) Joseph B. Lightfoot (1828-1889), editions of several of the Pauline Letters, 1865-1875; (9) Charles J. Ellicott (1819-1905), editions of several of the Pauline letters, 1867-1880; (10) Bernhard Weiss (§77), edition of the Gospel according to Matthew, 1876. Roughly speaking, Weymouth explained, his "resultant text" represented that in which the majority of these ten editors agreed. Along with the main text, so constructed, he showed in the margin the variants of the different editors and, for comparison, all the readings of the third edition of Robert Stephen in 1550 (§63) and variations in the second Elzevir edition of 1633 (§65), and some readings in the Complutensian Polyglot printed in 1514 (§60), and in the text published by Erasmus in 1516 (§61).

§79. In Germany, in turn, Eberhard Nestle (1851-1913), Professor in Tübingen and in Ulm, published at the Württembergische Bibelanstalt in Stuttgart in 1898 a Greek New Testament which was based upon a comparison of just three editions, namely, those of Tischendorf in his eighth major critical edition of 1869-1872 (§73), of Westcott and Hort in 1881 (§74), and of Weymouth in 1886 and 1892 (§78). At the foot of the page were shown also the readings placed by Westcott and Hort in their *Appendix,* and a number of other readings from various manuscripts, particularly readings in the Gospels and Acts from Codex Bezae (D) (Nestle, *Introduction,* pp. 23f.). From his third edition, published in 1901, onwards, however, Nestle used the text of Bernhard Weiss, which had been finished in the meantime (1894-1900) (§77), instead of Weymouth. Where at least two of these three editions agree, this reading is printed, and thus the text is constituted out of the majority or the consensus of HTW—to use the abbreviations by which Westcott and Hort, Tischendorf, and Weiss are referred to in the Nestle volume. Since Westcott and Hort gave preference to Codex Vaticanus (B), Tischendorf to Codex Sinaiticus (ℵ), and Weiss to Codex Vaticanus, the Nestle text tended to represent Codex Vaticanus and especially the concurrence of that manuscript and Codex Sinaiticus. With full awareness of this situation, the accompanying critical apparatus gave, in successive editions of the text, an ever increasing number of variant readings from the other manuscripts, and also even noted certain conjectures that were proposed for changing the text. After the death of Eberhard Nestle in 1913, the work was continued by his son, Erwin Nestle (born in 1883), an Instructor in Religion in Ulm; and he was joined in turn in 1952 by Kurt Aland, Director of the Institut für neutestamentliche Textforschung an der Westfälischen Wilhelms-Universität Münster/Westfalen. In particular the 13th edition by Erwin Nestle in 1927 represented a complete reworking of the materials; and in his 17th edition in 1941, and afterwards, a small number of variants have been placed in the text itself, even though they do not have the majority of HTW in their support (Metzger p. 144 n. 1). In 1963 the text was in its 25th edition, by Erwin Nestle and Kurt Aland; in 1969 the 26th edition was under preparation. Commonly known as "Nestle," or now as "Nestle-Aland," the work can be said to have provided the Textus Receptus of modern scholarship (Kurt Aland, "Studien zur Überlieferung des Neuen Testaments und Seines Textes," in ANT 2 [1967], pp. 58f.). In 1946 the Revised Standard Version of the New Testament was published as an authorized revision of the American Standard Version of 1901 (§76), which was a revision of the King James Version of 1611 (§65). For the new version no single printed edition of the Greek NT was adhered to, but the readings adopted are usually to be found in Westcott and Hort (cf. Colwell p. 85), or in the text or margin of the 17th edition of Nestle in 1941 (Luther A. Weigle in CHB p. 378). The New American Standard Bible—New Testament (abbreviated (NASB), published in 1960 (4th ed. 1963), was also based upon the American Standard Version but was a new translation, and in most instances the Greek text followed was that of the 23d edition of Nestle in 1957 (see the Preface to the NASB).

§80. Another new translation is that of The New English Bible—New Testament, which was published in 1961 by Oxford University Press and Cambridge University Press, on the 350th anniversary of the publication of the Authorized or King James Version in 1611. Again the translators did not follow any single previously printed Greek text, but made their own selection of preferred readings as they proceeded with the translation. Afterward, however, the text that was in fact translated was edited by R. V. G. Tasker and published by the Oxford and Cambridge University Presses in 1964. In the Introduction (pp. vii-ix) to this edition of the Greek text, it is stated that today, in view of the many manuscript discoveries that have been made, and the "mixed" character of many of the texts, no single witness or group of witnesses can be regarded as always reliable. Therefore, it is explained, the translators usually started with Nestle's text, and they gave some consideration to the antiquity and the geographical nature of the manuscript evidence; but they tried chiefly to judge each reading on its own intrinsic merits, by asking such questions as: "Which variant (or variants) is most likely to be due to the intentional or unintentional alteration of a scribe?" "Which variant would seem to be what the original author is most likely to have written?" "Which reading best accounts for the rise of the variants?" "Which is most likely to have suffered change at the hands of early copyists?" "And which seems most in keeping with the author's style and thought, and makes best sense in the context?" The total text which emerged as a result of this procedure, and which Tasker printed as the text translated in the NEB, is therefore an "eclectic" text, i.e., one "chosen out" of a variety of sources.

§81. In 1966 there was published simultaneously in New York by the American Bible Society, in London by the British and Foreign Bible Society, in Edinburgh by the National Bible Society of Scotland, in Amsterdam by the Netherlands Bible Society, and in Stuttgart by the Württemberg Bible Society, *The Greek New Testament,* edited by Kurt Aland, Matthew Black, Bruce M. Metzger, and Allen Wikgren (cf. G. D. Kilpatrick in JBL 85 [1966], pp. 479-481). This edition is specially intended as a basis for the work of Bible translators throughout the world, and the variant readings shown in the critical apparatus are chiefly those where the translation will be affected by the reading chosen. The number of variants is accordingly less than in Nestle, for example, but the evidence cited for the selected variants is very full. In addition the degree of certainty felt by the editors in placing a given reading in the text is indicated by letters: A means that the text is virtually certain, B that there is some degree of doubt, C that there is considerable degree of doubt, and D that there is a very high degree of doubt. A companion volume is to be published to explain the reasons for the decisions.[1] Because punctuation, largely lacking in ancient manuscripts (§24), also affects meaning and translation, an additional apparatus provides in some six hundred instances a survey of the punctuation adopted in fifteen modern editions and translations, five Greek, six English, two German, and two French (Moulton p. 52). In preparing this edition, the committee used the Westcott and Hort text as a basis, compared the text and apparatus in Nestle and several other editions, gathered fresh data of its own, and finally established the text on the basis of its own judgment of the several readings, thus the text is again "eclectic" (cf. §80). In 1966 a translation of this Greek text was also published by the American Bible Society, under the title *Good News for Modern Man, the New Testament in Today's English Version* (abbreviated TEV). A second edition of the Greek text of the Bible Societies is in preparation.[1] As both the Nestle-Aland text (§79) and the Bible Societies text go through successive editions it is expected that they will ultimately set forth the same text. Beyond this, in order to take yet more comprehensive account of all the textual materials that have become available since Tischendorf's last major critical apparatus (*editio octava critica maior*) in 1869 (§50), there are presently under way two large-scale long-range undertakings which aim to assemble a new critical apparatus of the Greek New Testament. The International Greek New Testament Project was

[1]The second edition of *The Greek New Testament* was published in 1968, and the third is expected. The companion volume, intended for use with the third edition but usable with the second, is *A Textual Commentary on the Greek New Testament,* by Bruce M. Metzger, published by the United Bible Societies in 1971.

launched in 1948 by British and American scholars, with Ernest C. Colwell as chairman. The intention was to proceed along the lines of work already begun by S. C. E. Legg, who published critical editions of the Gospel according to Mark in 1935, and of Matthew in 1940; and the first objective is the publication of a critical apparatus of the Gospel according to Luke. The readings are to be included of all available Lukan papyri (7) and uncials (57), of a selected number of manuscripts out of the 1348 Lukan minuscules, of 50 of the lectionary manuscripts, and of the main versions and church fathers (JBL 87 [1968], pp. 187-197; NTS 16 [1970], pp. 180-182). Likewise, in recognition of the fact that in Tischendorf's apparatus the papyri (except for the seventh-century $\mathfrak{P}^{11}$), 80 percent of the uncials, 95 percent of the minuscules, 99 percent of the lectionaries, and some of the versions, known today, were unused, and the church fathers were not yet available in modern critical editions (GCS, etc., cf. below §193), the making of a new Novi Testamenti Graeci Editio Maior was planned on the Continent of Europe in 1967 and 1968, and is now being carried forward by the Institut für Neutestamentliche Textforschung in Münster/Westfalen, the Vetus Latina Institut in Beuron, the Centre d'Analyse et de Documentation Patristiques in Strasbourg, the Institut orientaliste in Louvain, the Orientalisches Seminar of the University of Frankfurt am Main, the Pontificio Istituto Biblico in Rome, the École Biblique et Archéologique Française in Jerusalem, and the Rechenzentrum of the University of Tübingen. Here the 25th edition (1963, cf. §79) of Nestle-Aland provides the provisional basis, and the first objective is an edition of the Catholic Letters. The existence of three text forms—the Koine, the D-text (now sometimes considered a better designation than the looser term, Western), and the Egyptian (cf. §§84-86)—is recognized, and the early text back of them all is sought. All papyri and all uncials will be fully collated; important minuscules will be selected for inclusion on the basis of checking 1000 text passages; and lectionaries, versions, and church fathers will be included. The final edition will give the critically established text, a scheme showing the variants in plain relation to the text, and a full critical apparatus. The critical text, edited by Kurt Aland, should represent the form of the text with which, according to the best of present knowledge, the NT documents began their literary existence (NTS 16 [1970], pp. 163-177).

5. The Recognition of Text Types and the Evaluation of Textual Variants

§82. The foregoing survey makes it plain that the work of textual criticism with respect to the text of the NT is unending. It is also evident that two main approaches have been developed, one the attempt to recognize groups of witnesses and to establish the types of text they represent, the other the endeavor to assess each individual reading and to understand its place in the textual tradition.

Proceeding along lines pioneered by Bengel and others (§§69ff.), several notable suggestions have been made as to groups of manuscripts. Mention has already been made (§55) of the work of Hermann Freiherr von Soden, with particular respect to his entire new listing of the manuscripts. Along therewith he undertook also a new classification of text types (Souter pp. 120-124). In brief these were: (1) Koine, identified with the Greek letter Kappa for Κοινή, corresponding to the Syrian of Westcott and Hort (§75), and otherwise known as Byzantine; (2) Hesychian, abbreviated by the Greek letter Eta for Ἡσύχιος, since the recension is traced to Bishop Hesychius of Egypt (cf. §§71, 73), represented by B, א, the Coptic versions, etc., and corresponding to the Neutral and the Alexandrian text types of Westcott and Hort; (3) Jerusalem, indicated with the Greek letter Iota for Ἱεροσόλυμα, represented in D, etc., and corresponding roughly with the Western text of Westcott and Hort. Following in general the principle that the agreement of any two of the three groups pointed to the best reading, von Soden constructed the text that is found in Part II (*Text mit Apparat*, 1913) of his *Die Schriften des Neuen Testaments*. Of the entire enormous undertaking, Francis Crawford Burkitt wrote (in EB 3, p. 519): "This was an ambitious attempt to supersede Tischendorf in giving a complete conspectus of variants, including the newest discoveries, together with a new textual theory which necessitated a totally new notation for the documents. The new notation is almost incomprehensible in actual use, except to specialists, the textual theory has not commended itself to scholars, either in Germany or elsewhere, and there are grave inaccuracies in certain parts of the work. . . , which destroy confidence in statements about readings which otherwise cannot be controlled. It is therefore a work for specialists alone."

§83. Although he did not publish a critical Greek text, in his book on *The Four Gospels, A Study of Origins* (New York and London: Macmillan and Co., 1924, 4th impression revised, 1930) (cf. Taylor pp. 57-75), Burnett Hillman Streeter (1874-1934), Fellow in Queen's College, Oxford, pushed the idea of groups of manuscripts in the direction of the recognition of more local texts. It was his theory that certain groups of manuscripts could be recognized as representing the texts prevalent in different centers of the church. In brief, these texts are those of: (1) Alexandria, probably due to a revision by the Egyptian bishop Hesychius (d. 307) (cf. §§71, 73, 82), found in B, א, and their allies, equivalent to the Neutral and Alexandrian Texts of Westcott and Hort (§75); (2) Antioch, found in the Old Syriac; (3) Caesarea, found in what he identified as Family Theta (which includes the Koridethi codex [Θ] and the groups of minuscules known as fam. 1 and fam. 13 [cf. below §92]), and in Origen after he came to Caesarea in 231/232 (cf. §192); (4) Italy and Gaul, found in D and its allies; (5) Carthage, found in some Old Latin manuscripts; these last two texts (4 and 5) corresponding to the Western text of Westcott and Hort; and (6) Byzantium, probably produced by Lucian of Antioch (d. 312), found in A in the Gospels and in the mass of later uncials and minuscules, corresponding to the Syrian of Westcott and Hort, and finally to the Textus Receptus. Reversing the sequence, and simplifying the statement, there is a

Byzantine text, a Western text divided into two sub-families, an Eastern text divided into two sub-families, and an Alexandrian text. Of them all, the Alexandrian text, found in Codex Vaticanus and Codex Sinaiticus, is the best.

§84. While the work of Streeter (§83) was directed toward the Gospels and dealt with a supposed half-dozen local text types, some of relatively small compass, the investigation in this field by Hans Lietzmann (1875-1942), Professor of Church History at the University of Berlin, was directed toward the Pauline Letters and dealt with three major bodies of manuscripts, a large grouping now widely recognized and applicable, with modifications at particular points, to the whole NT. The *Einführung in die Textgeschichte der Paulusbriefe* by Lietzmann was published in conjunction with his *An die Römer* in his *Handbuch zum Neuen Testament* (abbreviated HNT) (Tübingen: J. C. B. Mohr [Paul Siebeck]), and accompanied the commentary in successive editions, the 2d in 1919, 3d in 1928, and 4th in 1933. His more detailed study of one individual manuscript of the Pauline Letters, *Zur Würdigung des Chester-Beatty-Papyrus der Paulusbriefe,* was published as a Sonderausgabe aus den Sitzungsberichten der Preussischen Akademie der Wissenschaften, Phil.-Hist. Klasse, 1934, XXV (Berlin: Verlag der Akademie der Wissenschaften). In these works Lietzmann presented this comprehensive view: The early papyri, of which the Chester Beatty Papyrus of the Letters of Paul ($\mathfrak{P}^{46}$), dating around 200, is an important example, show the kind of copies of NT books that were in circulation in the second and third centuries. As relatively early copies, they are free from many of the changes that come into later manuscripts; yet already changes and errors are in them, and no two are exactly alike. The manuscripts that were used by the church fathers of the third century (e.g., Clement of Alexandria [c. 200], and Origen [d. c. 253]), were of this sort. Such manuscripts also provided the basis for the Coptic translations in Egypt, and for Latin translations in the West. In the so-called Western text, this uncontrolled type of text is found at a further stage of development. Then, probably in the fourth century at Alexandria, and perhaps through the Egyptian bishop and martyr, Hesychius, mentioned by Jerome (cf. above §§71, 73, 82), a revision of the text was made. A number of the best papyri were probably brought together, their variations canceled out, and a good average text constructed. This became the official text of the Alexandrian patriarchate. But it was not stereotyped and, in the course of time, further changes were made in it, these changes consisting both in the making of more corrections and in the adding of material from other manuscripts. Thus, in B there are often "Western" readings; in A and C there are already readings that are also found in the Byzantine text. So, a text much like the later revision is found already in many of the early papyri and in the early Egyptian church fathers, Clement of Alexandria and Origen, and the revised text proper is found, with variations, in the four great uncials, B, א or S, A, and C, in the two translations into the most important Coptic dialects, the Sahidic (sa) in Upper Egypt and Bohairic (bo) in the

Delta, and in the later Egyptian church fathers, Athanasius (d. 373), Didymus the Blind (d. 398), and Cyril of Alexandria (d. 444). This is to be called the Egyptian (or Alexandrian) text, and because of its possible connection with Hesychius it may be designated with the sign 𝕳.

§85. The continued development of the uncontrolled text, apart from and without revision such as appears to be represented in the Egyptian text, is that which is represented, according to Lietzmann's view, in the so-called Western text. In Greek, the Western text is found chiefly in manuscripts that also contain the text in Latin, i.e., in bilingual manuscripts, notably in D or Codex Bezae, D^p or Codex Claromontanus, and G or Codex Boernerianus (ninth century). In Latin, it is found in fragments of the Old Latin or Itala translation, in Latin church fathers, including Cyprian, Augustine, Jerome, Ambrose, and Pelagius, and in Jerome's revision of the Old Latin translation known as the Vulgate. Eventually the readings of 𝕳 and of the Western text were brought together in a late and comprehensive form of the text which prevailed in the Byzantine world from Syria to Constantinople. This is the Common, Koine, or Byzantine text, designated by 𝕶. This text is found in three ninth-century uncials, K or Codex Mosquensis, L or Codex Angelicus, and P or Codex Porphyrianus, in the mass of minuscules, in the Peshitta Syriac translation of Bishop Rabbula c. 420, and the Gothic translation of Ulfilas c. 350, and in the church fathers, Chrysostom, Theodoret, Basil of Caesarea in Cappadocia (d. 380), and Ephraem the Syrian (d. 373). Of the three major families, concluded Lietzmann, the Koine is plainly secondary, the Western is old but its evaluation must proceed from inner criteria with respect to individual readings, and the Egyptian is most often basic, but even in its readings must also be judged finally on grounds of inner probability.

§86. The foregoing picture of the Egyptian (or Alexandrian), Western, and Koine (or Byzantine) text types (§§84-85) was wrought out by Lietzmann with respect, in the first instance, to the text of the Pauline Letters. When the entire NT is in view, the entire picture is more complex, yet at least the general conception of the three large groups of manuscripts is still widely held. Also a sharp definition of a so-called Hesychian revision (cf. §§71, 73, 82, 84) may be difficult to maintain, but at least some distinction between early Alexandrian and later Alexandrian manuscripts is recognizable. In what is at least widely accepted today, then, a comprehensive listing of the manuscripts in three major groups or text types appears as follows (the three portions of the table are adapted from Metzger pp. 216, 214, 213, and used by permission of Oxford University Press):

Alexandrian Witnesses

(1) Proto-Alexandrian:
𝔓^45 (in Acts) 𝔓^46 𝔓^66 𝔓^75 ℵ B Sahidic (in part), Clement of Alexandria, Origen (in part), and most of the papyrus fragments with Pauline text.

(2) Later Alexandrian:

C (in part) L T W (in Lk 1:1—8:12 and Jn 5:12—21:25) X (in part) Z Δ (in Mk) Ξ Ψ (in Mk; partially in Lk and Jn) 33 579 892 1241 Bohairic.

Acts: 𝔓⁵⁰ A C (in part) Ψ 33 81 104 326.

Pauline Letters: A C (in part) Hᵖ I Ψ 33 81 104 326 1739.

Catholic Letters: 𝔓²⁰ 𝔓²³ 𝔓⁷² 𝔓⁷⁴ A C (in part) Ψ 33 81 104 326 1739.

Revelation: A C (in part) 1006 1611 1854 2053 2344; less good 𝔓⁴⁷ א.

Western Witnesses

Gospels: D W (in Mk 1:1—5:30 and Jn 1:1—5:11) 0171, the Old Latin; Sinaitic Syriac (syrˢ) and Curetonian Syriac (syrᶜ) (in part), early Latin fathers, Tatian's *Diatessaron*.

Acts: 𝔓²⁰ 𝔓³⁸ 𝔓⁴⁸ D 383 614; Harclean Syriac margin (syrʰ ᵐᵍ), early Latin fathers, the *Commentary* of Ephraem (preserved in Armenian and partially in Syriac).

Pauline Letters: the Greek-Latin bilinguals Dᵖ Eᵖ Fᵖ Gᵖ; Greek fathers to the end of the third century; the Old Latin and early Latin fathers; Syrian fathers to about A.D. 450.

Koine or Byzantine Witnesses

Gospels: A E F G H K P S V W (in Mt and Lk 8:13—24:53) Π Ψ (in Lk and Jn) Ω and most minuscules.

Acts: Hᵃ Lᵃᵖ Pᵃ 049 and most minuscules.

Letters: Lᵃᵖ 049 and most minuscules.

Revelation: 046 051 052 and many minuscules.

§87. The foregoing table (§86) presupposes, of course, that the manuscripts placed in a common group have been compared and shown to be similar to each other in their readings. The process of comparison of one manuscript with another, which is called collation, has already been mentioned (§59), and it has been noted (§66) that, in practice, a manuscript is often collated with the Textus Receptus. Since the Textus Receptus is, in general, the latest form of the Byzantine text, this procedure serves to bring out the non-Byzantine readings in the manuscript being so collated. Again, the collation may be done with respect to a printed text, such as that of Nestle-Aland or the Bible Societies; and in this case the work will serve to make the readings in the manuscript available as additional items in the critical apparatus of that printed text. Or yet again, the manuscript may be collated with another single manuscript of outstanding importance. An example of this procedure may be seen in Sakae Kubo, 𝔓⁷² *and the Codex Vaticanus* (SD 27, Salt Lake City: University of Utah Press, 1965). Here the basic texts of 𝔓⁷² and of Codex Vaticanus were first established by the removal of those readings which are peculiar to the individual scribes of each manuscript, then these basic texts of the two manuscripts were compared with each other.

§88. As has been pointed out by many researchers (see, e.g., §85), even with the recognition of the existence of at least certain broad groups of manuscripts and the placing of an individual manuscript within such a group (§87), it is still finally necessary to judge each reading, where variants are found, on its own merits. The final result of such a process is to produce an "eclectic" or "chosen out" text (cf. §80). Such a text will probably not correspond fully with any single manuscript or group of manuscripts, but it will be the best that can be selected out of the many witnesses. As we have seen (§69), from Bengel onward the attempt has been made to state "canons" or rules by which to make selection among variant readings. A few of the rules that have chiefly commended themselves among the many that have been formulated are (Greenlee pp. 114f.), that that reading is often to be preferred which is (1) the shorter, (2) the harder, (3) the one from which the other readings could most easily have developed, and (4) the one most characteristic of the author of the document. As an example of the rule that a shorter reading is often to be preferred to a longer, the famous *comma Johanneum* (in I Jn 5:7-8, cf. above §62) may be recalled. The shorter reading, found in most of the older manuscripts and followed in the ASV, RSV, and NASB, affirms first (in verse 8) a threefold witness, which satisfies the requirements of the Law (Dt 17:6) and is valid among men, and then goes on (in verse 9) to the "greater" witness of God Himself. This is a logical sequence of thought. The longer reading, which Erasmus was finally persuaded to include in his text, and which is followed in the KJV, puts first (KJV verse 7) a statement about three (Father, Word, and Holy Ghost) that bear record in heaven, then comes to the three that bear witness in earth, and then returns to the witness of God. So the clear and natural sequence of the passage, which was surely original, is confused (A. E. Brooke, *Johannine Epistles,* ICC, p. 154). Yet even this rule, although it may often commend itself, cannot be followed automatically (cf. G. D. Kilpatrick in JBL 85 [1966], p. 480), and each case of variation must still be looked at for itself in the light of every possible kind of criterion. In the present book, in its latter part (§§96ff.), the procedure that is illustrated and implicitly commended is to search for the earliest available manuscript, even fragmentary, to try to understand the text it contains, including whatever may by intrinsic evidence appear already as corruption, and to go on to compare with it as many as possible of the witnesses that come after it, noticing, and trying to understand the reasons for, the further changes that come into view, thus in the end arriving at a hypothetical but not unsupported picture of the evolution of the text from its most nearly original discernible form to its latest existing variation. (See also §§218ff.)

Next (§§89ff.), now, a summary and systematic statement concerning the several categories of manuscripts and other witnesses that are presently available, will be useful.

C

The Witnesses

1. Introduction

§ 89. The following are systematic but concise lists of the NT manuscripts mentioned or discussed in the present book: first the manuscripts on papyrus, then those on parchment (unless otherwise specified), namely, the parchment uncials and the parchment minuscules. More extended but still concise lists may be found in the Introduction to *The Greek New Testament* of the Bible Societies (cf. above § 81), where are also lists of Greek lectionaries, ancient versions, and church fathers. For reference to other and more detailed listings, and for explanation of the manner of designating the manuscripts, see above § § 49-55. In the lists that follow are given for each item the designation (the Gregory-Aland symbol and sometimes the name), the content (cf. above § § 51, 53), the location and library number (if known), and the date according to present judgment (Roman numerals indicate centuries, e.g., III = third century, etc.).

2. Papyri

§ 90. For a longer list than that given here, and for more details concerning the papyri, see Kurt Aland, "Das Neue Testament auf Papyrus," in *Studien zur Überlieferung des Neuen Testaments* (ANT 2, 1967), pp. 91-136, and also Aland, *Kurzgefasste Liste*, pp. 29-33. In the following list the content of the papyri is indicated with these abbreviations: e = Gospels, a = Acts, p = Pauline Letters, c = Catholic Letters, r = Revelation.

Papyri

Symbol	Content	Location/Library No.	Date
$\mathfrak{P}^1$	e	Philadelphia, Univ. Mus. E 2746	III
$\mathfrak{P}^2$	e	Florence, Mus. Arch. Inv. No. 7134	VI
$\mathfrak{P}^3$	e	Vienna, Österr. Nat. Bibl. Pap. G. 2323	VI/VII
$\mathfrak{P}^{11}$	p	Leningrad, Offtl. Bibl. Gr. 258	VII
$\mathfrak{P}^{20}$	c	Princeton, Univ. Lib. Pr. Pap. AM 4117	III
$\mathfrak{P}^{23}$	c	Urbana, Univ. of Ill. Class. Mus. G.P. 1229	early III

Symbol	Content	Location/Library No.	Date
$\mathfrak{P}^{28}$	e	Berkeley, Pacif. Sch. Relig. Pal. Inst. Pap. 2	III
$\mathfrak{P}^{38}$	a	Ann Arbor, Univ. of Mich. Inv. No. 1571	about 300
$\mathfrak{P}^{45}$	ea	Dublin, A. Chester Beatty; and (Mt 25:41–26:39) Vienna, Österr. Nat. Bibl. Pap. G. 31974	III
$\mathfrak{P}^{46}$	p	Dublin, A. Chester Beatty; and Ann Arbor, Univ. of Mich. Inv. No. 6238	about 200
$\mathfrak{P}^{47}$	r	Dublin, A. Chester Beatty	late III
$\mathfrak{P}^{48}$	a	Florence, Bibl. Laurenziana PSI 1165	late III
$\mathfrak{P}^{50}$	a	New Haven, Yale Univ. Lib. P. 1543	IV/V
$\mathfrak{P}^{52}$	e	Manchester, J. Rylands Lib. Gr. P. 457	early II
$\mathfrak{P}^{60}$	e	New York, Pierpont Morgan Lib. P. Colt 4	VII
$\mathfrak{P}^{64}$	e	Oxford, Magdalen Coll. Gr. 18	about 200
$\mathfrak{P}^{66}$	e	Cologny/Geneva, Bibl. Bodmer P. Bodmer II; and (Jn 19:25-28, 31-32) Dublin, A. Chester Beatty	about 200
$\mathfrak{P}^{67}$	e	Barcelona, Fundación San Lucas P. Barc. 1 (belongs to $\mathfrak{P}^{64}$)	about 200
$\mathfrak{P}^{72}$	c	Cologny/Geneva, Bibl. Bodmer P. Bodmer VII, VIII	III/IV
$\mathfrak{P}^{74}$	ac	Cologny/Geneva, Bibl. Bodmer P. Bodmer XVII	VII
$\mathfrak{P}^{75}$	e	Cologny/Geneva, Bibl. Bodmer P. Bodmer XIV, XV	early III
$\mathfrak{P}^{76}$	e	Vienna, Österr. Nat. Bibl. Pap. G. 36102	VI
$\mathfrak{P}^{77}$	e	Oxyrhynchus Pap. 2683	late II
$\mathfrak{P}^{78}$	c	Oxyrhynchus Pap. 2684	III/IV

For $\mathfrak{P}^{79}$, $\mathfrak{P}^{80}$, and $\mathfrak{P}^{81}$ see above §54.

§91

The Witnesses

3. Parchment Uncials

§91. For longer lists than that given here, and for more details concerning the uncials, see Gregory, *Prolegomena*, pp. 345-450; Vogels, *Handbuch*, pp. 36-61; and Aland, *Kurzgefasste Liste*, pp. 37-57. In the following list the content of the uncials is indicated with these abbreviations: e = Gospels, a = Acts and Catholic Letters, p = Pauline Letters, r = Revelation. All are on parchment.

Uncials

Symbol/Name		Content	Location/Library No.	Date
ℵ	01	Sinaiticus	eapr	London, Brit. Mus. Add. 43725	IV
A	02	Alexandrinus	eapr	London, Brit. Mus. Royal I D. VIII	V
B	03	Vaticanus	eap	Rome, Bibl. Vaticana Gr. 1209	IV
C	04	Ephraemi Rescriptus	eapr	Paris, Bibl. Nat. Gr. 9	V (palimpsest)
D	05	Bezae Cantabrigiensis	ea	Cambridge, Univ. Libr. Nn. 2.41	VI
D	06	Claromontanus	p	Paris, Bibl. Nat. Gr. 107	VI

Symbol/Name		Content	Location/Library No.	Date
E	07 Basiliensis	e	Basel, Univ. Bibl. AN III 12	VIII
E	08 Laudianus	a	Oxford, Bodl. Libr. Laud. 35	VI
F	09 Boreelianus	e	Utrecht, Univ. Bibl. Ms. 1	IX
F	010 Augiensis	p	Cambridge, Trinity Coll. B. XVII. 1	IX
G	011 Wolfii A	e	London, Brit. Mus. Harley 5684; and (1 fol.) Cambridge, Trinity Coll. B. XVII. 20	IX
G	012 Boernerianus	p	Dresden, Sächs. Landesbibl. A 145b	IX
H	013 Wolfii B	e	Hamburg, Univ. Bibl. Cod. 91; and (1 fol.) Cambridge, Trinity Coll. B. XVII. 20, 21	IX
H	014 Mutinensis	a	Modena, Bibl. Estens. G. 196	IX
H	015 Coislinianus, Euthalianus	p	Athos, Laura; Kiev, Nat. Bibl. Petrov 26; Leningrad, Öfftl. Bibl. Gr. 14; Moscow, Hist. Mus. 563, Lenin Bibl. Gr. 166, 1; Paris, Bibl. Nat. Suppl. Gr. 1074, Coislin 202; Turin, Bibl. Naz. A. 1.	VI
I	016 Washingto-nensis	p	Washington, Freer Gall. 06.275	V
K	017 Cyprius	e	Paris, Bibl. Nat. Gr. 63	IX
K	018 Mosquensis	ap	Moscow, Hist. Mus. V. 93	IX
L	019 Regius	e	Paris, Bibl. Nat. Gr. 62	VIII
L	020 Angelicus	ap	Rome, Bibl. Angelica 39	IX
O	023 Sinopensis	e	Paris, Bibl. Nat. Suppl. Gr. 1286	VI
P	024 Guelpher-bytanus A	e	Wolfenbüttel, Herz. Aug. Bibl. Weissenburg 64	VI (palimpsest)
P	025 Porphyrianus	apr	Leningrad, Öfftl. Bibl. Gr. 225	IX (palimpsest)
S	028 Vaticanus	e	Rome, Bibl. Vatic. Gr. 354	949
T	029 Borgianus	e	Rome, Bibl. Vatic. Borg. Copt. 109	V
V	031 Mosquensis	e	Moscow, Hist. Mus. V. 9	IX
W	032 Washingto-nensis, Freerianus	e	Washington, Freer Gall. 06.274	V
X	033 Monacensis	e	Munich, Univ. Bibl. fol. 30	X
Z	035 Dublinensis	e	Dublin, Trinity Coll. K 3. 4	VI (palimpsest)
Γ	036 Tischendorf-ianus IV	e	Leningrad, Öfftl. Bibl. Gr. 33; Oxford, Bodl. Libr. Auct. T. infr. 2. 2	X
Δ	037 Sangallensis	e	St. Gall, Stiftsbibl. 48	IX
Θ	038 Koridethi	e	Tiflis, Grus. Mus. Gr. 28	IX
Ξ	040 Zacynthius	e	London, Brit. and For. Bibl. Soc. 24	VI (palimpsest)

Symbol/Name		Con-tent	Location/Library No.	Date
Π 041	Petropolitanus	e	Leningrad, Öfftl. Bibl. Gr. 34	IX
Ψ 044	Athous Laurae, Athusiensis	eap	Athos, Laura 172	VIII/IX
Ω 045	Athous Dionysiou	e	Athos, Dionysiu (10) 55	IX
046	Vaticanus	r	Rome, Bibl. Vatic. Gr. 2066	X
049		ap	Athos, Laura A′ 88	IX
051		r	Athos, Pantokratoros 44	X
052		r	Athos, Panteleimonos 99, 2	X
0165		a	Berlin, Staatl. Mus. P. 13271	V
0171		e	Florence, Bibl. Laurenziana PSI 2. 124	IV
0220		p	Jamaica Plain, Leland C. Wyman	III
0250		e	Cambridge, Westminster Coll. Cod. Climaci rescr.	VIII (palimpsest)

4. Minuscules

§92.   For longer lists than that given here, and for more details concerning the minuscules see Gregory, *Prolegomena,* pp. 457-686; Vogels, *Handbuch,* pp. 61-69; and Aland, *Kurzgefasste Liste,* pp. 61-202. In the following list the content of the minuscules is indicated with these abbreviations: e = Gospels, a = Acts and Catholic Letters, p = Pauline Letters, r = Revelation. All are on parchment except where otherwise indicated.

Minuscules

Symbol	Con-tent	Location/Library No.	Date
1	eap	Basel, Univ. Bibl. A.N. IV. 2	XII
1	r	Schloss Harburg (Donauwörth), Öttingen-Wallersteinsche Bibl. I, 1, 40, 1	XII
2	e	Basel, Univ. Bibl. A.N. IV. 1	XII
2	ap	Basel, Univ. Bibl. A.N. IV. 4	XII
3	eap	Vienna, Österr. Nat. Bibl. Suppl. Gr. 52	XII
13	e	Paris, Bibl. Nat. Gr. 50	XIII
33	eap	Paris, Bibl. Nat. Gr. 14	IX
61	eapr	Dublin, Trinity Coll. A 4. 21	XVI (paper)
81	ap	London, Brit. Mus. Add. 20003; Alexandria, Greek Patriarch. 59	1044
88	apr	Naples, Bibl. Naz. II. A. 7	XII
104	apr	London, Brit. Mus. Harley 5537	1087
112	e	Oxford, Bodl. Lib. E. D. Clarke 10	XI
181	apr	Rome, Bibl. Vatic. Reg. Gr. 179	XI (ap); XV (r)
203	apr	London, Brit. Mus. Add. 28816	1111
326	ap	Oxford, Lincoln Coll. Lat 82	XII
383	ap	Oxford, Bodl. Lib. E. D. Clarke 9	XIII

Symbol	Con-tent	Location/Library No.	Date
579	e	Paris, Bibl. Nat. Gr. 97	XIII
614	ap	Milan, Bibl. Ambros. E 97 sup	XIII
666	e	Cambridge, Mass., Harvard Univ. Lib. Ms. Gr. 1	XIII
892	e	London, Brit. Mus. Add. 33277	IX
1006	er	Athos, Iviron (56) 728	XI
1241	eap	Sinai, Cather. Monas. 260	XII
1244	ap	Sinai, Cather. Monas. 274	XI
1345	e	Jerusalem, Greek Patriarchal Lib. Saba 572	XIV (paper)
1611	apr	Athens, Nat. Bibl. 94	XII
1739	ap	Athos, Laura B ′64	X
1770	p	Athos, Laura Γ ′63	XI
1835	a	Madrid, Bibl. Nac. 4588	XI
1845	ap	Rome, Bibl. Vatic. Gr. 1971	X
1854	apr	Athos, Iviron (25) 231	XI
2004	pr	Escorial, T. III. 17	XII
2053	r	Messina, Bibl. Univ. 99	XIII
2304	e	Maywood, Ill., Theol. Sem. Gruber Ms. 50	XIII
2344	apr	Paris, Bibl. Nat. Coislin Gr. 18	XI
2646	e	Oxford, Christ Church, Wake 51	XII

Note that fam. 1 is a group of minuscules headed by 1, and fam. 13 a group headed by 13 (cf. above § 83).

5. Lectionaries

§93. For longer lists than that given here, and for more details concerning the lectionaries, see Gregory, *Prolegomena*, pp. 695-791; Vogels, *Handbuch*, pp. 69-73; and Aland, *Kurzgefasste Liste*, pp. 205-318. In the following list the content of the lectionaries is shown with the abbreviations: e = Gospels, a = Acts and Letters, both according to the order of readings in the Byzantine Church. All are on parchment and in minuscule script unless otherwise indicated.

Lectionaries

Symbol	Content	Location/Library No.	Date
l 1	e	Paris, Bibl. Nat. Gr. 278	X (Uncial)
l 2	e	Paris, Bibl. Nat. Gr. 280	X (Uncial)
l 1997	a	Manchester, J. Rylands Libr. Gr. 23	XIV (Paper)

6. Versions

§94. For the ancient translations or versions, Latin, Syriac, Coptic, etc., their names, manuscripts, and abbreviations, see Gregory, *Prolegomena*, pp. 803-1128; Vogels, *Handbuch*, pp. 73-133; and *The Greek New Testament* of the Bible Societies, pp. xxvi-xxx.

7. Church Fathers

§95. For the writers of the ancient church, whose quotations of the NT provide another witness to the text, see Gregory, *Prolegomena,* pp. 1131-1230; Vogels, *Handbuch,* pp. 133-152; and *The Greek New Testament* of the Bible Societies, pp. xxxi-xxxiv.

III. ENCOUNTER WITH MANUSCRIPTS

Introduction

§96. It will now be undertaken to deal directly with a number of the most interesting and important manuscripts, papyrus, parchment, and even paper, of the Greek NT. For verisimilitude, to give the reader as far as possible the sense of having the actual document in hand, the fragments or pages of these manuscripts are reproduced in photographs and, as far as the limits of the present book allow, these reproductions are in or near the original size. Since the oldest known portion of the text of the Greek NT is a small fragment of the Gospel according to John, and since altogether there are more portions of the text of the Gospel according to John in the early papyri than of any other book of the NT, the text passages studied will all be from that Gospel. In the first series of texts we will begin with the oldest known fragment of John ($\mathfrak{P}^{52}$), and go on to read in comparison with it the same passage in the oldest fairly extensively preserved copy of the same Gospel ($\mathfrak{P}^{66}$), and again in a much later and again quite fragmentary copy ($\mathfrak{P}^{60}$). In a second series, we will begin with a particular passage in the same fairly extensive copy of John ($\mathfrak{P}^{66}$), go on to the same passage in the next oldest fairly extensive copy of the same Gospel ($\mathfrak{P}^{75}$), and finally read the same passage as it is contained in one more relatively early papyrus ($\mathfrak{P}^{28}$), where the original document itself is available to the writer of the present book. In yet a third series, a longer section will be read, namely, the opening portion of the Gospel according to John, and the comparison of the text will be carried through from the early papyri, $\mathfrak{P}^{66}$ and $\mathfrak{P}^{75}$, to a number of the parchment manuscripts, uncial and minuscule (and in this case one manuscript of paper) as well. In all the examples, concrete instances of variation and peculiarity in individual manuscripts will be observed; in the last series variations in punctuation and wording that are of theological significance will be encountered and evaluated. Where it is necessary to restore the text in gaps in the manuscript in question, this is done from the best text as otherwise known and, for practical purposes, this is usually done from the text printed in *The Greek New Testament* published by the several Bible Societies in 1966 (§81).

A

A Sequence Beginning with
the Oldest Known Fragment ($\mathfrak{p}^{52}$)

1. Papyrus Rylands Greek 457 ($\mathfrak{p}^{52}$)

§97. Papyrus Rylands Greek 457 ($\mathfrak{p}^{52}$) (C. H. Roberts, *An Unpublished Fragment of the Fourth Gospel* [Manchester: The Manchester University Press, 1935]) (Fig. 3) is a small piece of papyrus, 3.5 by 2.3 inches in size, with seven lines of writing on each side. It was one of a large number of papyri acquired in Egypt in 1920 by Bernard P. Grenfell, and placed in The John Rylands Library in Manchester, England. The group as a whole consists of literary texts and documents of the Ptolemaic and Roman periods, and was stated to have come from the Fayum or from Oxyrhynchus. The text is

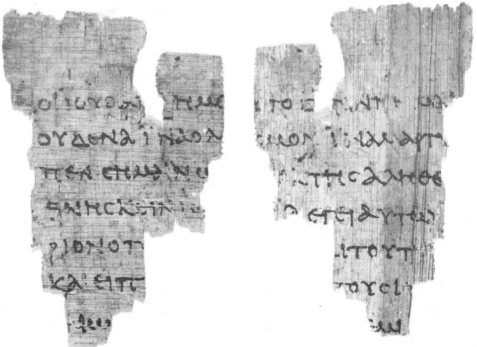

Figure 3. Papyrus Rylands Greek 457 ($\mathfrak{p}^{52}$), *recto:* John 18:31-33; *verso:* John 18:37-38. *Reproduced at actual size.*

written in dark ink on light-colored good-quality papyrus. At the right side of the *verso* an additional vertical strip of papyrus has been affixed, perhaps to strengthen the sheet where it was folded. When the text is deciphered (below) it is seen that it continues from the *recto* to the *verso,* with a gap corresponding to the amount of the page that is missing at the bottom. This was, therefore, a leaf in a codex. The top margin of the piece is preserved, and a portion of the inner margin (at the left on the *recto*). Therefore we have the writing preserved beginning with the top line on each side: on the *recto* we have the first part of each line, on the *verso* the last portion of each line. From what is missing it can be determined that each page must have had originally about 18 lines altogether, with 30-35 letters per line.

§98. The script of $\mathfrak{P}^{52}$ is in uncial letters, written informally but carefully. At least in some cases, the words appear to be slightly separated. There are no accents or breathings, and no marks of punctuation, but the dieresis (§24) is employed (sometimes improperly as in ἵνα in Line 2 on each side, although there one might almost wish to see it as a rough breathing and acute accent, which would of course be correct if it could only be assumed that such marks were, after all, sometimes used already at such an early date). No *nomina sacra* (§25) occur, so it cannot be determined if abbreviations were employed. Paleographically, the way individual letters are formed has been compared (Roberts, *op. cit.,* pp. 13-16) most closely with papyri of the end of the first or beginning of the second century, among them ones bearing dates corresponding to A.D. 94 and A.D. 127. It is probable, therefore, that the present papyrus also belongs at the end of the first or beginning of the second century, at all events hardly later than A.D. 125. Since the text is of the Gospel according to John (see below), the papyrus is evidence that that Gospel was circulating in Egypt already at this date. As a copy of such date of a portion of a NT text, the papyrus is our presently earliest known fragment of any part of the NT.

§99. Let it be supposed, now, that this fragment of papyrus has just been recovered from the sands of Egypt. The handwriting has been noted as uncial, and evidently early in date, although more precise placement chronologically will await comparison with other manuscripts (cf. §98). Now it is desired to find out what is contained in the text. First, therefore, the legible uncial letters are copied out, with an effort to recognize spaces between words, and the lines of writing are numbered (by fives).

$\mathfrak{P}^{52}$

recto

```
ΟΙ ΪΟΥΔΑΙ    ΗΜΕ
ΟΥΔΕΝΑ ΪΝΑ Ο Λ
ΠΕΝ CΗΜΑΙΝω
ΘΝΗCΚΕΙΝ ΙC
5   ΡΙΟΝ Ο Π
```

KAI ЄΙΠ
ΙѠ

verso

ΤΟ Γ   Ν   ΑΙ
ϹΜΟΝ ÏΝΑ ΜΑΡΤ
ΤΗϹ ΑΛΗΘЄ
ЄΓЄΙ ΑΥΤѠ
5   Ι ΤΟΥΤ
ΟΥϹ Ι
ΜΙ

§100. For easier recognition, the uncial text may next be written in the characters in which Greek is more frequently printed today (at the same time omitting the diereses).

recto

οι ιουδαι   ημε
ουδενα ινα ο λ
πεν σημαινω
θνησκειν ισ
5   ριον ο π
και ειπ
ιω

verso

το γ   ν   αι
σμον ινα μαρτ
της αληθε
εγει αυτω
5   ι τουτ
ους ι
μι

§101. It may now be observed that the fragment has preserved intact a number of small connectives, prepositions, articles, and negatives, but that otherwise there are no two complete consecutive words on the entire piece. At the same time sufficient portions of other words are preserved that by supplying what we may guess were the missing letters (shown here within square brackets) we can recognize, with considerable probability, the following terms:

οἱ Ἰουδαῖ[οι]	the Jews
σημαίνω[ν]	signifying
[ἀπο]θνῄσκειν	to die
γ[εγέν]ν[ημ]αι	have been born
[κό]σμον	world
μαρτ[ ]	bear witness
τῆς ἀληθε[ίας]	of the truth
[λ]έγει αὐτῷ	said to him

§102. Short as it is, this list shows several different possibilities of damage and loss in the text of an ancient manuscript. The end of a word may be missing, or the beginning of it, or portions in the middle. In attempting to supply the missing portions, one may, of course, go astray; and until some longer context can be established, it will be particularly easy to supply endings that are wrong as to number or case of nouns, and tense of verbs. Indeed one might even go astray as to whether a word is a noun or a verb. Provisional errors of this sort will not be too serious, however, and can be corrected later. What is important is to recognize the main words, irrespective of the particular endings by which they must be made to fit into sentences, and this can be done if main root portions of them are preserved or can be restored with considerable certainty.

§103. For example, in the sixth word in the list above (§101), it can be recognized with much probability that μαρτ- is the main part of the Greek word from which English "martyr" is derived. In Greek are the verbs μαρτυρέω and μαρτύρομαι, both of which mean "to bear witness" or "to give testimony," and the nouns which have related meanings, μαρτυρία, "testimony," μαρτύριον, "that which serves as testimony," and μάρτυς, "one who bears witness," often meaning "one who bears witness unto death," i.e., "martyr." Ultimately, when the context is reconstructed, it can be seen that the complete word here was probably μαρτ[υρήσω], which is the first person singular future indicative of μαρτυρέω. For the moment it is sufficient to establish that the meaning of "bear witness" is represented by a word at this point in the text.

§104. Given, then, this sequence of recognizable words not too far apart on the front and back of a fragment of papyrus—"the Jews . . . signifying . . . to die . . . have been born . . . world . . . bear witness . . . of the truth . . . said to him"—one may recall or, with some searching, find in the Gospel according to John the passage in which these words occur in the same sequence. Citing the places by the chapter and verse divisions with which we are familiar, and underscoring the same key words, it is noted that 18:31 mentions "*the Jews*"; 18:32 refers to the word of Jesus which He spoke "*signifying* by what kind of death He was about *to die*"; 18:37 quotes Jesus as saying, "For this I *have been born,* and for this I have come into the *world,* to *bear witness* to the truth. Every one who is *of the truth* hears My voice"; and 18:38 states that Pilate "*said to him.* . . ."

§105. At this point we may, therefore, proceed to fill out the gaps in the papyrus from the text of the Gospel according to John as otherwise known, i.e., as printed in *The Greek New Testament* of the Bible Societies (cf. §§81, 96), for the portion that is in question, namely, John 18:31-33, 37-38. In so doing it is remembered that, as the intact margins show (§97), the papyrus preserves the first part of its lines of writing on the *recto,* but the last part on the *verso.* When the full text is supplied, with punctuation, capitalization, and verse numbers, from the source indicated, the result is as follows:

recto (Jn 18:31-33)

οἱ Ἰουδαῖ[οι], Ἡμε[ῖν οὐκ ἔξεστιν ἀποκτεῖναι]
οὐδένα· 32 ἵνα ὁ λ[όγος τοῦ Ἰησοῦ πληρωθῇ ὃν εἶ-]
πεν σημαίνω[ν ποίῳ θανάτῳ ἤμελλεν ἀπο-]
θνήσκειν. 33 Ἰσ[ῆλθεν οὖν πάλιν εἰς τὸ πραιτώ-]
5 ριον ὁ Π[ιλᾶτος καὶ ἐφώνησεν τὸν Ἰησοῦν]
καὶ εἶπ[εν αὐτῷ, Σὺ εἶ ὁ βασιλεὺς τῶν Ἰου-]
[δα]ίω[ν; 34 ἀπεκρίθη Ἰησοῦς, Ἀπὸ σεαυτοῦ]

verso (Jn 18:37-38)

[λεύς εἰμι. ἐγὼ εἰς τοῦ]το γ[εγέν]ν[ημ]αι
[καὶ ⟨εἰς τοῦτο⟩ ἐλήλυθα εἰς τὸν κό]σμον, ἵνα μαρτ[υ-]
[ρήσω τῇ ἀληθείᾳ· πᾶς ὁ ὢν ἐκ] τῆς ἀληθε-
[ίας ἀκούει μου τῆς φωνῆς.] 38 λέγει αὐτῷ
5 [ὁ Πιλᾶτος, Τί ἐστιν ἀλήθεια; Κα]ὶ τοῦτ[ο]
[εἰπὼν πάλιν ἐξῆλθεν πρὸς τ]οὺς Ἰ[ου-]
[δαίους, καὶ λέγει αὐτοῖς, Ἐγὼ οὐδε]μί[αν]

The translation, in accordance with the NASB, and in approximately equivalent lines, is

recto (Jn 18:31-33)

The Jews (said to him), "We are not permitted to put any one to death"; 32 that the word of Jesus might be fulfilled, which He spoke, signifying by what kind of death He was about to die. 33 Pilate therefore entered again into the Praeto-
5 rium, and summoned Jesus,
and said to Him, "You are the King of the Jews?" 34 Jesus answered, "Are you saying this on your own initiative"

verso (Jn 18:37-38)

"I am a king. For this I have been born,
and for this I have come into the world, to bear witness to the truth. Every one who is of the truth hears My voice." 38 Pilate said to Him,
5 "What is truth?" And when he had said this,
he went out again to the Jews,
and said to them, "I find no"

§106. In the Greek text we note variations in spelling from what is now usual practice, namely, ἡμεῖν for ἡμῖν (*recto* Line 1), and ἰσῆλθεν for εἰσῆλθεν (*recto* Line 4). Whether the name of Jesus (Ἰησοῦ, *recto* Line 2; Ἰησοῦν, *recto* Line 5; Ἰησοῦς, *recto* Line 7) was abbreviated cannot be known, since the name falls only at the point of gaps in the papyrus. The precise points at which the text of the papyrus ended in Line 7 on each side, and at which it began in Line 1 on the *verso*, are, of course hypothetical. As restored, there are from 31 to 35 letters to the line in the first six lines on the *recto;* 29 or 30 letters to the line in Lines 1, 3, 4 and 5 on the *verso*. A question arises as to Line 2 on the *verso*. As restored, this line

§106

A Sequence Beginning with 𝔓⁵²

contains 38 letters. This seems an excessive number in comparison with the restored lines in the rest of the papyrus, particularly in comparison with the other restored lines on the *verso*. If the words εἰς τοῦτο ("for this") were not in Line 2 in the papyrus, then this line, as restored, would also consist of 30 letters. It appears probable, therefore, that these two words were not contained in the papyrus, and this probability has been indicated above (§105) by enclosing them within angled brackets. Since the manuscripts represented by the text in *The Greek New Testament* of the Bible Societies contain the words, the question is whether they were original or not. In Line 1 of the *verso* the papyrus has the same two words along with all the other manuscripts. The possibility is, therefore, that the omission (which we are assuming) of the same two words in Line 2 of the papyrus is simply an accidental slip. On the other hand, our papyrus is a very early witness, and it is possible that the repetition of the two words as found in the other manuscripts is the result of a later alteration. Without the two words in Line 2, the text would read: "For this I have been born and have come into the world. . . ."

2. Papyrus Bodmer II ($\mathfrak{P}^{66}$)

§107. Papyrus Bodmer II ($\mathfrak{P}^{66}$) (Victor Martin, *Papyrus Bodmer II, Evangile de Jean chap. 1-14* [Bibliotheca Bodmeriana V, 1956]; *Papyrus Bodmer II, Supplément, Evangile de Jean chap. 14-21* [1958], 2d ed. by Victor Martin and J. W. B. Barns [1962]; cf. J. N. Birdsall, *The Bodmer Papyrus of the Gospel of John* [London: The Tyndale Press, 1960]) is a codex of the Gospel according to John, well preserved in the first part, very fragmentary in the last part, which belongs to the *Bibliothèque Martin Bodmer* in Cologny/ Geneva, Switzerland. The codex consists of 75 leaves and 39 unidentified fragments, and probably (Aland in ANT 2, p. 132) was made up originally out of 39 sheets of papyrus, folded and arranged in quires to make 78 leaves and 156 pages. At the outset there is an unwritten leaf which provides a front cover. The written pages are numbered, and the page numbers are preserved and legible in the upper outside corner of most of the pages of the first fourteen chapters of the Gospel. The sequence of numbers runs consecutively from Page α ʹ (Page 1) to Page λδ ʹ (34), which ends in Jn 6:11; then pages 35-38 are missing; and after that the manuscript continues from Page λθ ʹ (39), beginning in Jn 6:35, to Page ρη ʹ (108), ending with 14:26.

Up to this point, and with the exception of the two missing leaves (Pages 35-38), the intact character of the manuscript is amazing. The leaves are nearly rectangular and quite small, being about 6.4 inches high and 5.6 inches wide. Individually the leaves are so well preserved that there are rarely more than a few letters missing on a page. From this point on, however, the balance of the manuscript is very fragmentary. On what must be a portion of Page ρθ ʹ = 109 (the page number is missing) is contained some of Jn 14:29-30. More or less fragmentary pages, and groups of fragments which have been carefully reassembled, continue into Jn 21 and to the point where a tiny piece contains only one last and legible page number, ρνδ ´ = 154. Of these portions one fragment, with parts of Pages 139f. and of Jn 19:25-28, 31-32, is in Dublin in the collection of A. Chester Beatty. In addition there are 39 small fragments, each containing only a few letters, which, because they preserve so little, it has not been possible to replace in correct sequence in the manuscript.

§108. On the pages of $\mathfrak{P}^{66}$ the number of lines of text per page runs from 14 on Page 149 (ρμθ´) to 25 on Page 1 (α´), and the number of letters in a line of text runs from 18 to 28. The handwriting is a good literary uncial, to which a date around A.D. 200 is usually assigned (§90), although some would place it earlier, in the middle or even in the first half of the second century (so Herbert Hunger, director of the papyrological collections in the National Library at Vienna, see Metzger p. 40 n. 1). There is rudimentary punctuation with a high point at the end of sentences and a double point at the end of sections. The dieresis is used frequently over Iota and Upsilon. The words θεός, Ἰησοῦς, κύριος, and Χριστός are always abbreviated, and so also sometimes are ἄνθρωπος, πατήρ, πνεῦμα, and υἱός. There are numerous obvious errors in the manuscript, but most of these have been corrected, many of the corrections perhaps having been made by the scribe himself during the course of his work. This, it has been suggested, may indicate that the manuscript was written by a commercial copyist.

§109. For the portion of the text of the Gospel according to John that was studied in $\mathfrak{P}^{52}$ (Jn 18:31-33, 37-38) (§105) we turn in $\mathfrak{P}^{66}$ to Page 131 (ρλα´), a broken *verso* page with Jn 18:29-33 (Fig. 4), and Page 133 (ρλγ´), also a broken *verso* page with Jn 18:37–19:1 (Fig. 5). Condensing the several steps that were worked through separately with $\mathfrak{P}^{52}$, we may here proceed directly through those steps to the end result and present a transcription and restoration of the text of $\mathfrak{P}^{66}$ in the relevant passages as follows:

$$\mathfrak{P}^{66}$$

Page 131 (Jn 18:31-33)

οἱ Ἰ[ου-]
[δαῖοι, Ἡμῖν οὐκ ἔξεστιν] ἀπο[κτεῖ-]
10 [ναι οὐδένα· 32 ἵνα ὁ λ]όγος τοῦ ἰ[ῦ]
[πληρωθῇ ὃν εἶ]πεν σημαίνω[ν]
[ποίῳ θανάτῳ ἤμε]λλεν ἀπο-
[θνῄσκειν. 33 Εἰ]σῆλθ[εν οὖν] πάλ[ιν]
[εἰς τὸ πραιτώ]ριον ὁ [Πειλᾶ]τος [καὶ]
15 [ἐφώνησεν τ]ὸ[ν] ιν [καὶ εἶ]πεν

Page 133 (Jn 18:37-38)

[ἐ- (this must have been the last letter on Page 132)]
[λ]ήλυθ[α] εἰς τ[ὸν κόσμ]ον, [ἵνα μαρτυ-]
ρή[σω τῇ] ἀληθεί[ᾳ]· πᾶς ὁ [ὢ]ν ἐκ τῆ[ς]
ἀληθί[ας] ἀκούει μου τῆς φωνῆς.

38 λέγει ο[ὖν] αὐτῷ Πειλᾶτος, Τί ἐστῑ
ἀλήθι[α]; Καὶ τοῦτο εἰπὼν πάλ[ιν]
ἐξῆλ[θεν π]ρὸς τοὺ[ς] Ἰουδαίους,
[καὶ λέγει αὐτοῖς, Ἐγ]ὼ οὐδεμίαν ε[ὑ-]
[ρίσκω] α[ἰτία]ν ἐν αὐτῷ.

Page 131 (Jn 18:31-33)

The Jews (said
to him), "We are not permitted to put any one
to death"; 32 that the word of Jesus
might be fulfilled, which He spoke, signifying
by what kind of death He was about to
die. 33 Pilate therefore entered again
into the Praetorium, and
summoned Jesus, and said

Figure 4. Papyrus Bodmer II ($\mathfrak{P}^{66}$), Page 131: John 18:29-33. *Reproduced at actual size.*

Page 133 (Jn 18:37-38)

"I have come into the world, to bear
witness to the truth. Every one who is of the
truth hears My voice."
38 Pilate therefore said to Him, "What is
5   truth?" And when he had said this,
he went out again to the Jews,
and said to them, "I find no
guilt in Him."

§109

*A Sequence
Beginning with
𝔓⁵²*

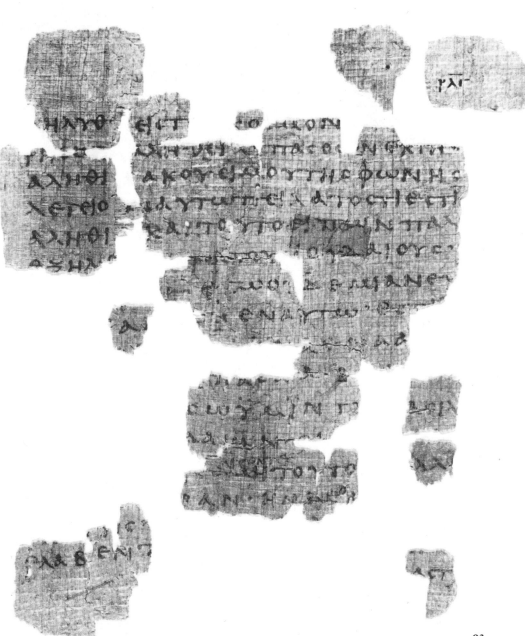

93

Figure 5.   Papyrus Bodmer II (𝔓⁶⁶), Page 133: John 18:37-19:1. *Reproduced at actual size.*

§110. In the Greek text it is to be noted that on Page 131 the name of Jesus is abbreviated, $\overline{\iota\upsilon}$ for Ἰησοῦ in Line 10, and $\overline{\iota\upsilon}$ for Ἰησοῦν in Line 15. On Page 133, at the end of Line 4, the final Nu of ἐστιν is abbreviated by a horizontal line extending from the top of the preceding letter, thus ἐστῑ. On Page 133, Line 2, the word for "truth" is spelled ἀλήθεια. The same spelling was evidently used in 𝔓⁵² (§105 *verso* Line 3), and is now considered normal. But in Lines 3 and 5 of Page 133, the writer of 𝔓⁶⁶ changes to the spelling ἀλήθια. On Page 133 Line 4, the name of Pilate is spelled Πειλᾶτος, a form preferred by Tischendorf, and Westcott and Hort (cf. Gregory, *Prolegomena,* pp. 84f.). In 𝔓⁵² the name fell in a gap in the papyrus; in the restoration above (§105 *verso* Line 5) the alternate spelling, Πιλᾶτος, preferred by Nestle-Aland and *The Greek New Testament* of the Bible Societies, was used. As to the use of the article with the name of Pilate, which was presupposed in the restoration of 𝔓⁵² above, here in 𝔓⁶⁶ the article is used with the name on Page 131 Line 14, but not on Page 133 Line 4. On Page 133 Lines 7-8, the word order of 𝔓⁶⁶ is Ἐγὼ οὐδεμίαν εὑρίσκω αἰτίαν ἐν αὐτῷ, "I find no guilt in him." In 𝔓⁵² only the first two words are preserved, and the rest of the sentence is lost. Elsewhere an alternate order is found, and is preferred in *The Greek New Testament* of the Bible Societies, namely, Ἐγὼ οὐδεμίαν εὑρίσκω ἐν αὐτῷ αἰτίαν, "I find in him no guilt," a difference in order which makes, at the most, only a slight change in emphasis. Finally there is one actually observable variant between the present text and that in 𝔓⁵². 𝔓⁵², *verso* Lines 4-5, reads: λέγει αὐτῷ [ὁ Πιλᾶτος], "Pilate said to Him." 𝔓⁶⁶, Page 133 Line 4, reads: λέγει ο[ὖν] αὐτῷ Πειλᾶτος, "Pilate therefore said to Him." The use of οὖν, "therefore," to indicate a response is fairly characteristic of the Gospel according to John (e.g., Jn 4:9, 48; 6:53, etc.), so it could be original here in 𝔓⁶⁶. On the other hand, it is perhaps more probable that it would be added by a scribe who was already well familiar with this usage in the Gospel, than that it would be omitted if it stood already in the text from which he was copying. If the latter explanation is adopted, then 𝔓⁵² remains both the older and the better (in this one very slight point) copy of the very small portion of the Gospel according to John which it contains.

3. Papyrus Colt 4 (𝔓⁶⁰)

§111. In dealing directly with some of the oldest manuscripts of the Greek New Testament we have made a beginning with the very oldest known fragment of all, namely, 𝔓⁵², containing Jn 18:31-33, 37-38, and then have gone on to the second oldest known manuscript in which the same passage is contained, namely, 𝔓⁶⁶, and have noted the characteristics of the text of this very limited passage in these two most ancient witnesses. Now one more step in this same sequence may be taken by looking at the same passage as it is preserved in one more papyrus of much later date, namely, in 𝔓⁶⁰. 𝔓⁶⁰ is the designation of a manuscript also known as Papyrus Colt 4, which is in The Pierpont Morgan Library in New York City. The Colt

Papyri were found in 1936-1937 by the Colt Archaeological Expedition under H. Dunscombe Colt, working at Nessana in the Negeb in southern Palestine. This site, known today as 'Auja-el-Hafir, was a stopping point on the caravan route from Aqabah to Gaza, was fortified as early as the second century B.C., and flourished in the sixth and seventh centuries of the Christian era. The papyri had been buried in the collapse of a room annexed to a small church, and consisted of a considerable body of both nonliterary and literary documents.

§112. Among the literary documents (*Excavations at Nessana*, 2, *Literary Papyri,* by Lionel Casson and Ernest L. Hettich [Princeton: Princeton University Press, 1950]) are three with NT texts, namely, $\mathfrak{P}^{59}$ and $\mathfrak{P}^{60}$ with parts of the Gospel according to John, and $\mathfrak{P}^{61}$ with portions of seven of the Pauline Letters. Paleographically, the first two papyri are written in a careful upright uncial and the third in a similar but more ornate hand. Similar handwriting is found in two dated Easter letters, one of about A.D. 719, the other of either 577 or 672 (*ibid.,* pp. 81f.), and, by comparison, it is judged probable that $\mathfrak{P}^{59}$ and $\mathfrak{P}^{60}$ are of the seventh century in date, and that $\mathfrak{P}^{61}$ is a little later, say around A.D. 700. $\mathfrak{P}^{60}$, selected for consideration here, consists of twenty consecutive leaves, half or two-thirds intact, with text extending from Jn 16:29 to 19:26. The pages are about 3.5 by 3 inches in size, or smaller, each with one column of writing. There are from 14 to 22 letters to the line, and the number of lines to the page appears to have varied from 5 to 18 or 20. Only the upper portion of each page is preserved but, even so, in some cases the text does not run down as far as the break. Also each page starts, or appears to have started when intact, with a new sentence or new thought. In $\mathfrak{P}^{59}$ the page was laid out in the same way, and there on some pages is also preserved, beneath the main text, the word ερμηνυα (a variant spelling of ἑρμηνεία [Gregory, *Prolegomena,* p. 88], meaning "interpretation" or "explanation"), together with a line or so of summary of the text above. It appears, therefore, that the pages of $\mathfrak{P}^{59}$ were arranged to contain the amount of text to which the ἑρμηνεῖαι at the bottom referred, and $\mathfrak{P}^{60}$ was probably arranged in the same way (*ibid.,* pp. 80f., 94f.).

§113. We are interested now to read the portions of text preserved in $\mathfrak{P}^{60}$ which correspond most nearly in extent to what is contained in $\mathfrak{P}^{52}$, namely, Jn 18:31-33, 37-38. These portions are found on three of the pages of $\mathfrak{P}^{60}$, reproduced among a number of pages from this manuscript in Figs. 6 and 7 (cf. Casson and Hettich, *op. cit.,* pp. 105-107). The fragmentary page in the upper left-hand corner of Fig. 6 is Folio 13 *verso,* and contains Jn 18:31 in seven lines of writing, the last line almost completely lost. In the first line the initial letter (Epsilon) of the first word (Εἶπεν), which is also the first word of the verse, is enlarged and set in the margin to mark the beginning of a section. The portion of Jn 18:31 with which $\mathfrak{P}^{52}$ began (§105) was copied here in the last part of Line 5, which is now lost, in Line 6 which is preserved in a few letters, and in Line 7 which is almost completely lost. Also the continuation of the text on

Figure 6. Papyrus Colt 4 ($\mathfrak{P}^{60}$), Upper left, Folio 13 *verso:* John 18:31-32; Left-center, Folio 15 *verso:* John 18:37. *Fragments reproduced at actual size.*

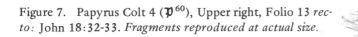
Figure 7. Papyrus Colt 4 ($\mathfrak{P}^{60}$), Upper right, Folio 13 *recto:* John 18:32-33. *Fragments reproduced at actual size.*

the other side of this same fragment shows that Line 7 must have contained, at the end, the first word of the following verse, Jn 18:32. Restored, this part of the text of the fragment is:

$$\mathfrak{P}^{60}$$

Folio 13 *verso* (Jn 18:31-32)

5   [οἱ Ἰου-]
     [δ] αῖοι [Ἡμῖν οὐκ ἔξεστιν]
     [ἀποκτεῖναι οὐδένα · 32 ἵνα]

The continuation of the text (Jn 18:32-33) is found on the other side (Folio 13 *recto*) of the same fragment, and this is to be seen in the upper right-hand corner of Fig. 7. Here seven lines of writing are, at least to some extent, legible.

Folio 13 *recto* (Jn 18:32-33)

     [ὁ λόγος τ] οῦ ω̄ πληρωθ [ῇ]
     [ὃν εἶπεν σ] ημένων
     [ποίῳ θα] νάτῳ ἤμελλ [εν]
     [ἀποθνή] σκιν. 33 Ἐξῆλθεν
5   [οὖν εἰς] τὸ πραιτώρ [ιον]
     [πάλιν κα] ὶ εἶπεν αὐ [τῷ, Σὺ]
     [εἶ ὁ βασιλεὺς τ] ῶν [Ἰουδαίων;]

As for the portion of Jn 18:37-38 contained in $\mathfrak{P}^{52}$, the nearest equivalent in $\mathfrak{P}^{60}$ is the portion of Jn 18:37 found on Folio 15 *verso*. This page is the fragment in the left-center of Fig. 6. Seven lines of writing are recognizable, although the fifth of these is almost entirely illegible.

Folio 15 *verso* (Jn 18:37)

             [ἐγὼ εἰς του-]
     το γεγένν [ημαι καὶ εἰς τοῦ]
     το ἐλήλυ [θα εἰς τὸν κόσμον,]
5   [ἵνα μαρτυρήσω τῇ ἀλη-]
     [θ] εία · [πᾶς] ὁ ὢ [ν ἐκ τῆς]
     [ἀλ] ηθεί [ας]

Folio 13 *verso* (Jn 18:31-32)

5   The
     Jews (said to him), "We are not permitted
     to put any one to death"; 32 that

Folio 13 *recto* (Jn 18:32-33)

     the word of Jesus might be fulfilled,
     which He spoke, signifying
     by what kind of death He was about
     to die. 33 He went out
5   therefore into the Praetorium
     again, and said to Him, "You
     are the King of the Jews?"

Folio 15 *verso* (Jn 18:37)

"For this I
have been born, and for this
I have come into the world,
to bear witness to the
truth. Every one who is of the
truth"

§ 114

§ 114.   Minor points to be noted in 𝔓60 in comparison with 𝔓52 (§ 105) and 𝔓66 (§ 109) are: on Folio 13 *recto,* Line 1, the abbreviation of the name of Jesus, $\overline{\iota\omega}$ for Ἰησοῦ, as in 𝔓66; Line 2, the spelling σημένων as compared with σημαίνων in 𝔓52 and 𝔓66; and, Line 4, the spelling ἀποθνήσκιν as compared with ἀποθνήσκειν in 𝔓52. The major discrepancy occurs on the same Folio 13 *recto,* in Lines 4ff., giving the text of Jn 18:33. If the same verse be copied from the restored text of 𝔓52 and 𝔓66 in lines corresponding as nearly as possible with the lines of 𝔓60, we have the following comparison:

Jn 18:33

𝔓52

Ἰσ[ῆλθεν οὖν πάλιν]
[εἰς τὸ πραιτώ]ριον ὁ Π[ιλᾶτος καὶ ἐφώνησεν]
[τὸν Ἰησοῦν] καὶ εἶπ[εν αὐτῷ, Σὺ]
[εἶ ὁ βασιλεὺς τῶν Ἰουδα]ίω[ν;]

𝔓66

[Εἰ] σῆλθ[εν οὖν] πάλ[ιν]
[εἰς τὸ πραιτώ]ριον ὁ [Πειλᾶ]τος [καὶ ἐφώνησεν]
[τ]ὸ[ν] $\overline{\iota\omega}$ [καὶ εἶ]πεν

𝔓60

Ἐξῆλθεν
[οὖν εἰς] τὸ πραιτώρ[ιον]
[πάλιν κα]ὶ εἶπεν αὐ[τῷ, Σὺ]
[εἶ ὁ βασιλεὺς τ]ῶν [Ἰουδαίων;]

𝔓52 and 𝔓66

Pilate therefore entered again
into the Praetorium, and summoned
Jesus, and said to Him, "You
are the King of the Jews?"

𝔓60

He therefore went out
into the Praetorium
again, and said to Him, "You
are the king of the Jews?"

As compared with $\mathfrak{P}^{52}$ and $\mathfrak{P}^{66}$ (as far as the latter extends), $\mathfrak{P}^{60}$ has written ἐξῆλθεν, "went out," instead of εἰσῆλθεν, "went into," or "entered into," changed the position of πάλιν, "again," and, after that word, omitted the entire statement, ὁ Πιλᾶτος καὶ ἐφώνησεν τὸν Ἰησοῦν, "and Pilate summoned Jesus." These are surely all mistakes of the scribe of $\mathfrak{P}^{60}$ (cf. Casson and Hettich, *op. cit.* p. 106).

§115.   The three papyri noted in this sequence, $\mathfrak{P}^{52}$ (§105), $\mathfrak{P}^{66}$ (§109), and $\mathfrak{P}^{60}$ (§113), are all fragmentary and there are many gaps in their respective texts. Yet when the three are brought together, the sheer chance of where the preserved portions and the gaps fall often makes it possible to restore surprisingly complete sequences of words. For a single example, take Line 2 of $\mathfrak{P}^{52}$. Here the words and letters that are actually preserved are ουδενα ινα ο λ. If we look at this point in $\mathfrak{P}^{66}$ (Page 131 Line 10) we find preserved and clearly legible ογος του ῑ. Again if we look at the same point in $\mathfrak{P}^{60}$ (Folio 13 *recto*, Line 1) we find ου ῶ πληρωθ. The three portions may be brought together thus:

$\mathfrak{P}^{52}$ ουδενα ινα ο λ
$\mathfrak{P}^{66}$ ογος του ι
$\mathfrak{P}^{60}$ ου ῶ πληρωθ

Thus we are actually given in the three papyri almost the whole of what must have been the complete original Line 2 of $\mathfrak{P}^{52}$, and we have only to supply five letters at the end to connect the text perfectly with the next line (Line 3) of $\mathfrak{P}^{52}$, as follows:

Jn 18:31-32

οὐδένα · 32 ἵνα ὁ λόγος τοῦ ῶ πληρωθ [ῇ ὃν εἶ-]
πεν. . . .

"any one (to death);" 32 that the word of Jesus might be fulfilled which He spoke. . . .

This, on a small scale, illustrates why it is such a hopeful undertaking, in the endeavor to recover the earliest possible copies of the NT, to gather together and carefully compare all the available NT papyri, even the tiniest fragments. Altogether, also, the sequence of the three passages in the three papyri has provided an initial introduction to the direct reading of the ancient NT manuscripts, and to the kind of matters that must be dealt with in such reading.

B

A Sequence Extending to a Relatively Early and
Immediately Available Fragment ($\mathfrak{p}^{28}$)

1. Papyrus Bodmer II ($\mathfrak{p}^{66}$)

§116. In this second series we begin with a particular passage in
our oldest relatively extensively preserved copy of the Gospel according to John ($\mathfrak{p}^{66}$), go on to approximately the same passage in our
next oldest relatively extensive copy of the same Gospel ($\mathfrak{p}^{75}$), and
finally read the passage in a papyrus fragment ($\mathfrak{p}^{28}$) where the
original document itself is in the museum with which the present
writer is associated, so that he can have it immediately in hand as he
copies and discusses the text. Since the sequence is directed toward
the immediate encounter with the actual in-hand piece of papyrus
($\mathfrak{p}^{28}$), the text that that fragment contains is looked at in the first
two witnesses as well. This text is Jn 6:8-12, 17-22. $\mathfrak{p}^{66}$ or Papyrus
Bodmer II is the manuscript at which we look first. This codex has
already been described above (§107), and its early date, perhaps
around A.D. 200 or even as early as the middle or first half of the
second century, noted (§108).

§117. The nearest equivalent to the passage contained in $\mathfrak{p}^{28}$
(namely, Jn 6:8-12, 17-22), which is preserved in $\mathfrak{p}^{66}$, is to be found
on the page of the manuscript numbered λδ´ = 34 (Fig. 8). This page
in $\mathfrak{p}^{66}$ contains Jn 6:5-11; after it, two leaves, which must have
contained Jn 6:11-35, are missing from the manuscript. As may be
seen in the photograph, this is a *recto* page; at the end of Line 9 is a
damaged portion where the horizontal fibers of this side are broken
away and show the underlying vertical fibers. The place just mentioned is virtually the only place on the entire page where any of the
text is destroyed. The page number ΛΔ is preserved at the upper
left-hand corner. The margins are intact, and the length of the lines
can be seen. There are 20 lines of writing on the page, and the
number of letters per line runs from 19 (plus two written in above
the line) in Line 16, to 26 in Lines 3 and 12, all within the number
of letters per line (18 to 28) in the manuscript as a whole (§108).
Additional letters are written in above the line in Lines 5, 16, and 18,
and the probability that such corrections were made in the manu-

script by the original scribe himself has already been spoken of (§108).

§118. With a page so well intact as this, it is now possible to proceed immediately to transcribe the text, including the corrections, and supplying the evidently missing letters in the one gap. The part of the text with which we are concerned, corresponding as nearly as possible and as far as it goes with what is contained in 𝔓²⁸ (Jn 6:8-12, 17-22), begins at the end of Line 7 (Jn 6:8) and continues through Line 20 which breaks off in Jn 6:11.

𝔓⁶⁶

Page 34 (Jn 6:8-11)

8 λέγει αὐ-
τῷ εἷς ἐκ τῶν μαθητῶν αὐτοῦ,
᾽Ανδρέας ὁ ἀδελφὸς [Σίμωνος]
10 Πέτρου, 9 ῎Εστιν παιδάριον ὧδε ὃς
{ς} ἔχει πέντε ἄρτους κριθίνους
καὶ δύο ὀψάρια· ἀλλὰ τί ἐστιν ταῦτα εἰς τοσούτους; 10 εἶπεν οὖν ὁ ι̅ς̅,
Ποιήσαται τοὺς α̅ν̅ο̅υ̅ς̅ ἀναπε
15 σῖν. ἦν δὲ χόρτος πολὺς ἐν
τῷ τόπῳ. ἀνέπεσαν οὖν οἱ ἄνδρες τὸν ἀριθμὸν ὡσὶ πεντακισχίλιοι. 11 ἔλαβεν οὖν τοὺς ἄρτους ὁ ι̅ς̅ καὶ εὐχαριστήσας ἔδω-
20 κεν τοῖς ἀνακειμένοις, ὁμοίως

Page 34 (Jn 6:8-11)

8 Said to
him, one of His disciples,
Andrew, Simon Peter's
10 brother, 9 "There is a lad here, who
has five barley loaves,
and two fish; but what are these
for so many people?" 10 Jesus therefore said,
"Have the people sit
15 down." Now there was much grass in
the place. So the men sat
down, in number about five
thousand. 11 Jesus therefore took the
loaves; and having given thanks, he gave
20 to those who were seated; likewise

§119. To be noted in the Greek text are the abbreviations of the name of Jesus (I̅C̅ = ᾽Ιησοῦς) in Lines 13 and 19, and of the word "men" or "people" (A̅N̅O̅Y̅C̅ = ἀνθρώπους) in Line 14. Along with the loss of the end of Line 9 due to the break in the papyrus, there is also some damage to the tops of the letters at the end of Line 10, but it still appears quite plain that in the last word the two letters OC = ὃς ("who") are to be read. Therefore the additional Sigma which

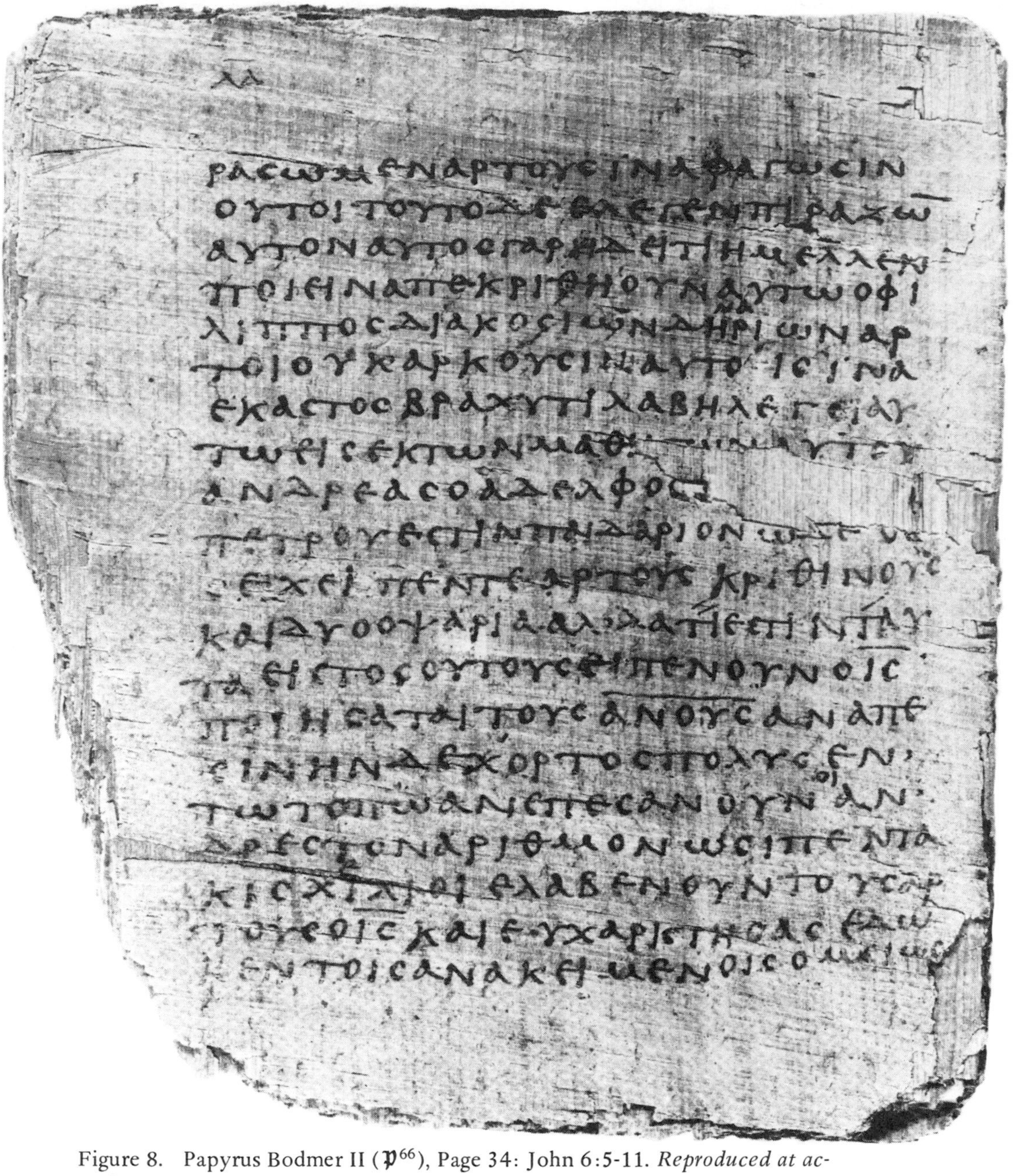

Figure 8.   Papyrus Bodmer II ($\mathfrak{P}^{66}$), Page 34: John 6:5-11. *Reproduced at actual size.*

appears at the beginning of Line 11 is superfluous, and is so indicated in the transcription. It looks, however, as if the scribe himself may have tried to erase the mistaken letter. In Line 16 οἱ ("the") was omitted, and then written in above the line. In Line 18 the letter ε is written in above the word πεντακισχίλιοι ("five thousand"), evidently to make a familiar variant spelling of χίλιοι as χείλιοι. Also in Line 14 we have ποιήσαται for ποιήσατε, second person plural first

103

aorist imperfect active of ποιέω, "to make or have"; in Lines 14-15 ἀναπεσῖν for ἀναπεσεῖν, second aorist infinitive of ἀναπίπτω, which means literally "to fall back," and is used as an equivalent for ἀνακλίνομαι, "to recline for a meal," here to recline on the ground; and in Line 17 ὡσί for ὡσεί, "about" (in number).

2. Papyrus Bodmer XV ($\mathfrak{P}^{75}$)

§120. $\mathfrak{P}^{75}$ is the designation for Papyrus Bodmer XIV-XV (Victor Martin and Rodolphe Kasser, *Papyrus Bodmer XIV, Evangile de Luc chap. 3-24* and *Papyrus Bodmer XV, Evangile de Jean chap. 1-15* [Bibliotheca Bodmeriana, 1961]), a codex with 51 surviving leaves containing parts of Luke 3–24 and of John 1–15. The pages were originally about 10.2 by 5.1 inches in size (26 X 13 cm., reduced to 22.5 X 11.5 cm. in the photographic reproduction by Martin and Kasser), and in much of the manuscript are very well preserved, although in other parts reduced to fragments which had to be fitted back together again. Each page is written in a single column of from 38 to 45 lines, with 25 to 36 letters in a line. The handwriting is a clear upright uncial and, on the basis of comparison with Oxyrhynchus Papyri 2293 (second century), 2322 (second or early third century), 2370 (c. A.D. 200) and other manuscripts, is attributed to a date between A.D. 175 and 225 (Martin and Kasser, *Papyrus Bodmer XIV,* p. 13), thus is nearly as old as $\mathfrak{P}^{66}$ (§108).

§121. In the case of $\mathfrak{P}^{75}$ the pages of the codex are not numbered. The text with which we are concerned, corresponding to what is available on $\mathfrak{P}^{28}$ (Jn 6:8-12, 17-22), is found on the page that appears as Plate 75 in the publication of *Papyrus Bodmer XV* by Martin and Kasser, and is reproduced in our Fig. 9. This page, now in fragmentary condition, contained Jn 6:7-22. Lines 1-15 correspond to Jn 6:8-12, and Lines 27-44 correspond to Jn 6:17-22. They may be transcribed and restored as follows:

$$\mathfrak{P}^{75}$$

Page containing Jn 6:7-22
Lines 1-15 (Jn 6:8-12)

               8 λέγει αὐτ[ῷ εἷς ἐκ]
 [τῶν] μαθητῶν αὐτοῦ, Ἀνδρέας ὁ ἀδελ-
 [φὸς Σί]μονος Πέτρου, 9 Ἔστιν παιδάριον
 ὧδε [ὃς ἔ]χει ε̄ ἄρτους κριθίνους καὶ β̄ ὀψά-
5 [ρ]ια· ἀ[λλὰ] ταῦτα τί ἐστιν εἰς τοσούτους;
 10 [ε]ἶπεν [ὁ ι̅ς̅], Ποιήσατε τοὺς α̅ν̅ο̅υ̅ς̅ ἀναπε-
 [σεῖν. ἦν δὲ χόρτος πολὺς ἐν τῷ] τόπῳ.
 [ἀνέπεσαν οὖν οἱ ἄνδρες τὸν ἀριθμὸν ὡς]
 πεντ[ακισχίλιοι. 11 ἔλαβεν οὖν τοὺς ἄρ]τους
10 [ὁ ι̅ς̅ καὶ εὐχαριστήσας] ἔδω-
 [κ]εν [τοῖς ἀνακειμένο]ις, ὁμοίως καὶ
 [ἐκ] τῶ[ν ὀψαρίων ὅ]σον ἤθελο[ν.] 12 ὡς [δὲ]
 [ἐνεπλήσθησαν λέγ]ει τοῖς μαθη[ταῖς αὐ-]
 [τ]οῦ, Συναγάγε[τε τὰ περισσεύσαντα] κλά-

Figure 9. Papyrus Bodmer XV ($\mathfrak{P}^{75}$): John 6:7-22.
Approximately actual size.

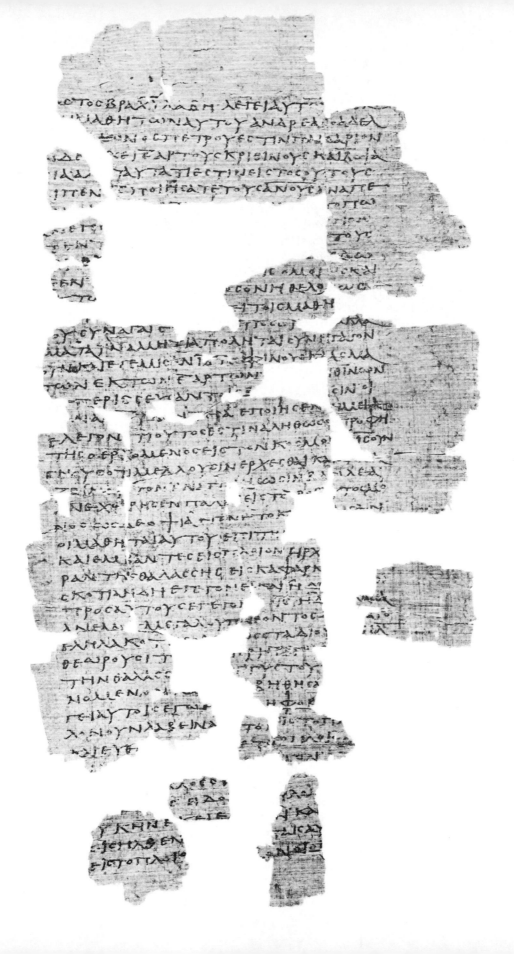

ετοσβραχ̣ι̣λαεμ λετει αυτ̣[
τιλαδητωναυτουανδρεα . . δλε[
. . εωνοσεστερουεστιναγα . αριον[
. . δε   ξει γαρτουσκρισ̣ινουσκαιϲαδα[
ιδα[ταυταπεστινεισ̣το̣σ̣ουτους̣[
ιττεν   ε̣στοιησατετουσανουσανατε[
                                          . . . τω[
                                          . . . . . [
                                          του[

                      . . ι̣ . . . . . οσκ̣[
              εσονημβελ̣ω ωϲ[
              . . τοισμαθη[
                      . . ωϲ̣[κα[
γ̣ευναγα̣σ   λ̣ . . εγνειϲ̣του[
καται̣ λναλιη̣σ̣ιαπολησ̣ταϲ̣ευ̣η̣σ̣ισ̣του[
γ̣ν̣ωλαϲ̣ελλισεντοιστ̣ . εινουσ̣εϲ̣λα[
τωνεκτωνϲ̣εαρτων . . ε   . . θ̣ινω̣ν[
        περισσ̣εω̣αντ . . . . ε   σιν ο̣[
        . λα   . . ι̣ . . . . ελα εποιησεν̣   . . ρο̣φη[
ελειον   πο̣υτοσεστινα̣λα̣ληθ̣ω̣ϲ̣   . . ̣̣ιϲ̣ω̣ν̣[
τηϲο̣εϲ̣ . αλμενοσεισ̣τονκ̣ . ελ̣α[
ετ̣ . νΰϲ̣οτιαλλαλοϲιν ερχεσθ̣α̣ . κα[
ϲε . λα . . . . τον̣ . ναϲ̣ . . . . . ωϲ̣ιν̣ . χ̣ιλεα[
νεχ̣ . ρ̣μεντπαυ̣ . . . . ειϲ̣τ̣ε̣   . . αιν[
διο . . τοϲ̣αϲω . . . + . λα̣ . τ̣ιτ̣ε̣τ̣ . . [
οιμαθηταιαυτ̣ουεπιτ̣ι[
καιθελαντεσειστ̣πλοιον ηρχ̣[
ρανττϲθαλασσησ̣εισκαφαρνα̣[
ϲκ̣οτιαηδηε̣τ̣ . . . ονε̣ . . . ν η̣ . α̣[
ττροϲα̣υτουϲετ̣εγε̣ . . . . ον̣τοϲ̣ . . . [
λ̣νεμ̣α . . . λιε . . ιϲ̣ . . . . . . τ̣λ̣α̣ι̣[
εληλακοτ̣[σ̣[
θεωρουϲιτ̣[τ̣ . υ̣σ̣τ̣ . [
τηνθαλασϲ[η̣ημε̣α[
γ̣αλλεν̣ . . . . [η̣οε̣[
γ̣εταυτο̣ϲε̣γ̣ . [τ̣[
λ̣ . ιογνλαϲ̣εινα[το̣ι̣ . [τ̣ι̣τ̣ι
διευ[ϲ̣ . ̣ . ι̣ . νο̣ . . [

                . . οεϲ̣[
                . . λ̣δ̣[. ̣ . α̣[
                . . ϲ̣ιε[. . ι̣ϲ̣α̣ . [
γ̣κμ̣ηε̣[. . ϲ̣α̣ε̣[
ϲ̣ξεηλθεν[. . λ̣νοϲε̣[
ειϲ̣τοττλο̣ι̣ο̣[

15   [σ]ματα, ἵνα μή τι ἀπόληται.

Lines 27-44 (Jn 6:17-22)

17 καὶ ἐμβάντες εἰς πλοῖον ἤρχ[οντο πέ-]
ραν τῆς θαλάσσης εἰς Καφαρν[αούμ. καὶ]
σκοτία ἤδη ἐγεγόνει καὶ ʹἤδ[η' οὔπω]
30   πρὸς αὐτοὺς ἐγεγόν[ει ὁ] ι̅ς̅. 18 ἡ δ[ὲ θάλασσα]
ἀνέμ[ου] μεγάλου πνέοντος [διεγείρ]ατο.
19 ἐληλακότ[ες οὖν ὡ]ς σταδίου[ς κ̅ε̅], ἠ̅λ̅
θεωροῦσι τ[ὸν ι̅ν̅ πε]ριπ[ατοῦντα ἐπὶ]
τὴν θάλασσ[αν καὶ ἐ]γγὺς τοῦ [πλοίου γι-]
35   νόμενον, [καὶ ἐφο]βήθησα[ν. 20 ὁ δὲ λέ-]
γει αὐτοῖς, Ἐγώ ε[ἰμι, μ]ὴ φοβ[εῖσθε. 21 ἤθε-]
λον οὖν λαβεῖν α[ὐ]τὸ[ν ε]ἰς τὸ π[λοῖον,]
καὶ εὐθ[έως ἐγένετο] τὸ πλοῖον [ἐπὶ]
[τῆς γῆς εἰς ἣν ὑπῆγ]ον. 22 [Τῇ ἐπαύρι-]
40   [ον ὁ ὄχ]λος ὁ[ἑστηκὼς πέραν τῆς θα-]
[λάσση]ς εἶδο[ν ὅτι π]λοι[άριον ἄλλο]
[ο]ὐκ ἦν ἐκεῖ ε[ἰ μὴ ἕ]ν, καὶ [ὅτι οὐ συ-]
[ν]εισῆλθεν [τοῖς μαθη]ταῖς αὐ[τοῦ ὁ]
[ι̅ς̅] εἰς τὸ πλοῖο[ν ἀλλὰ μ]όνοι οἱ [μαθηταί]

Page containing Jn 6:7-22
Lines 1-15 (Jn 6:8-12)
          8 Said to him one of
His disciples, Andrew, Simon
Peter's brother, 9 "There is a lad
here, who has five barley loaves, and two
5   fish; but what are these for so many people?"
10 Jesus said, "Have the people sit
down." Now there was much grass in the place.
So the men sat down, in number about
five thousand. 11 Jesus therefore took the loaves;
10   and having given thanks, He gave
to those who were seated; likewise also
of the fish as much as they wanted. 12 And when
they were filled, He said to His disciples,
"Gather up the left-over frag-
ments that nothing may be lost."

Lines 27-44 (Jn 6:17-22)
17 and after getting into a boat, they started to cross
the sea to Capernaum. And
it had already become dark, and Jesus had not yet
30   come to them. And the sea
began to be stirred up because a strong wind was blowing.
19 When therefore they had rowed about 25 or 30 stadia,
they beheld Jesus walking on
the sea, and drawing near to the boat;
35   and they were frightened. 20 But He
said to them, "It is I; do not be afraid." 21 They were

willing therefore to receive Him into the boat;
and immediately the boat was at
the land to which they were going. 22 The next
day the multitude that stood on the other side of the
sea saw that there was no other small boat
there, except one, and that Jesus had not
entered with His disciples
into the boat, but that His disciples had gone away alone.

40

§122.   To be noted in the Greek text of $\mathfrak{P}^{75}$ are the following points. In Jn 6:9 instead of the Greek words πέντε and δύο, as in $\mathfrak{P}^{66}$, this scribe uses the Greek numerals $\bar{\epsilon}$ and $\bar{\beta}$ for "five" and "two" in Line 4, and also in Jn 6:19 uses $\overline{\kappa\epsilon}$ (as must undoubtedly be supplied in the space available) and $\bar{\lambda}$ for 25 and 30 in Line 32. In Jn 6:10 where $\mathfrak{P}^{66}$ reads, "Jesus therefore said," $\mathfrak{P}^{75}$ omits οὖν in Line 6 and reads, "Jesus said." As the available space indicates, the name of Jesus was undoubtedly abbreviated here (Line 6) ($\overline{\iota\varsigma}$), as in $\mathfrak{P}^{66}$, and the name is in fact preserved in the abbreviated form elsewhere on the same page (Line 30). In this same verse and line, $\mathfrak{P}^{75}$ also abbreviates ἀνθρώπους as $\overline{ανους}$, the same as $\mathfrak{P}^{66}$. In Jn 6:17 and Line 29, the scribe of $\mathfrak{P}^{75}$ wrote a second ἤδη ("already") after καί ("and") and in front of οὔπω ("not yet"), so that the sentence read, "And it had already become dark, and Jesus had already not yet come to them," probably an inadvertent repetition of the first "already," then went back and put two curving marks (the second supplied in our restoration where the papyrus is broken) above the second and mistaken ἤδη to cancel it. In the same verse in Line 30, probably also by an inadvertent repetition of ἐγεγόνει from Line 29 ("And it had already become dark"), the scribe writes this same third person singular pluperfect middle form of γίνομαι, properly meaning "to come to be," where $\mathfrak{P}^{28}$ (see below §124) and most other manuscripts will be found more properly to have ἐληλύθει, the third person singular pluperfect of the verb ἔρχομαι, meaning "to come." In Jn 6:18 and Line 30, $\mathfrak{P}^{75}$ has ἡ δέ where $\mathfrak{P}^{28}$ and most other manuscripts have ἥ τε, without appreciable change of meaning. In Jn 6:19 and Line 34, $\mathfrak{P}^{75}$ has ἐπὶ τὴν θάλασσαν (accusative case) where most other manuscripts have the more usual genitive of place for "on the sea," ἐπὶ τῆς θαλάσσης. In spite of these several variations as compared with $\mathfrak{P}^{66}$, and in spite of a few obvious errors, it is evident that, at least in these sections, $\mathfrak{P}^{75}$ is in close agreement with $\mathfrak{P}^{66}$.

3. Pacific School of Religion Papyrus 2 ($\mathfrak{P}^{28}$)

§123.   Pacific School of Religion Papyrus 2 comes from Oxyrhynchus, and in that series is Oxyrhynchus Papyrus 1596 (Bernard P. Grenfell and Arthur S. Hunt, *The Oxyrhynchus Papyri*, XIII [London: The Egypt Exploration Fund, 1919], pp. 8-10). In the international listing it is designated as $\mathfrak{P}^{28}$. The papyrus is shown in photographs made by infrared light in Fig. 10, the *recto* with Jn

Figure 10. Pacific School of Religion Papyrus 2 (OP 1596, 𝔓²⁸), *recto:* John 6:8-12; *verso:* John 6:17-22. *Approximately actual size.*

6:8-12 at the left, and the *verso* with Jn 6:17-22 at the right. The size of the fragment is about 4.2 by 2.1 inches. The lower margin is preserved, and the outer margin (at the right on the *recto,* at the left on the *verso*) is also intact or almost intact in the lower half of the fragment. The writing was in one column on the page. Eleven lines are preserved on the *recto,* twelve on the *verso,* with the extreme bottom portions of a few letters of one more line showing at the top of the *verso.* The original pages had probably 25 or 26 lines of writing, with 28 to 38 letters per line. The handwriting is a medium-sized, somewhat irregular and slanting uncial. The date is probably in the third century (Aland, ANT 2, p. 116).

§ 124.   The transcription and restoration of the *recto* (Jn 6:8-12) and *verso* (Jn 6:17-22) of 𝔓²⁸ follow.

𝔓²⁸

recto (Jn 6:8-12)

[Σίμω]νος Πέτρο[υ,]

[9 "Εστιν παιδάριον ὧδε ὃς ἔχ]ει πέντε ἄρτους [κρι-]
[θίνους καὶ δύο ὀψάρια·ἀλλ]ὰ ταῦτα τί ἐστιν ε[ἰς]
[τοσούτους; 10 εἶπεν ὁ ι̅ς̅, Ποιήσ]ατε τοὺς ἀνθρώπου[ς]

5   [ἀναπεσεῖν. ἦν δὲ χόρτο]ς πολὺς ἐν τῷ τό[πῳ.]
     [ἀνέπεσαν οὖν οἱ ἄ]νδρες τὸν ἀριθ[μὸν]
     [ὡς πεντακισ]χίλειοι. 11 [ἔ]λεβεν ο[ὖν]

     [τοὺς ἄρτους ὁ ι̅ς̅ κα]ὶ ε[ὐχα]ριστήσας ἔδ[ω-]
     [κεν τοῖς ἀνακειμ]ένοις, ὁμοίως καὶ ἐ[κ]
10   [τῶν ὀψαρίων ὅσο]ν ἤθελον. 12 ὡς δὲ
     [ἐνεπλήσθησαν] λέγει τοῖς μαθηταῖς α[ὐτοῦ]

verso (Jn 6:17-22)

     [κα]ὶ σκοτία ἤδ[η ἐγεγόνει καὶ οὔπω πρὸς αὐτοὺς]
     [ἐλ]ηλύθει ὁ ι̅ς̅. 18 ἤ τε θ[άλασσα ἀνέμου μεγά-]
     [λο]υ πνέοντος [δ]ιεγε[ίρετο. 19 ἐληλακότες οὖν]
     [ὡ]ς σταδίους εἴκοσι π[έντε ἢ τριάκοντα θεωροῦσιν]
5   [τὸ]ν ι̅ν̅ περιπατο[ῦντα ἐπὶ τῆς θαλάσσης]
     [κ]αὶ ἐγγὺς τοῦ πλο[ίου γινόμενον, καὶ]
     ἐφοβήθησαν. 20 ὁ δ[ὲ λέγει αὐτοῖς, Ἐγώ εἰμι,]
     μὴ φοβεῖσθ[αι.] 21 ἤθ[ελον οὖν λαβεῖν αὐτὸν
     εἰς τὸ πλοῖον, καὶ ε[ὐθέως ἐγένετο τὸ πλοῖον]
10   ἐπὶ τῆς γῆς εἰς ἢ[ν ὑπῆγον. 22 Τῇ ἐπαύ-]
     ριον ὁ ὄχλος ὁ ἐσ[τηκὼς πέραν τῆς θαλάσσης]
     ἴδεν ὅτι πλοιάριον [ἄλλο οὐκ ἐκεῖ εἰ μὴ ἕν]

recto (Jn 6:8-12)

            [Andrew,] Simon Peter's [brother, said to Him,]
     9 "There is a lad here, who has five barley loaves
     and two fish; but what are these for
     so many people?" 10 Jesus said, "Have the people
5   sit down." Now there was much grass in the place.
     So the men sat down, in number
     about five thousand. 11 Jesus therefore took
     the loaves; and having given thanks, He gave
     to those who were seated; likewise also of
10   the fish as much as they wanted. 12 And when
     they were filled, He said to His disciples,

verso (Jn 6:17-22)

     And it had already become dark, and Jesus had not yet
     come to them. 18 And the sea began to be stirred up because
     a strong wind was blowing. 19 When therefore they had rowed
     about twenty-five or thirty stadia, they beheld
5   Jesus walking on the sea,
     and drawing near to the boat; and
     they were frightened. 20 But He said to them, "It is I;
     do not be afraid." 21 They were willing therefore to receive Him
     into the boat; and immediately the boat was
10   at the land to which they were going. 22 The next
     day the multitude that stood on the other side of the sea
     saw that there was no other small boat there, except one

§125. In $\mathfrak{P}^{28}$ the scribe uses words for numbers in Jn 6:9, *recto*
Line 2, and Jn 6:19, *verso* Line 4, as $\mathfrak{P}^{66}$ (§118) did in Jn 6:9, rather
than numerals like $\mathfrak{P}^{75}$ (§121) used in Jn 6:9 and 19. In Jn 6:9, *recto*   **109**

Line 3, $\mathfrak{P}^{28}$ writes ταῦτα τί ἐστιν, the same as $\mathfrak{P}^{75}$, rather than τί ἐστιν ταῦτα, as in $\mathfrak{P}^{66}$. In Jn 6:10, *recto* Line 4, $\mathfrak{P}^{28}$ writes out the word ἀνθρώπους in full rather than using the abbreviation $\overline{ανους}$ as in both $\mathfrak{P}^{66}$ and $\mathfrak{P}^{75}$. The name of Jesus is abbreviated as $\overline{IC}$ in both $\mathfrak{P}^{66}$ and $\mathfrak{P}^{75}$, appearing in intact portions of the *verso* of $\mathfrak{P}^{28}$ in Line 2 (Jn 6:17) as $\overline{IC}$ = Ἰησοῦς and in Line 5 (Jn 6:19) as $\overline{IN}$ = Ἰησοῦν. In Jn 6:11 in Line 7 of the *recto* $\mathfrak{P}^{28}$ has ἔλεβεν, "took," rather than the more usual spelling ἔλαβεν, which was in both $\mathfrak{P}^{66}$ and $\mathfrak{P}^{75}$. Also in Jn 6:19 in Line 6 of the *verso* $\mathfrak{P}^{28}$ has ἐνγύς rather than the more usual spelling ἐγγύς, which is in $\mathfrak{P}^{75}$. In both of these cases the spelling by $\mathfrak{P}^{28}$ no doubt corresponded with the usual pronunciation. In Jn 6:17 in Line 2 of the *verso* $\mathfrak{P}^{28}$ writes correctly ἐληλύθει rather than the erroneous second ἐγεγόνει of $\mathfrak{P}^{75}$ (cf. §122). In Jn 6:18 in Line 2 of the *verso* $\mathfrak{P}^{28}$ has ἤ τε rather than the ἡ δέ of $\mathfrak{P}^{75}$ (cf. §122), and is in agreement in this point with most of the later manuscripts. In Jn 6:22 in Line 12 of the *verso* $\mathfrak{P}^{28}$ has ἴδεν, doubtless as the equivalent of εἶδεν, which is the third person singular second aorist indicative active of ὁράω, "to see," rather than εἶδον, which is the third person plural of the same verb, and is found in $\mathfrak{P}^{75}$ and most of the other manuscripts. Such are the minor variations in the preserved text of $\mathfrak{P}^{28}$. But at one point there is also a question as to the restoration. In Jn 6:19 in Lines 4-5 of the *verso,* the restoration we have given makes Line 4 contain 40 letters, or perhaps 39 if the last word was written with a stroke extending horizontally from the top of the preceding letter in place of the final ν, as was sometimes done (cf. §110 and see Casson and Hettich, *Excavations at Nessana,* 2, p. 82), i.e., θεωροῦσῑ. With either 40 or 39 letters, the otherwise apparently normal maximum of 38 letters per line in $\mathfrak{P}^{28}$ (§123) is exceeded. This difficulty could be avoided if it is supposed that the article τόν was omitted in front of the name of Jesus at the beginning of Line 5 and that the ν that appears there is in fact the final letter of -σιν, the last syllable of θεωροῦσιν carried over from the end of the preceding line. But perhaps the slight excess in the preceding line is not impossible even if the article is retained at the beginning of Line 5. Here again, then, in spite of some variations of $\mathfrak{P}^{28}$ from $\mathfrak{P}^{75}$ and $\mathfrak{P}^{66}$, it is still, in the main, a witness to the very same text.

C

A Sequence Extending from the Papyri to the
Parchments, and from the Uncials to the
Minuscules, and Grouped
by Theoretical Text Types

1. Introduction

§ 126. The small portion of text studied in the first sequence
above (§ § 97-115) was selected because this was the portion preserved in the oldest known fragment of the Greek New Testament,
namely, Papyrus Rylands Greek 457 ($\mathfrak{P}^{52}$), which contains Jn 18:31-
33, 37-38. The small portion of text studied in the second sequence
(§ § 116-125) was chosen because this is the portion preserved in the
immediately available fragment, Pacific School of Religion Papyrus 2
(OP 1596; $\mathfrak{P}^{28}$), which contains Jn 6:8-12, 17-22. In a third sequence, now, we will, for reasons already given (§ 96), continue in
the Gospel according to John, but will select a passage that consti-
tutes a considerable section in the book, namely, the passage with
which the Gospel opens, the prologue (Jn 1:1-18). We will also read
this passage in a somewhat larger number of witnesses, beginning
with the papyri and going on into the parchments (and even one
paper manuscript), and reading not only uncial but also minuscule
script. For some sense of order and grouping among this larger
number of manuscripts, they will be taken up in a sequence corresponding to recognition of Alexandrian witnesses, Western witnesses,
and Koine or Byzantine witnesses (cf. § 86); but the variants at any
given point will be looked at not only in terms of hypothetical text
type but also from the point of view of intrinsic probability (cf.
§ 88). In the first two sequences above (§ § 97-125) not a few
variations among the several manuscripts were observed, but they
were of minor sort, as are most of the variations found in textual
criticism, the sort of variations that are apparently almost inevitable
in the copying of manuscripts, involving such matters as differences
in spelling or order of words, and relatively obvious mistakes. In the
third sequence, now, however, the variations that will be encoun-

tered will be not only more of this sort already met but also at least some that have an actual and important bearing on the understanding and meaning of the passage in question (particularly in Jn 1:3-4 and 1:18). Remembering (cf. §96) that we are deliberately directing our attention to Greek manuscripts that contain the Gospel according to John (particularly Jn 1:1-18), and that we are following the hypothetical three large text types outlined above (§86), we begin with the Alexandrian witnesses, and specifically the Proto-Alexandrian which are, for John, the papyri $\mathfrak{P}^{66}$ and $\mathfrak{P}^{75}$, and the parchment B. For the Western witnesses we use ℵ, D, and W, for along with the well-known Western manuscript D, ℵ has been shown to agree with D and to have a Western text in Jn 1:1–8:38 (although being, as is more commonly known, Alexandrian thereafter), while W also has Western readings in Jn 1:1–5:11 (W^{supp}) as well as elsewhere (although it also has yet other sections which are Alexandrian and Byzantine). For the Koine or Byzantine witnesses we use A, which belongs to this text family in the Gospels, and two of the numerous minuscules, namely, Codex 666 and Codex 1345. Codex 1345 also gives an intimation of the nature of the lectionaries (which we will not take up as such) for, although not a lectionary manuscript proper, it does have the lections marked. Beyond that we shall give only some examples of the kind of evidence to be found further in the versions (examples in the Itala and Vulgate) and the church fathers (examples in Irenaeus and Origen). Finally, at the end of this sequence, and to the extent that it has provided limited but relevant evidence, we shall draw our own conclusions as to the most probably original text in the two passages (Jn 1:3-4 and 1:18) where the variants have the largest bearing on the understanding and meaning of the text. We proceed now to the papyri ($\mathfrak{P}^{66}$ and $\mathfrak{P}^{75}$) and the parchment (B) that are Proto-Alexandrian witnesses.

(a) *Proto-Alexandrian Witnesses*

(a) *Papyri*

2. Papyrus Bodmer II ($\mathfrak{P}^{66}$)

§127. Papyrus Bodmer II ($\mathfrak{P}^{66}$), already described (§§107-108), is a remarkably early manuscript, dating around A.D. 200 or, perhaps, even as much earlier as the middle or first half of the second century, and is remarkably well preserved, containing the first fourteen chapters of the Gospel according to John almost intact, and the balance of the book in fragments. In the small portions already studied, namely, Jn 6:8-11 (§118) and 18:31-33, 37-38 (§109), it has also exhibited a text that appears to have been copied and corrected with relative care as compared, for example, with some evident errors in $\mathfrak{P}^{75}$ (Papyrus Bodmer XV, A.D. 175-225, §122) and more in $\mathfrak{P}^{60}$ (Papyrus Colt 4, seventh century, §114). Because of the early date of $\mathfrak{P}^{66}$, therefore, and because of what, by the above sampling, appears to be the relatively good character of its text, it may be taken as providing the base text of Jn 1:1-18, with which the several other manuscripts in the present sequence will be compared. Accordingly, our first task is to read this portion of 𝔓⁶⁶. In this case we shall revert to the initial procedure employed with 𝔓⁵² (§99) and copy the uncial text, as nearly as we can make it out, just as it is.

§128. The upper outside corner of the first written leaf of 𝔓⁶⁶, where the page number would normally stand (§107), is broken away; but the sequence of completely legible page numbers that soon follows makes it plain that we have here Pages *a'* and *β'*, i.e., 1 and 2. At the top of Page 1 (Fig. 11), in the first written line, there is the title of the Gospel with dashed horizontal lines above and below it, εὐαγγέλιον κατὰ Ἰωάννην, Gospel according to John. Below that, twenty-five lines of writing contain the text of the first chapter of the Gospel extending into the fourteenth verse and, on Page 2 (Fig. 12), twenty-three lines of writing continue the text almost to the end of verse 21. The uncial text of Jn 1:1-18, as it stands on the two pages, is as follows. Spacing is introduced between words. Punctuation, which consists of a high point, and dieresis over initial Iota and over Upsilon, is reproduced as it stands in the manuscript. Gaps in the text are, for the moment, not supplied.

§128

A Sequence Grouped by Text Types

𝔓⁶⁶

Page 1 (Jn 1:1-14)

```
   ΕΝ ΑΡΧΗ ΗΝ Ο ΛΟΓΟϹ · ΚΑΙ Ο ΛΟΓΟϹ ΗΝ ΠΡΟϹ ΤΟ
   ΚΑΙ Θ̅Ϲ̅ ΗΝ Ο ΛΟΓΟϹ · ΟΥΤΟϹ ΗΝ ΕΝ ΑΡΧΗ ΠΡΟϹ Τ
   ΠΑΝΤΑ ΔΙ ΑΥΤΟΥ ΕΓΕΝΕΤΟ · ΚΑΙ ΧΩΡΙϹ Α
5  ΕΓΕΝΕΤΟ ΟΥΔΕΝ Ο ΓΕΓΟΝΕΝ ΑΥΤΩ ΖΩ
   ΚΑΙ Η ΖΩΗ ΗΝ ΤΟ ΦΩϹ ΤΩΝ ΑΝΘΡΩΠΩ̅
   ΚΑΙ ΤΟ ΦΩϹ ΕΝ ΤΗ ϹΚΟΤΙΑ ΦΑΙΝΕΙ · ΚΑΙ Η
   ϹΚΟΤΙΑ ΑΥΤΟ ΟΥ ΚΑΤΕΛΑΒΕΝ ·
   ΓΕΝΕΤΟ ΑΝΘΡΩΠΟϹ ΑΠΕϹΤΑΛΜΕΝΟϹ ΠΑ
10 ΡΑ Θ̅Υ̅ ΟΝΟΜΑ ΑΥΤΩ ϊΩΑΝΝΗϹ ΟΥΤΟϹ ΗΛ
   ΘΕΝ ΕΙϹ ΜΑΡΤΥΡΙΑΝ ϊΝΑ ΜΑΡΤΥΡΗϹΗ
   ΠΕΡΙ ΤΟΥ ΦΩΤΟϹ · ϊΝΑ ΠΑΝΤΕϹ ΠΙϹΤΕΥ
   ϹΩϹΙΝ ΔΙ ΑΥΤΟΥ · ΟΥΚ ΗΝ ΕΚΕΙΝΟϹ ΤΟ
   ΦΩϹ ΑΛΛΑ ϊΝΑ ΜΑΡΤΥΡΗϹΗ ΠΕΡΙ ΤΟΥ
15 ΦΩΤΟϹ ΗΝ ΤΟ ΦΩϹ ΤΟ ΑΛΗΘΙΝΟΝ Ο ΦΩ
   ΤΙΖΕΙ ΠΑΝΤΑ ΑΝΘΡΩΠΟΝ ΕΡΧΟΜΕΝΟ
   ΕΙϹ ΤΟΝ ΚΟϹΜΟΝ · ΕΝ ΤΩ ΚΟϹΜΩ ΗΝ Κ
   Ο ΚΟϹΜΟϹ ΔΙ ΑΥΤΟΥ ΕΓΕΝΕΤΟ ΚΑΙ Ο ΚΟϹ
   ΜΟϹ ΑΥΤΟΝ ΟΥΚ ΕΓΝΩ ΕΙϹ ΤΑ ϊΔΙΑ ΗΛΘ
20 ΚΑΙ ΟΙ ϊΔΙΟΙ ΑΥΤΟΝ ΟΥ ΠΑΡΕΛΑΒΟΝ · ΟϹΟ
   ΔΕ ΕΛΑΒΟΝ ΑΥΤΟ͞Ν ΕΔΩΚΕΝ ΑΥΤΟΙ Ε
   ΞΟΥϹΙΑΝ ΤΕΚΝΑ Θ̅Υ̅ ΓΕΝΕϹΘΑΙ ΤΟΙϹ
   ΠΙϹΤΕΥΟΥϹΙΝ ΕΙϹ ΤΟ ΟΝΟΜΑ ΑΥΤΟΥ ΟΙ
   Κ ΕΞ ΑΙΜΑΤΩΝ ΟΥΔΕ ΕΚ ΘΕΛΗΜ
25 ϹΑΡΚΟϹ ΟΥΔΕ ΕΚ ΘΕΛΗΜΑΤΟϹ ΑΝ
   ΑΛΛΑ ΕΚ Θ̅Υ̅ ΕΓΕΝΝΗΘΗϹΑΝ ΚΑΙ
```

Page 2 (Jn 1:14-18)

```
   ΑΡΞ ΕΓΕΝΕΤΟ ΚΑΙ ΕϹΚΗΝΩϹΕΝ ΕΝ ΗΜ
```

ΚΑΙ ΕΘΕΑϹΑΜΕΘΑ ΤΗΝ ΔΟΞΑΝ ΑΫΤΟΫ
ΞΑΝ ωϹ ΜΟΝΟΓΕΝΟΫϹ ΠΑΡΑ ΠΡϹ ΠΛΗ
ΧΑΡΙΤΟϹ ΚΑΙ ΑΛΗΘΙΑϹ · ΪωΑΝΝΗϹ ΜΑ
5 ΤΫΡΙ ΠΕΡΙ ΑΫΤΟΫ ΚΑΙ Κ ΕΚΡΑΓΕΝ ΛΕ
ΟΫΤΟϹ ΗΝ ΟΝ ΕΙΠΟΝ Ο ΟΠΙϹω ΜΟΫ ΕΡΧ
ΜΕΝΟϹ ΕΜΠΡΟϹΘΕΝ ΜΟΫ ΓΕΓΟΝΕΝ
ΤΙ ΠΡωΤΟϹ ΜΟΫ ΗΝ · ΟΤΙ ΕΚ ΤΟΫ ΠΛΗΡω
ΜΑΤΟϹ ΑΫΤΟΫ ΗΜΕΙϹ ΠΑΝΤΕϹ ΕΛΑΒ
10 ΜΕΝ ΚΑΙ ΧΑΡΙΝ ΑΝΤΙ ΧΑΡΙΤΟϹ · ΟΤΙ
ΜΟϹ ΔΙΑ ΜωΫϹΕωϹ ΕΔΟΘΗ · Η ΧΑΡ
ΔΕ ΚΑΙ ΑΛΗΘΙΑ ΔΙΑ ΙΫ ΧΫ ΕΓΕΝΕΤ

Figure 11.   Papyrus Bodmer II ($\mathfrak{P}^{66}$), Page 1: John 1:14. *Reproduced at actual size.*

ΘΝ ΟΥΔΕΙϹ ΕѠΡΑΚΕΝ ΠѠΠΟΤΑΙ · Μ
ΝΟΓΕΝΗϹ ΘϹ Ο ѠΝ ΕΙϹ ΤΟΝ ΚΟΛΠΟΝ Τ
ΠΡϹ ΕΚΙΝΟϹ ΕΞΗΓΗϹΑΤΟ ·

§129. In the foregoing text a few letters are missing at the right end of many of the lines on Pages 1 and 2 (in the latter case due especially to the vertical strips of strengthening fibers which have been overlaid), and a very few more letters are missing at the left end of some of the lines on both pages, particularly Page 2. These can easily be supplied, and will be added in the complete transcription and restoration of the text which follows. At the end of Line 6 on

Figure 12. Papyrus Bodmer II (𝔓⁶⁶), Page 2: John 1:14-21. *Reproduced at actual size.*

Page 1 there is a horizontal stroke extending from over the last letter, and this indicates that a final Nu is to be supplied (cf. §125), thus, ἀνθρώπων. Throughout the text abbreviations are employed for God ($\overline{\theta\varsigma}$, $\overline{\theta\upsilon}$, $\overline{\theta\nu}$), Father ($\overline{\pi\rho\varsigma}$), and Jesus Christ ($\overline{I\upsilon}$ $\overline{X\upsilon}$), and these words are also written out in full in the following transcription. On Page 1, in Lines 4, 13, and 18, the final Alpha of διά ("through") is dropped before the following Alpha (in the word αὐτοῦ), and will be shown with the apostrophe which is now customary. In Line 5 it is obvious that the word ἐν ("in") is needed before αὐτῷ ("him"), and it was probably omitted by accident because the scribe had just written a word ending with the same two letters (γέγονεν). That the end of Line 8 (after κατέλαβεν, "comprehend") is left blank shows that this is the termination of a paragraph. At the beginning of the next paragraph (Jn 1:6) at the beginning of the next line (Line 9) we are able to read only γένετο. The initial Epsilon of the full word, ἐγένετο ("there came"), could have been omitted by mistake, but more probably was set out into the left margin (where it has now been lost by the dilapidation of the papyrus) on purpose to mark the beginning of a new paragraph. Similar examples of the placement in the margin of an initial letter of what could be a paragraph appear elsewhere in the manuscript (Page 3 Line 7, etc.). At the end of Line 17 there is a Kappa with a stroke to the right and below; this must stand for καί. On Page 2, at the end of Line 1 it can no longer be made out whether there was written ἡμεῖν or ἡμῖν ("us"); the latter would now be the more usual spelling. In Line 4 we have ἀληθίας, and in Line 12 ἀλήθια, where the more usual spellings would now be ἀληθείας and ἀλήθεια. In Line 5 μαρτυρῖ corresponds to μαρτυρεῖ ("bore witness"); in Line 13 πώποται would more usually be spelled πώποτε. Again, in Line 5, in the word κέκραγεν ("cried out") the scribe evidently wrote an additional wrong letter (between the first Kappa and Epsilon), then later he or his corrector erased it, leaving an empty space within the word. Also in Line 6 the article ὁ which goes with the participle ἐρχόμενος ("he who comes") was omitted at the first writing, then afterward put in above the line. Taking account of the foregoing observations, we shall now set forth the completed text of $\mathfrak{P}^{66}$ in Jn 1:1-18, including the changes by the corrector, restoring the missing places, writing out the abbreviations, and bringing the spelling into accord with what is now customary usage. As for punctuation, there is some in $\mathfrak{P}^{66}$, but unfortunately it is completely lacking at the very point where it would be most helpful in determining the sense, namely, in Line 5 of Page 1 (Jn 1:3). At this point, where judgment will be only provisional until evidence in other manuscripts is noted, our punctuation is that of Nestle-Aland, *Novum Testamentum Graece,* 25th ed. 1963, and Aland, *Synopsis,* 2d ed. 1964, while the rest of our punctuation is that of *The Greek New Testament* of the Bible Societies. The text as thus reconstituted and punctuated, and with breathing and accents, which we will consider as being, in our terms and for the purposes of a base with which to compare other manuscripts, the real text of $\mathfrak{P}^{66}$, follows:

𝔓⁶⁶

Page 1 (Jn 1:1-14)

εὐαγγέλιον κατὰ Ἰωάννην
1 Ἐν ἀρχῇ ἦν ὁ λόγος, καὶ ὁ λόγος ἦν πρὸς τὸ[ν θεόν,]
καὶ θεὸς ἦν ὁ λόγος. 2 οὗτος ἦν ἐν ἀρχῇ πρὸς τ[ὸν θεόν.]
3 πάντα δι᾿ αὐτοῦ ἐγένετο, καὶ χωρὶς α[ὐτοῦ]
5   ἐγένετο οὐδὲν ὃ γέγονεν. 4 [ἐν] αὐτῷ ζω[ὴ ἦν,]
καὶ ἡ ζωὴ ἦν τὸ φῶς τῶν ἀνθρώπων·
5 καὶ τὸ φῶς ἐν τῇ σκοτίᾳ φαίνει, καὶ ἡ
σκοτία αὐτὸ οὐ κατέλαβεν.
6 ἐγένετο ἄνθρωπος ἀπεσταλμένος πα-
10   ρὰ θεοῦ, ὄνομα αὐτῷ Ἰωάννης· 7 οὗτος ἦλ-
θεν εἰς μαρτυρίαν, ἵνα μαρτυρήσῃ
περὶ τοῦ φωτός, ἵνα πάντες πιστεύ-
σωσιν δι᾿ αὐτοῦ. 8 οὐκ ἦν ἐκεῖνος τὸ
φῶς, ἀλλὰ ἵνα μαρτυρήσῃ περὶ τοῦ
15   φωτός. 9 Ἦν τὸ φῶς τὸ ἀληθινόν, ὃ φω-
τίζει πάντα ἄνθρωπον, ἐρχόμενον
εἰς τὸν κόσμον. 10 ἐν τῷ κόσμῳ ἦν, καὶ
ὁ κόσμος δι᾿ αὐτοῦ ἐγένετο, καὶ ὁ κόσμος αὐτὸν οὐκ ἔγνω. 11 εἰς τὰ ἴδια ἦλθ[εν,]
20   καὶ οἱ ἴδιοι αὐτὸν οὐ παρέλαβον. 12 ὅσο[ι]
δὲ ἔλαβον αὐτόν, ἔδωκεν αὐτοῖς ἐ-
ξουσίαν τέκνα θεοῦ γενέσθαι, τοῖς
πιστεύουσιν εἰς τὸ ὄνομα αὐτοῦ, 13 οἳ [οὐ-]
κ ἐξ αἱμάτων οὐδὲ ἐκ θελήμ[ατος]
25   σαρκὸς οὐδὲ ἐκ θελήματος ἀν[δρὸς]
ἀλλὰ ἐκ θεοῦ ἐγεννήθησαν. 14 Καὶ [ὁ λόγος]

Page 2 (Jn 1:14-18)

[σ]ὰρξ ἐγένετο καὶ ἐσκήνωσεν ἐν ἡμ[ῖν,]
καὶ ἐθεασάμεθα τὴν δόξαν αὐτοῦ, [δό-]
ξαν ὡς μονογενοῦς παρὰ πατρός, πλή[ρης]
χάριτος καὶ ἀληθείας. 15 Ἰωάννης μα[ρ-]
5   τυρεῖ περὶ αὐτοῦ καὶ κέκραγεν λέ[γων,]
Οὗτος ἦν ὃν εἶπον, Ὁ ὀπίσω μου ἐρχ[ό-]
μενος ἔμπροσθέν μου γέγονεν, [ὅ-]
τι πρῶτός μου ἦν. 16 ὅτι ἐκ τοῦ πληρώματος αὐτοῦ ἡμεῖς πάντες ἐλάβ[ο-]
10   μεν, καὶ χάριν ἀντὶ χάριτος· 17 ὅτι [ὁ νό-]
μος διὰ Μωυσέως ἐδόθη, ἡ χάρ[ις]
δὲ καὶ ἀλήθεια διὰ Ἰησοῦ Χριστοῦ ἐγένετ[ο.]
18 θεὸν οὐδεὶς ἑώρακεν πώποτε· μ[ο-]
νογενὴς θεὸς ὁ ὢν εἰς τὸν κόλπον τ[οῦ]
15   πατρὸς ἐκεῖνος ἐξηγήσατο.

Page 1 (Jn 1:1-14)

Gospel according to John

1 In the beginning was the Word, and the Word was with God,
and the Word was God. 2 He was in the beginning with God.
3 All things came into being through Him; and apart from Him
5   nothing came into being that has come into being. 4 In Him was life
and the life was the light of men.
5 And the light shines in the darkness; and the
darkness did not comprehend it.
6 There came a man, sent from
10   God, whose name was John. 7 He came
for a witness, that he might bear witness
of the light, that all might believe through him. 8 He was not the
light, but came that he might bear witness of the
15   light. 9 There was the true light which,
coming into the world, enlightens every man.
10 He was in the world, and
the world was made through Him, and the world
did not know Him. 11 He came to His own,
20   and those who were His own did not receive Him. 12 But as
many as received Him, to them He gave the
right to become children of God, even to those
who believe in His name: 13 who were born
not of blood, nor of the will
25   of the flesh, nor of the will of man,
but of God. 14 And the Word

Page 2 (Jn 1:14-18)

became flesh, and dwelt among us,
and we beheld His glory, glory
as of the Only Begotten from the Father, full
of grace and truth. 15 John bore
5   witness of Him, and cried out, saying,
"This was He of whom I said, 'He who comes after
me is become before me, for
He existed before me.' " 16 For of His full-
ness we all received,
10   and grace for grace. 17 For the
law was given through Moses; but grace
and truth were realized through Jesus Christ.
18 No man has seen God at any time; only
begotten God, who is in the bosom of the
15   Father, He has explained Him.

3. Papyrus Bodmer XV ($\mathfrak{P}^{75}$)

§ 131. With the text of $\mathfrak{P}^{66}$, a remarkably early and, insofar as
we have sampled it, an apparently quite carefully copied manuscript,
established in the foregoing fashion (§ 130) for Jn 1:1-18, it is now

Figure 13. Papyrus Bodmer XV ($\mathfrak{P}^{75}$): Luke 24:51-53 and John 1:1-16. *Approximately actual size.*

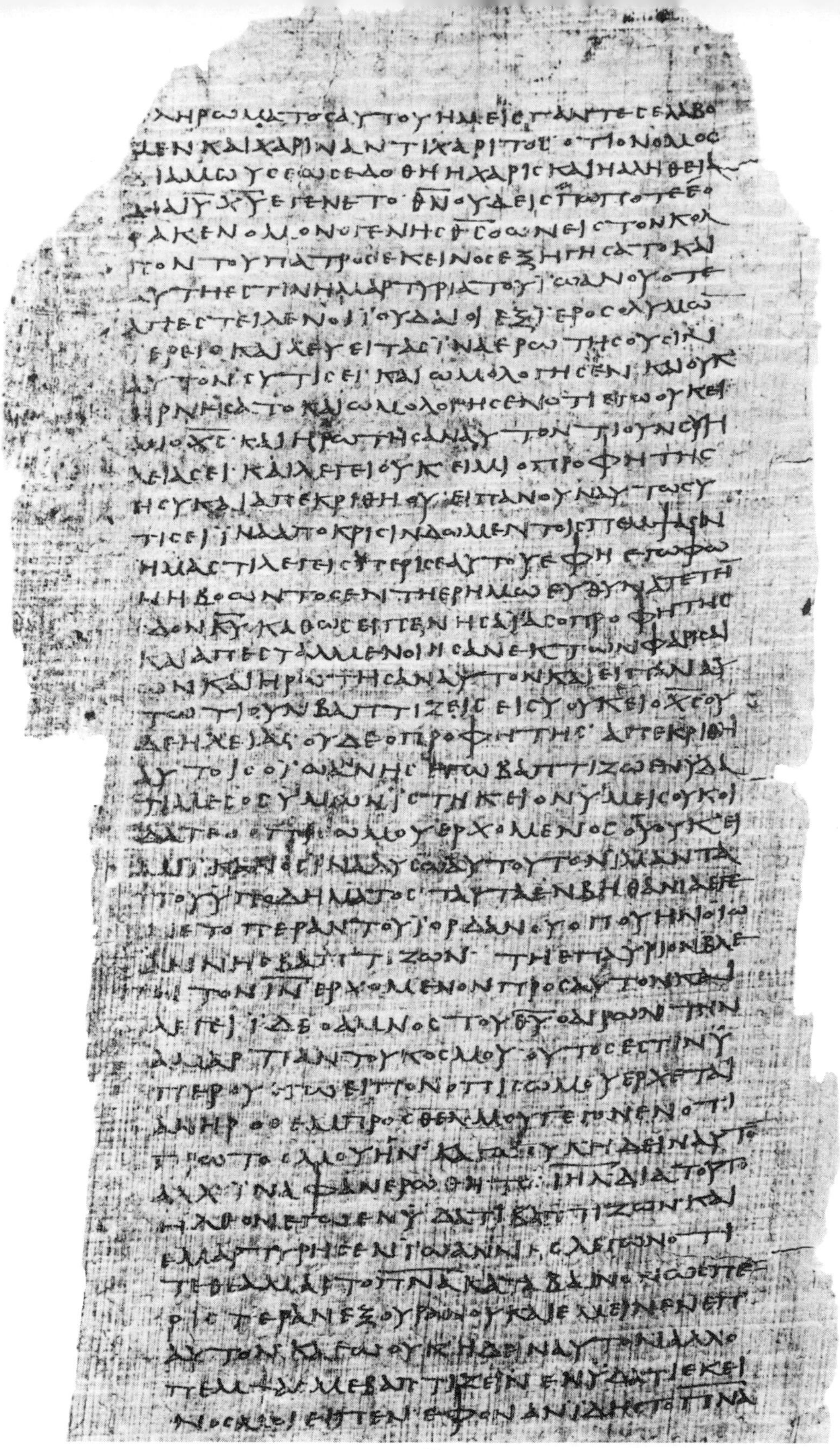

Figure 14. Papyrus Bodmer XV ($\mathfrak{P}^{75}$): John 1:16-33. *Approximately actual size.*

readily possible to read the same passage in the other manuscripts we chose to investigate (§126) and compare their texts with this text. For comparison of the other texts with the text of 𝔓⁶⁶, it may now be assumed that there is general familiarity, from the detailed transcriptions and restorations made hitherto, with the various problems of differences in spelling, use of abbreviations, recognition of obvious mistakes, etc.; and we may plan to pass over such matters or handle them in passing as a matter of course, in order to concentrate chiefly on only a few major problems which actually involve the meaning and interpretation of the text in significant points. In actual fact there are in Jn 1:1-18 just two textual problems of chief importance (in 1:3-4 and 1:18), with which we will be mainly concerned, and a few others of lesser importance which we will notice. Our next step is a comparison, of the sort just indicated, of 𝔓⁷⁵ with 𝔓⁶⁶. It will be remembered that 𝔓⁷⁵ is a codex dating probably between A.D. 175 and 225 (§120) and, although containing some obvious errors, tending on the whole, as far as we have seen, to agree very closely with 𝔓⁶⁶ (§122).

§132. On the page of 𝔓⁷⁵ shown in Fig. 13, the Gospel according to Luke ends with its title in a colophon near the top of the page; then, after a short space, comes in two lines the title of the Gospel according to John (εὐαγγέλιον / κατὰ Ἰωάνην). Following this, on the same page, are thirty more lines of writing which contain Jn 1:1-15 and the first three words of 1:16. In Line 10 of the text of John (counting inclusively from the title lines) it may be noted that the first letter (π) of the line is set out to the left into the margin. This marks the first full line of the sentence that began in the preceding line, ἐγένετο ἄνθρω/πος κτλ., "There came a man, etc.," and is the beginning of a new paragraph (Jn 1:6, cf. the same paragraph beginning in 𝔓⁶⁶, see above §129). On the next page of 𝔓⁷⁵, shown in Fig. 14, the balance of Jn 1:16-18 occupies the first six lines of the page.

§133. The first place to make a comparison of importance of 𝔓⁷⁵ with 𝔓⁶⁶ is in Jn 1:3-4. Looking back first at 𝔓⁶⁶ (Page 1 Lines 4-6, see above §128), the uncial text and punctuation of this passage are as follows:

𝔓⁶⁶

Page 1 (Jn 1:3-4)

ΠΑΝΤΑ ΔΙ ΑΥΤΟΥ ΕΓΕΝΕΤΟ· ΚΑΙ ΧΩΡΙC Α
5   ΕΓΕΝΕΤΟ ΟΥΔΕΝ Ο ΓΕΓΟΝΕΝ ΑΥΤΩ ΖΩ
ΚΑΙ Η ΖΩΗ ΗΝ ΤΟ ΦΩC ΤΩΝ ΑΝΘΡΩΠΩ‾

Restoring the letters obviously missing at the end of the lines, supplying one word probably omitted by mistake in Line 5, and adding breathings and accents, but for the moment supplying no punctuation in addition to what is contained in the manuscript itself (namely, a high point in Line 4), the text is as follows:

πάντα δι' αὐτοῦ ἐγένετο· καὶ χωρὶς α[ὐτοῦ]
5 ἐγένετο οὐδὲν ὃ γέγονεν [ἐν] αὐτῷ ζω[ὴ ἦν]
καὶ ἡ ζωὴ ἦν τὸ φῶς τῶν ἀνθρώπων

In order to read this text it is necessary to supply one more punctuation stop in addition to the stop the manuscript itself exhibits in Line 4, and the stop that is obvious at the end of Line 6. The required additional stop must go in Line 5, but there are two possible places where it can go. In our reconstruction of the text of 𝔓⁶⁶ above (§130) we chose, provisionally, to place the stop after ὃ γέγονεν. This punctuation results in the translation found in many English versions, as follows:

Jn 1:3-4

KJV
3 All things were made by him; and without him
was not any thing made that was made. 4 In him was life;
and the life was the light of men.

ASV
3 All things were made through him; and without him
was not anything made that hath been made. 4 In him was life;
and the life was the light of men.

RSV
3 all things were made through him, and without him
was not anything made that was made. 4 In him was life,
and the life was the light of men.

NASB
3 All things came into being through Him; and apart from Him
nothing came into being that has come into being. 4 In Him
was life; and the life was the light of men.

But it is also grammatically possible to place the stop, instead, after οὐδέν, and, strictly speaking, there is nothing in 𝔓⁶⁶ to say that this is not an equally good choice. This punctuation results in the translation recognized in several English versions, for example:

ASV margin
3 All things were made through him; and without him
was not anything made. That which hath been made 4 was life
in him; and the life was the light of men.

RSV margin
3 all things were made through him, and without him
was not anything made. That which has been made 4 was life
in him, and the life was the light of men.

§134. In 𝔓⁷⁵, in Lines 5-7 (Fig. 13, counting lines from the title at the beginning of the Gospel), the same passage (Jn 1:3-4) reads as follows, first in the uncial text, and then in the restored text:

Jn 1:3-4

5   ΠΑΝΤΑ ΔΙ ΑΥΤΟΥ ΕΓΕΝΕΤΟ ΚΑΙ ΧΩΡΙC
ΑΥΤΟΥ ΕΓΕΝΕΤΟ ΟΥΔΕ ΕΝ·Ο ΓΕΓΟΝΕΝ ΕΝ ΑΥΤΩ
ΖΩΗ ᴴΝ ΚΑΙ Η ΖΩΗ ΗΝ ΤΟ ΦΩC ΤΩΝ A̅N̅W̅N̅

5   πάντα δι᾽ αὐτοῦ ἐγένετο καὶ χωρὶς
αὐτοῦ ἐγένετο οὐδὲ ἕν· ὃ γέγονεν ἐν αὐτῷ
ζωὴ ἦν καὶ ἡ ζωὴ ἦν τὸ φῶς τῶν ἀνθρώπων

Here, in Jn 1:3-4 and in Line 6 of 𝔓⁷⁵, two matters call for notice in comparison with the same passage in 𝔓⁶⁶. The first is this: whereas 𝔓⁶⁶ reads the word οὐδέν ("nothing," or "not anything"), 𝔓⁷⁵ has οὐδὲ ἕν, which means "not one thing," or "no single thing." This simply makes more emphatic the statement already embodied in the sentence. Supposing that the punctuation stop is still to be placed after ὃ γέγονεν, the text results that, in fact, is found in Nestle-Aland (25th ed. 1963) and in the margin of *The Greek New Testament* edited by R. V. G. Tasker (cf. above §80), as follows:

Jn 1:3-4

Nestle-Aland, and Tasker margin

3 πάντα δι᾽ αὐτοῦ ἐγένετο, καὶ χωρὶς
αὐτοῦ ἐγένετο οὐδὲ ἓν ὃ γέγονεν. 4 ἐν αὐτῷ
ζωὴ ἦν, καὶ ἡ ζωὴ ἦν τὸ φῶς τῶν ἀνθρώπων.

If, in the translation of this text, οὐδὲ ἕν is treated as simply the equivalent of οὐδέν and rendered as "not anything" or "nothing," then the English versions already quoted in §133 suffice for the translation of this text too. If it is desired to emphasize the literal meaning of οὐδὲ ἕν ("not one thing," or "no single thing"), then the translation of The New English Bible, with the reading it recognizes in the margin, may be preferred:

Jn 1:3-4

NEB margin

3 through him all things came to be; no single created thing came into being without him. 4 There was life in him, and that life was the light of men.

§135. The second matter to notice in Line 6 in this passage in 𝔓⁷⁵ is, however, that there is now, in fact, a mark of punctuation in the line, namely, a high point after οὐδὲ ἕν and before ὃ γέγονεν. Yet it must be plainly noted that this mark of punctuation was probably not a part of the text as it was first copied in the manuscript. Note, for comparison, that farther down on the same page, in Line 9, there is another high point, which comes after the word κατέλαβεν, "comprehend." At this place, however, the scribe has almost certainly written the high point at the same time that he was writing the rest of the line, for he has left adequate room for the mark. But in Line 6 this is not the case. Rather in Line 6 the high point has been put in between two words (between ἕν and ὅ) where no extra space was originally left for it at all. Therefore in the original text of 𝔓⁷⁵, as well as in 𝔓⁶⁶ (§133), there was probably no punctuation at all in the line to which our present inquiry relates; and the full stop, which is required at the one place or the other in the line to make the passage intelligible, could have been equally well considered to belong at either place. What 𝔓⁷⁵ does, then, is to give us a mark of punctuation at the place where the person who inserted this high point understood or believed that it should go. There is also an addition to the original text in Line 7 on the same page, in the form of the addition of a letter that was erroneously omitted in the original copying. The first word in the line (ζωή, "life") ended with the letter Eta, and the second word (ἦν, "was") began with the same letter. The original scribe, by a natural type of mistake, omitted the second Eta. This is then put in above the line to make the necessary correction. Because the Eta inserted above the line is written slightly differently and more heavily than the Eta in the line, it may be supposed that this correction was made by a person other than the original scribe. Presumably this corrector was also the person who inserted the mark of punctuation in Line 6, but this cannot be known for sure. It is also to be remembered that this punctuation is provided here in 𝔓⁷⁵ in a manuscript that reads οὐδὲ ἕν ("no single thing") rather than οὐδέν ("nothing") as in 𝔓⁶⁶. Since οὐδὲ ἕν is a usual sentence-ending in Greek (cf. Rom 3:10, and below §209), the very existence of these words (rather than οὐδέν) in this manuscript could have been a factor in making the interpretation of the sentence provided by the insertion of the high point immediately after these words. At all events, in the punctuation as it stands in 𝔓⁷⁵ we have one possible interpretation of how the line in question is to be read. With respect to 𝔓⁷⁵ in its original form, however, as also with respect to 𝔓⁶⁶, this interpretation is not necessarily binding, for probably 𝔓⁷⁵ in its original form, like 𝔓⁶⁶, had no punctuation at all at the place in question. But if the interpretation by the corrector of 𝔓⁷⁵ is accepted, then we have here the text (§134) that is, in fact, printed in *The Greek New Testament* edited by R. V. G. Tasker, and in *The Greek New Testament* of the Bible Societies, and translated in the New English Bible, as follows:

Jn 1:3-4

The Greek New Testament, ed. Tasker
The Greek New Testament, Bible Societies

3 πάντα δι' αὐτοῦ ἐγένετο, καὶ χωρὶς
αὐτοῦ ἐγένετο οὐδὲ ἕν. ὃ γέγονεν 4 ἐν αὐτῷ
ζωὴ ἦν, καὶ ἡ ζωὴ ἦν τὸ φῶς τῶν ἀνθρώπων.

NEB

3 through him all things came to be; no single thing
was created without him. All that came to be 4 was alive
with his life, and that life was the light of men.

§136. The second place of importance to make a comparison of $\mathfrak{p}^{75}$ and $\mathfrak{p}^{66}$ is in Jn 1:18. Again looking first at $\mathfrak{p}^{66}$, we have the following text in its original uncial form (§128) and in our restoration (§130), the latter corresponding with the text printed in Nestle-Aland and in *The Greek New Testament* of the Bible Societies.

Jn 1:18

$\mathfrak{p}^{66}$

Page 2

$\overline{\Theta N}$ ΟΥΔΕΙϹ ΕѠΡΑΚΕΝ ΠѠΠΟΤΑΙ· Μ
ΝΟΓΕΝΗϹ $\overline{\Theta C}$ Ο ѠΝ ΕΙϹ ΤΟΝ ΚΟΛΠΟΝ Τ
15    $\overline{\Pi PC}$ ΕΚΙΝΟϹ ΕΞΗΓΗϹΑΤΟ·

θεὸν οὐδεὶς ἑώρακεν πώποτε· μ[ο-]
νογενὴς θεὸς ὁ ὢν εἰς τὸν κόλπον τ[οῦ]
15   πατρὸς ἐκεῖνος ἐξηγήσατο.

No man has seen God at any time; only
begotten God, who is in the bosom of the
15   Father, He has explained Him.

This English translation corresponds literally to the Greek, but may not bring out the full meaning of the sentence. Note that μονογενής ("only begotten") may also be translated "only" or "unique" (cf. Dale Moody in JBL 72 [1953], pp. 213-219), and that the following word θεός ("God") is without the article. For comparison, Jn 1:1 is to be recalled, where θεός appears once with the article and once without it (καὶ ὁ λόγος ἦν πρὸς τὸν θεόν, καὶ θεὸς ἦν ὁ λόγος). Here also the usual English translation ("and the Word was with God, and the Word was God") is not incorrect, but may fall short of reproducing the subtle difference between the use of the same noun, once with the article and once without. That difference is maintained and shown, at least in paraphrase, in *The New English Bible:* "The Word dwelt with God, and what God was, the Word was." In Jn 1:18 the word God (θεόν) occurs at the beginning of the sentence, indeed, without the article, but in a context that calls unmistakably for the regular translation, in the general sense, "God." But in the position after μονογενής, θεός is without the article. Here, as the comparison with the anarthrous θεός in 1:1 suggests, a different shade of meaning may be recognized. Like the NEB translation of 1:1 (just above), this meaning is brought out by the NEB translation or paraphrase at the margin of 1:18, as follows:

Jn 1:18

NEB margin

No man has ever seen God; but
the only one, himself God, the nearest to
the Father's heart, has made him known.

Perhaps even better, and closer to the NEB translation itself in 1:1, is the rendering in *Good News for Modern Man, The New Testament in Today's English Version* (cf. §81):

TEV

No one has ever seen God.
The only One, who is the same as God and is at
the Father's side, has made him known.

Such appears to be the meaning of the Greek, as well as it can be expressed in English, of Jn 1:18 in $\mathfrak{P}^{66}$.

§137. Proceeding now to $\mathfrak{P}^{75}$, we have the text of Jn 1:18 as follows in Lines 4-6 of the page shown in Fig. 14.

$\mathfrak{P}^{75}$

Jn 1:18

$\overline{\Theta N}$ OYΔEIC ΠΩΠOTE EO
5   PAKEN O MONOΓENHC $\overline{\Theta C}$ O ΩN EIC TON KOΛ
ΠON TOY ΠATPOC EKEINOC EΞHΓHCATO

θεὸν οὐδεὶς πώποτε ἑό-
5   ρακεν ὁ μονογενὴς θεὸς ὁ ὢν εἰς τὸν κόλπον τοῦ πατρὸς ἐκεῖνος ἐξηγήσατο

No man has at any time seen
5   God; the only begotten God, who is in the bosom of the Father, He has explained Him.

Aside from the minor matters of the spelling of ἑόρακεν (instead of ἑώρακεν), and the reversal of order of this word and πώποτε ("at any time has seen" instead of "has seen at any time"), the significant difference in the text of Jn 1:18 in $\mathfrak{P}^{75}$ is that the article (ὁ) stands here before μονογενὴς θεός. This provides a statement that the only begotten God, or the only God, is in the bosom of the Father, i.e., of God. Such a statement seems to blur the fine distinction in the text as preserved in $\mathfrak{P}^{66}$ (§136), but it will be repeated in other manuscripts (§158) and will, in turn, provide the basis for yet a further change which will be found in yet later manuscripts (§170).

§138. At this point the significant variations dealt with above (§§134f. and 136f.) in the text of $\mathfrak{P}^{75}$ as compared with the text of $\mathfrak{P}^{66}$ may be recorded summarily in a form like that of a simple text-critical apparatus (for standard form in collation see Greenlee pp. 136f.). The small letter c after $\mathfrak{P}^{75}$ means the corrector of that manuscript.

Jn
1:3-4   οὐδὲν ὃ γέγονεν $\mathfrak{P}^{66}$
οὐδὲ ἓν ὃ γέγονεν $\mathfrak{P}^{75}$
οὐδὲ ἕν· ὃ γέγονεν $\mathfrak{P}^{75c}$

1:18   μονογενὴς θεός $\mathfrak{P}^{66}$
ὁ μονογενὴς θεός $\mathfrak{P}^{75}$

4. Codex Vaticanus (B)

§139. According to the theoretical outline of text types shown above (§86), the two papyri just dealt with, $\mathfrak{P}^{66}$ and $\mathfrak{P}^{75}$ (§§127-138), belong to the Proto-Alexandrian witnesses. In the same group of Proto-Alexandrian witnesses are also the two oldest parchment manuscripts, Codex Sinaiticus (‭א‬) and Codex Vaticanus (B), both of the mid fourth century in date. With respect to Codex Sinaiticus, however, this statement about the text type to which it belongs must be qualified. In most of the NT it does belong to the Alexandrian group, but in Jn 1:1–8:38 it has been shown (see below §146) to exhibit a text with many affinities with the Western text. Therefore, precisely at the point with which we are dealing, namely, Jn 1:1-18, Codex Sinaiticus is to be considered as a Western witness rather than an Alexandrian. It will be taken up, accordingly, at the appropriate point below. Thus we turn now to Codex Vaticanus.

§140. The manuscript commonly known as Codex Vaticanus is preserved in the Biblioteca Apostolica Vaticana in the Città del Vaticano, where it bears the number Vaticano Greco 1209. In the several internationally used systems of notation (§§48ff.) it is designated as B, **03**, and δ1. The codex was already in the Vatican Library when the first catalogue of that library was issued in 1475. In 1720 a collation of the manuscript was obtained for the Greek New Testament proposed by Richard Bentley (§68). In 1809 the codex was carried off as a prize of war by Napoleon to Paris, and it remained there until returned to the Vatican in 1815. While at Paris, the manuscript was studied by Leonhard Hug, a Roman Catholic professor from Tübingen, and its great age and value were recognized for the first time (§71). In 1843 Tischendorf studied the codex in Rome under restricted circumstances. In 1857 Angelo Mai published a first edition of the manuscript, and this was replaced by a better one by Vercellone, Cozza-Luzi, Sergio, and Fabiani in 1868-1881. A photographic edition was issued in 1904 in Milan as Volume 4 of the *Codices e Vaticanis selecti phototypice expressi iussu Pii P. P. IX consilio et opera curatorum Bybliothecae Vaticanae.*

§141. In its original form Codex Vaticanus was a complete Bible, containing both the OT and the NT. Of the 759 leaves that are preserved, 617 belong to the OT, 142 to the NT. The OT is almost complete (FHRJ pp. 23f.). The NT contains the Four Gospels, Acts, the Catholic Letters, and the Pauline Letters as far as Heb 9:14; lacking after that is the rest of that letter, and also the Pastoral Letters, the Letter to Philemon, and the Revelation of John (FHRJ p. 41). The leaves of the manuscript are about 10.8 inches on each side. Each page is written in brown ink, with three columns of text, 40 to 44 lines to the column, and usually 16 to 18 letters to the line. A sharp point was used to draw horizontal lines for guiding the writing; on some pages the letters are written on the line, elsewhere the guidance line runs halfway between two lines of writing. The letters are remarkably even uncials, except that sometimes smaller letters are crowded in at the end of lines, usually, it seems, in order to finish a word or to allow the next line to begin with a consonant. The words are written continuously without separation, and there is almost no punctuation, although initial Iota and Upsilon are marked with the diercsis, and sacred names are abbreviated. Old Testament quotations are marked with a horizontal caret (>). Chapter divisions (cf. §27), largely peculiar to this manuscript, are marked in the margin with Greek letters. Under the first letter of the line in which such a division begins, a horizontal line extends outward into the margin. One scribe wrote the OT portion of the manuscript, another scribe the NT portion. One corrector went through the manuscript very soon after the time of the original writing. A second corrector worked at a much later date, probably the tenth or eleventh century. The latter traced over the pale letters with fresh ink, omitting letters and words he believed to be incorrect, and also adding accents and breathings. The original handwriting of the manuscript is usually assigned to a date about the middle of the fourth century. The general nature of the NT text (§139) suggests Alexandria as a place of origin. In about A.D. 340 Athanasius of Alexandria prepared and sent to the Emperor Constans (337-350), at the latter's request, "parchment codices (πύκτια) containing the holy Scriptures" (Athanasius, *Defence before Constantius* 4, NPNFSS IV, p. 239), and this codex, it has been suggested, could have been one of those volumes (Vogels, *Handbuch,* p. 39 n. 1). Also it may be noted that, insofar as the manuscript is intact, it contains all the books that are enumerated as canonical in the list published by Athanasius in his *Festal Letter* in 367 (FHRJ p. 26).

§142. For the passage Jn 1:1-18, with which we are presently concerned, we turn in Codex Vaticanus to the two pages shown in Figs. 15 and 16, the former containing Lk 24:32-53 and Jn 1:1-14, the latter Jn 1:14-41. Some points of general interest may be noted first. In the first column of Jn, which is the third column on the page in Fig. 15, the title of the Gospel, κατὰ Ἰωάνην, "according to John," stands at the top between crosses. Three more crosses and a horizontal bar stand over the text proper, and this begins with an ornamental letter Eta set in the left margin. Also in the left margin, opposite Line 12 of the text (counting the lines of the text proper, not including the title), the letter Beta marks the beginning of the second of the chapters into which the Gospel is divided (cf. §141). This chapter begins with the word that ends Line 12 and carries over into Line 13, namely, ἐγένε/το, "There came"; and thus this new paragraph begins at the same point (Jn 1:6) as was also indicated for a paragraph beginning in 𝔓⁶⁶ (§129) and in 𝔓⁷⁵ (§131). In the text proper, in Jn 1:4 the original scribe wrote, καὶ ἡ ζωὴ ἦν τὸ φῶς, "and the life was the light," omitting (in Line 9), probably by sheer inadvertence, τῶν ἀνθρώπων, "of men"; and the omitted words have been added by the corrector in the right margin, with a mark (⁒) to show where they are to be inserted in the line. In like fashion in Jn 1:13 the original scribe wrote οὐδὲ ἐκ θελήματος σαρκός, "nor of the will of the flesh," but omitted the following very similar phrase, οὐδὲ ἐκ θελήματος ἀνδρός, "nor of the will of man"; and the corrector added the words in the right margin directly at the end of Line 38. In the second column of Jn, which is the first column on the page in Fig. 16, in Line 4 (Jn 1:14) the original scribe wrote χάριτος ἀληθείας, "grace truth," without the connecting καί, "and"; and this omitted word was put in by the corrector between the words and above the line. In Line 7 (Jn 1:15) the scribe wrote ὁ εἶπον instead of ὃν εἶπον, "of whom I said," and the corrector wrote in the missing Nu, required to make the correct grammatical form, above the line.

Figure 15.   Codex Vaticanus (B): Luke 24:32-53 and John 1:1-14. *Actual size 10.8 × 10.8 in.*

§143. Turning now to the places in Codex Vaticanus that correspond to the places where significant variations were noted in the text in $\mathfrak{P}^{66}$ and $\mathfrak{P}^{75}$, we have the following reading in Jn 1:3-4.

B

Jn 1:3-4 (Fig. 15, Column 3 Lines 5-8)

5   ΠΑΝΤΑ ΔΙ ΑΥΤΟΥ ΕΓΕΝΕ
    ΤΟ ΚΑΙ ΧΩΡΙϹ ΑΥΤΟΥ ΕΓΕ
    ΝΕΤΟ ΟΥΔΕ ΕΝ Ο ΓΕΓΟΝΕ
    ΕΝ ΑΥΤΩ ΖΩΗ ΗΝ . . .

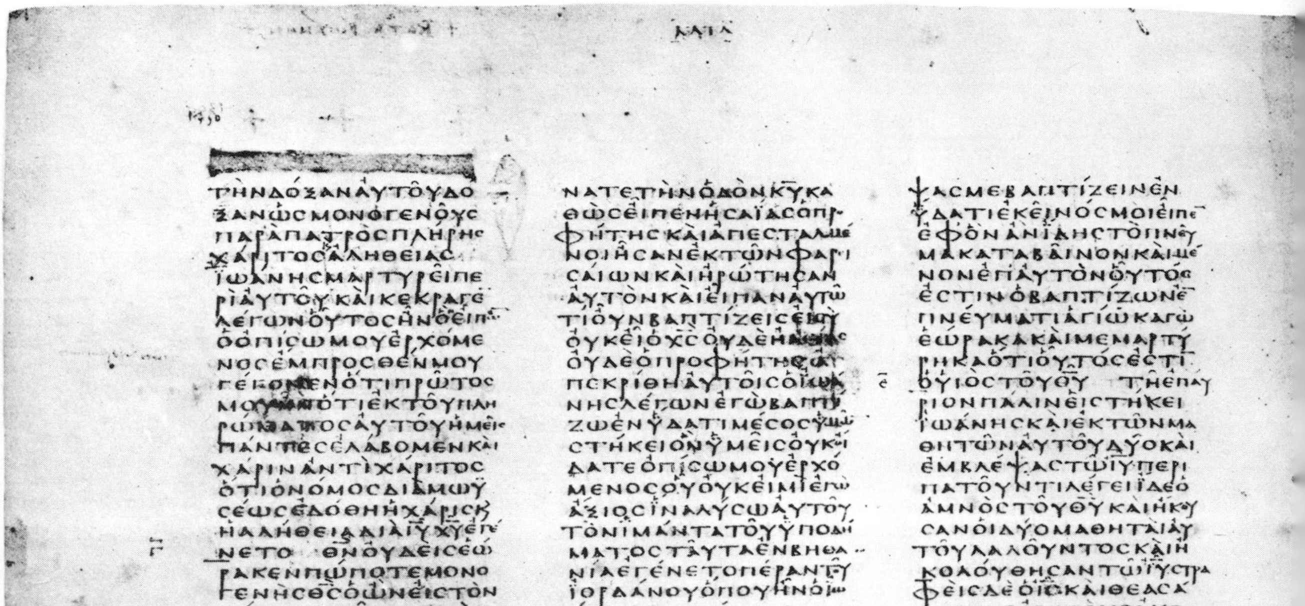

Figure 16.   Codex Vaticanus (B): John 1:14-41. *Actual size 10.8 × 10.8 in.*

5 πάντα δι᾽ αὐτοῦ ἐγένε-
το καὶ χωρὶς αὐτοῦ ἐγέ-
νετο οὐδὲ ἕν ὃ γέγονεν
ἐν αὐτῷ ζωὴ ἦν . . .

§144

*A Sequence
Grouped by
Text Types*

Here we have οὐδὲ ἕν ὃ as in 𝔓⁷⁵ (§134), rather than οὐδὲν ὃ as in 𝔓⁶⁶ (§133); but in the absence of all punctuation, whether by the original scribe or by a corrector, it is not possible to know for sure where the break is intended to come. If it is thought most likely that Line 7 should be read through to the end, and the break made there, then we have the same reading that is possible in 𝔓⁶⁶ (§133) and in 𝔓⁷⁵ if the punctuation mark inserted by the corrector of 𝔓⁷⁵ is disregarded (§134):

Jn 1:3-4

NASB

5   3 All things came into being through Him;
and apart from Him nothing (*or* NEB, no single thing)
came into being that has come into being.
4 In Him was life . . .

§144. As for the reading with which we are concerned in Jn 1:18, this verse is found in Lines 18-22 of the first column of the page shown in Fig. 16. The last part of the last word of the preceding verse (ἐγέ/νετο, "were realized") occupies the first part of Line 18, and then there is a space before the next sentence begins. The letter Gamma in the left margin opposite this line indicates that a new chapter division, the third, begins at this point. The text is:

B

Jn 1:18 (Fig. 16, Column 1 Lines 18-22)

Θ̄Ν ΟΥΔΕΙϹ ΕΩ
ΡΑΚΕΝ Π̄ΩΠΟΤΕ ΜΟΝΟ
20   ΓΕΝΗϹ Θ̄Ϲ Ο ΩΝ ΕΙϹ ΤΟΝ
ΚΟΛΠΟΝ ΤΟΥ ΠΑΤΡΟϹ
ΕΚΕΙΝΟϹ ΕΞΗΓΗϹΑΤΟ

     θεὸν οὐδεὶς ἐώ-
ρακεν πώποτε· μονο-
20   γενὴς θεὸς ὁ ὢν εἰς τὸν
κόλπον τοῦ πατρὸς
ἐκεῖνος ἐξηγήσατο.

Here the text is identical with that in 𝔓⁶⁶ (and not that in 𝔓⁷⁵, §137), and may be rendered in the same fashion (§136):

Jn 1:18

     No man has
seen God at any time; only
20   begotten God, who is in the
bosom of the Father,
He has explained Him.

131

No one has ever
seen God. The only
20 One, who is what God is, and who is near the
Father's side,
has made him known.

§145. The evidence of Codex Vaticanus (B) may be added, therefore, to our summary statement (§138) as follows:

Jn
1:3-4 οὐδὲν ὃ γέγονεν 𝔭⁶⁶
       οὐδὲ ἓν ὃ γέγονεν 𝔭⁷⁵ B
       οὐδὲ ἕν· ὃ γέγονεν 𝔭⁷⁵ᶜ
1:18   μονογενὴς θεός 𝔭⁶⁶ B
       ὁ μονογενὴς θεός 𝔭⁷⁵

Thus, although Codex Vaticanus is a manuscript of the fourth century, it is evident that it transmits a type of text that is much older. As far as our sampling goes, it is essentially the same text that is found in 𝔭⁶⁶ and 𝔭⁷⁵; and that text reaches well back into the second century, as the dates of those papyri show (cf. Calvin L. Porter in JBL 81 [1962], pp. 363-376, who demonstrates the close relationship of 𝔭⁷⁵ and Codex Vaticanus at many other points).

(b) *Western Witnesses*

5. Codex Sinaiticus (א)

§146. In terms of the theory of text types sketched above (§86), three of the Proto-Alexandrian witnesses have now been looked at, namely, 𝔭⁶⁶, 𝔭⁷⁵, and B, all presenting very much the same text, yet with variations that are not unimportant. Without going on into the Later Alexandrian witnesses as such, we turn next to notice three of the witnesses that, at least in the portion of their text with which we are concerned (namely, Jn 1:1-18, cf. §126), fall into the group of Western witnesses, namely, Codex Sinaiticus (א), Codex Bezae, and Codex Washingtonensis (W). Of the three, Codex Bezae (D), a bilingual Greek-Latin manuscript (§§160f.), is commonly recognized as a leading witness to the Western text; but there are special circumstances with respect to the other two manuscripts. In common understanding, and in respect to most of its contents, Codex Sinaiticus (א) belongs to the Alexandrian family and appears, indeed, in the table above (§86) as a Proto-Alexandrian manuscript along with the early papyri, Codex Vaticanus, etc. But in the first part of the Gospel according to John, specifically in Jn 1:1–8:38, it has been shown that there are a large number of agreements between Codex Sinaiticus and Codex Bezae, and that, in that portion of the Gospel, Codex Sinaiticus is to be considered as transmitting a Western text (Gordon D. Fee in NTS 15 [1968], pp. 23-44). Since we are presently concerned with a section of the Gospel according to John

(1:1-18) that falls within that portion of the manuscript, it is evident that we will deal with Codex Sinaiticus (in this passage) among the Western witnesses, and indeed, in view of the relatively early date of this manuscript, will take it up as the first in this group. As to Codex Washingtonensis (W), the situation is also complicated, even more so than with respect to Codex Sinaiticus. While the details will be explained more fully below (§167), it has already appeared in the table above (§86) that Codex Washingtonensis is assigned in several of its portions to all three of the major groupings of text types, Alexandrian, Western, and Byzantine. In Jn 1:1–5:11 (which includes the passage with which we are concerned, 1:1-18), the manuscript actually contains both Alexandrian and Western readings; with respect to this portion of the manuscript, since it does contain Western readings, we have chosen to show it in the table, and to take it up here, as a Western witness. Now we proceed further with Codex Sinaiticus.

§147. Codex Sinaiticus (ℵ [sometimes S, see §51], 01, δ2) was discovered by Tischendorf in 1844 and 1859 in the Monastery of Saint Catherine at Mount Sinai (FLAP pp. 435f.), and is now in the possession of the British Museum in London. The first forty-three pages found (in 1844), with the text of the OT in Greek, were published in Leipzig in 1846 under the title, *Codex Friderico Augustanus.* The entire manuscript was published in St. Petersburg (Leningrad) in 1862 (on the 1000th anniversary of the founding of the Russian Empire) in an edition called *Bibliorum Codex Sinaiticus,* for which special type was made to resemble the original letters in the manuscript as closely as possible. A photographic facsimile of the manuscript was made by Kirsopp Lake and published by Oxford University Press, the NT in 1911, the OT in 1922.

§148. Of the original codex, which must have contained at least 730 leaves, only 390 (including those at Leipzig) remain today—242 in the OT, and 148 in the NT. Although a considerable part of the OT is lost (FHRJ p. 25), the NT is well preserved; it contains the Gospels, the Pauline Letters (including Hebrews between II Th and I Tim), Acts, the Catholic Letters, and Revelation, and in addition, at the end, the Letter of Barnabas and the Shepherd of Hermas (FHRJ p. 41). The leaves of the codex are about 15 inches high by 13.5 or 14 inches broad. The writing, in pale brown ink, is in four columns on the page, with 48 lines to the column, and usually 12 to 16 letters to the line. The pages are ruled with a sharp point, and the letters are written on the line. The words are written continuously, but there is some punctuation with high and middle points and colon (for an example of the colon see Fig. 17, Column 1 Line 43). Initial Iota and Upsilon have the dieresis, and *nomina sacra* are abbreviated. There are no accents or breathings. At the end of a line, some letters are often crowded in in smaller size, as in Codex Vaticanus (§141). Sections of the text are often indicated by stopping the writing at the end of the preceding section even though an entire line is not filled out, and then moving the first letter of the new section slightly into the margin.

§149. The date of the copying of the manuscript is probably in the middle of the fourth century, approximately contemporary with, or only slightly later than, Codex Vaticanus. Three scribes are identified (largely on the basis of individual peculiarities in spelling) as having written the manuscript, the one known as Scribe A being the one who copied most of the NT. Interestingly enough, it appears (largely from the phonetic errors that occur) that a part of the OT was taken down from dictation, but that the NT was copied from a written exemplar (Christian Tindall, *Contributions to the Statistical Study of the Codex Sinaiticus* [Edinburgh and London: Oliver and Boyd, 1961], p. 17). Running throughout the entire manuscript is a series of quire numerations (the quires are of 4 sheets, 8 leaves, and 16 pages each). The small letters of these numbers, surmounted by a wavy stroke, appear in the upper left-hand corner of the first page of each quire. This numeration was probably contemporary with the original copying of the manuscript, although the writer of the numbers cannot be identified with any of the scribes of the text. Curiously enough, a whole quire (No. $\overline{o\gamma}$ = 73) is allowed for in the sequence of numbers, but is not found in the manuscript, so that the Gospel according to Matthew begins with quire No. $\overline{o\delta}$ = 74 after the OT ends (with the book of Job) with quire No. $\overline{o\beta}$ = 72. Perhaps the omitted quire was intended to contain the Eusebian canon-tables for the NT (cf. above §29), but was never actually written. A second series of quire numbers, running continuously from the OT into the NT, was added, probably in the eighth century; and these numbers appear in the upper right-hand corner of the pages to which they belong. In this series the Gospel according to Matthew begins, properly, with quire No. $\overline{o\gamma}$ = 73. Although the canon-tables of Eusebius are not actually found in the manuscript, the numbers of his sections and canons are found in the margin throughout the NT, and were probably copied in by a hand other than that of the original scribe, but contemporary with him. Altogether, from the fourth century to the twelfth, perhaps as many as nine correctors worked on the manuscript (J. J. M. Milne and T. C. Skeat, *Scribes and Correctors of the Codex Sinaiticus* [London: British Museum, 1938], pp. 22f., 40-50); and in Tischendorf's edition 14,800 places are enumerated where some alteration has been made to the text (H. J. M. Milne and T. C. Skeat, *The Codex Sinaiticus and the Codex Alexandrinus* [London: British Museum, 1938], p. 16).

§150. The page of Codex Sinaiticus containing the opening portion (1:1-39) of the Gospel according to John is reproduced in Fig. 17. The title of the Gospel is at the head of Column 1: κατὰ Ἰωάννην, "according to John." The number in the upper right-hand corner of the page ($\overline{o\theta}$ = 79) is one of the eighth-century quire numerations (see above §149, and cf. Milne and Skeat, *Scribes and Correctors of the Codex Sinaiticus,* pp. 7f., 107). The section of the Gospel with which we are occupying ourselves, namely, Jn 1:1-18, is contained in Column 1 and in Lines 1-40 in Column 2.

§151. Apart from the two passages of special interest, Jn 1:3-4 and 1:18 (see below §§155-159), we notice first several items of interest, minor variations, and corrections, elsewhere in the whole section, Jn 1:1-18. At Jn 1:6, in Column 1 Line 19 of the text, the already familiar point of a paragraph-beginning (see above §129 [𝔓^{66}], §131 [𝔓^{75}], §142 [B]) is marked by placing the first letter of the line slightly into the left-hand margin, where also are the letters for the Eusebian section and canon (cf. above §29), $\frac{\overline{\mathrm{B}}}{\Gamma}$, marking Section No. 2 in this Gospel, and Canon No. 3 in the tables of Eusebius. Here, in Lines 19-23, Jn 1:6 reads as follows:

§151

A Sequence Grouped by Text Types

Figure 17. Codex Sinaiticus (א): John 1:1-38. *Actual size 15 X 14 in.*

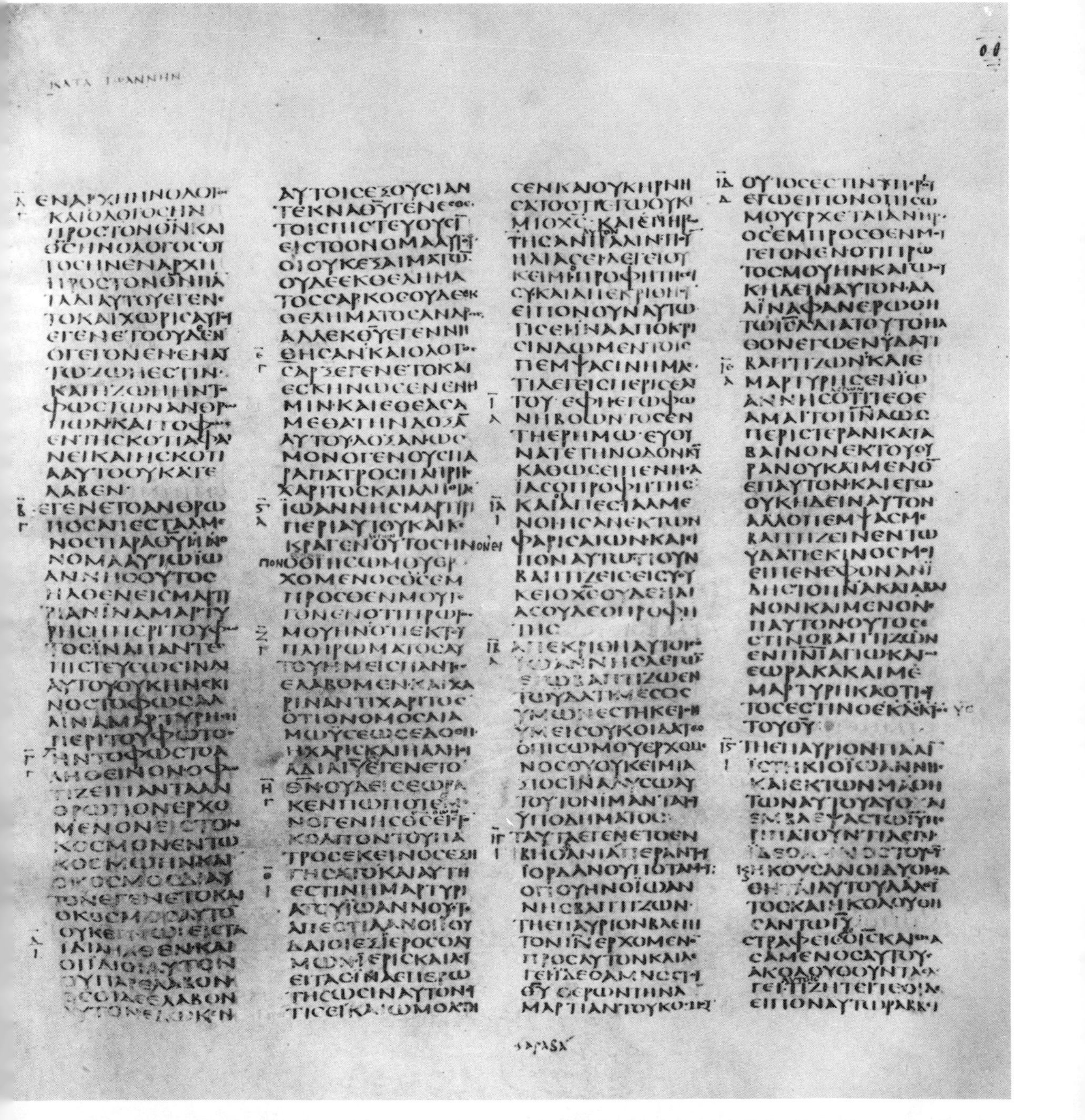

Jn 1:6

20   ΕΓΕΝΕΤΟ ΑΝΘΡΩ
ΠΟC ΑΠΕϹΤΑΛΜᵉ
ΝΟϹ ΠΑΡΑ Θ̄Ῡ Η̄Ν°
ΝΟΜΑ ΑΥΤΩ Ϊω
ΑΝΝΗϹ

The text of the original scribe was, therefore:

ἐγένετο ἄνθρω-
20   πος ἀπεσταλμέ-
νος παρὰ θεοῦ, ἦν ὄ-
νομα αὐτῷ Ἰω-
άννης

There came a man,
20   sent
from God, his
name was
John.

The word ἦν ("was") in Line 21 is, however, an addition to the text as it is found in 𝔓⁶⁶ (§130), 𝔓⁷⁵, and B, and an addition, moreover, that complicates rather than improves the grammar. A corrector has, therefore, put two dots over the two letters of this word to indicate that it should be deleted.

§152.   In Jn 1:10, in Lines 40-41 of Column 1, the original scribe wrote the word for "Him" in the accusative case (αὐ/τόν) rather than the genitive (αὐτοῦ), which is the more usual case to go with διά to say "through" in the sense of "by means of," and which is the case actually found in 𝔓⁶⁶ (§130), 𝔓⁷⁵, and B. A corrector has, therefore, marked the word for alteration. In Jn 1:13, the text of 𝔓⁶⁶ (§130), 𝔓⁷⁵, and B as corrected (§142) reads: οὐδὲ ἐκ θελήματος ἀνδρός, "nor of the will of man." Here the original scribe of Codex Sinaiticus wrote (in Column 2, Lines 7-8), οὐδὲ θελήματος ἀνδρός, and later a corrector squeezed in the missing ἐκ ("of") at the end of Line 7.

§153.   In Jn 1:15, 𝔓⁶⁶ (with minor correction, §§129-130), 𝔓⁷⁵, and B (with minor correction, §142), all read as follows (writing the text in lines to correspond as closely as possible with the lines in Codex Sinaiticus):

𝔓⁶⁶, 𝔓⁷⁵, B

Jn 1:15

Ἰωάννης μαρτυρεῖ
περὶ αὐτοῦ καὶ κέ-
κραγεν λέγων, Οὗτος ἦν ὃν εἶπον,
Ὁ ὀπίσω μου ἐρ-
χόμενος ἔμ-
προσθεν μου γέ-
γονεν, κτλ.

John bore witness
of Him, and cried
out, saying, "This was He of whom I said,
'He who comes
after me is
become before
me, etc.' "

In Codex Sinaiticus the corresponding text stands as follows (Column 2 Lines 19-25):

א

Jn 1:15

    ΙѠΑΝΝΗϹ ΜΑΡΤΥΡΙ
20 ΠΕΡΙ ΑΥΤΟΥ ΚΑΙ Κε
               _{ΛΕΓѠΝ}
    ΚΡΑΓΕΝ ΟΥΤΟϹ ΗΝ ^{ΟΝ ΕΙ}
  ^{ΠΟΝ} Ο ΟΠΙϹѠ ΜΟΥ ΕΡ
    ΧΟΜΕΝΟϹ Ο̇Ϲ ΕΜ
    ΠΡΟϹΘΕΝ ΜΟΥ Γε
25 ΓΟΝΕΝ

The original text was, therefore:

    Ἰωάννης μαρτυρῖ
20 περὶ αὐτοῦ καὶ κέ-
    κραγεν, Οὗτος ἦν
    ὁ ὀπίσω μου ἐρ-
    χόμενος ὃς ἔμ-
    προσθεν μου γέ-
25 γονεν

    John bore witness
20 of Him, and cried
    out, "This was
    He who comes after
    me who is
    become before
25 me"

This form of the text was presumably produced in order to simplify somewhat the rather involved grammatical form of the sentence as seen in the other manuscripts ($\mathfrak{P}^{66}$, $\mathfrak{P}^{75}$, B); but the corrector preferred to bring it into harmony with the other and older reading, and did so by writing in λέγων ("saying") above Line 21, adding ὃν εἷ/πον ("of whom I said") at the end of Line 21 and the beginning of Line 22, and deleting (with two dots) ὅς ("who") in Line 23. Thus the resultant text was identical with the text in $\mathfrak{P}^{66}$, $\mathfrak{P}^{75}$, and B.

§154. In Jn 1:17, $\mathfrak{P}^{66}$, $\mathfrak{P}^{75}$, and B all read that "grace and truth were realized through Jesus Christ" (διὰ Ἰησοῦ Χριστοῦ in $\mathfrak{P}^{66}$; ΔΙΑ Ι͞Υ Χ͞Υ = διὰ Ἰησοῦ Χριστοῦ in $\mathfrak{P}^{75}$ and B). In Codex Sinaiticus (Column 2 Line 34) the original scribe writes only ΔΙΑ Ι͞Υ ("through Jesus"), and the corrector squeezes in above the line the omitted X̄T̄ ("Christ").

§155. Now we turn to the two passages in which the most significant variations have been found in the manuscripts studied hitherto, namely, Jn 1:3-4 and 1:18. In Jn 1:3-4, in Column 1 Lines 6-14, Codex Sinaiticus provides this text:

ℵ

Jn 1:3-4

ΠᾹ
ΤΑ ΔΙ ΑΥΤΟΥ ΕΓΕΝε
ΤΟ ΚΑΙ ΧΩΡΙϹ ΑΥΤΟΥ
ΕΓΕΝΕΤΟ ΟΥΔΕΝ˙
10   Ο ΓΕΓΟΝΕΝ˙ΕΝ ΑΥ
ΤΩ ΖΩΗ ΕϹΤΙΝ˙
ΚΑΙ Η ΖΩΗ ΗΝ Τ°
ΦΩϹ ΤΩΝ ΑΝΘΡω
ΠΩΝ˙

There is no question as to the words that were written by the original scribe, and it appears probable that the middle points of punctuation in Lines 10, 11, and 14 are also a part of the original text, or at least the points that were first put in to accompany the original text. Therefore we read:

3 πάν-
τα δι' αὐτοῦ ἐγένε-
το, καὶ χωρὶς αὐτοῦ
ἐγένετο οὐδὲν
10   ὃ γέγονεν. 4 ἐν αὐ-
τῷ ζωή ἐστιν.
καὶ ἡ ζωὴ ἦν τὸ
φῶς τῶν ἀνθρώ-
πων.

3 All
things came into being through
Him; and apart from Him
nothing came into being
10   that has come into being. 4 In Him
is life.
And the life was the
light of
men.

As far as Verse 3 is concerned, then, this reading provides the same words as in 𝔓[66], and the punctuation that it was surmised might be most readily assumed for that unpunctuated text (§§129, 130, 133).

§156. A corrector, however, has written in above Line 9 an additional Epsilon to change οὐδέν into οὐδὲ ἕν, and probably has at the same time written the high point of punctuation which appears dimly above and to the right of the final Nu of those two words. Thus the corrector has given us the same two words (οὐδὲ ἕν) that are found in 𝔓⁷⁵ and B (§145), and the same punctuation that was supplied by the corrector in 𝔓⁷⁵ (§135). Therewith, disregarding the other punctuation, we read:

א Corrector

Jn 1:3-4

3 πάν-
τα δι' αὐτοῦ ἐγένε-
το, καὶ χωρὶς αὐτοῦ
ἐγένετο οὐδὲ ἕν.
10   ὃ γέγονεν 4 ἐν αὐ-
τῷ ζωή ἐστιν.
καὶ ἡ ζωὴ ἦν τὸ
φῶς τῶν ἀνθρώ-
πων.

3 All
things came into being through
Him; and apart from Him
no single thing came into being.
10   What has come into being 4 is
life in Him.
And the life was the
light of
men.

§157.   As far as verse 4 is concerned, it is notable that א reads ἐν αὐτῷ ζωή ἐστιν, "In Him is life," rather than ἐν αὐτῷ ζωὴ ἦν, "In Him was life." The latter reading (with ἦν) was supposed in our restoration of 𝔓⁶⁶ (§130), although the verb is there actually lost in a gap in the papyrus, and is the reading found in the otherwise oldest manuscripts, 𝔓⁷⁵ (§134) and B (§143). It is plausible to think that this change from the imperfect tense (referring to the past) to the present tense goes well with the punctuation just observed in §156, so that the sentence declares that all that which has come into being *is* life in Him (rather than *was* life in Him) (cf. EGT I, p. 684). Yet in the present instance the ἐστιν is a part of the text of the original scribe, prior to the work of the corrector who provided the reading οὐδὲ ἕν and the unmistakable stop at that point. Perhaps this argument suggests that the text copied by the original scribe of א was anyway understood to stop there. In that case the stop after ὃ γέγονεν would have to be understood as a later and incorrect interpretation. But if the stop after ὃ γέγονεν belongs with the original text, or if it is a correct interpretation thereof, then we can perhaps understand the use of the present tense rather than the imperfect as follows: that an affirmation about the life that is in the Word is more appropriately stated in terms of a timeless present than of a time that is in any sense past. All in all it seems best to take the reading in §155 (". . . apart from Him nothing came into being that has come into being. In Him is life. . . .") as most probably representing the original meaning of Codex Sinaiticus, a reading that, in Verse 3, coincides with what may be most probable for $\mathfrak{P}^{66}$ also (§129).

§158.   In Jn 1:18 we have read the following text in the manuscripts already studied (the lines are written now to correspond with the lines in ℵ):

Jn 1:18

$\mathfrak{P}^{66}$ (§136) and B (§144)

θεὸν οὐδεὶς ἐώρα-
κεν πώποτε· μο-
νογενὴς θεὸς ὁ ὢν εἰς τὸν
κόλπον τοῦ πα-
τρὸς ἐκεῖνος ἐξη-
γήσατο.

No man has seen God
at any time; only
begotten God, who is in the
bosom of the
Father, He has ex-
plained Him.

$\mathfrak{P}^{75}$ (§137)

θεὸν οὐδεὶς πώποτε
ἐόρακεν· ὁ μο-
νογενὴς θεὸς ὁ ὢν εἰς τὸν
κόλπον τοῦ πα-
τρὸς ἐκεῖνος ἐξη-
γήσατο.

No man has at any time
seen God; the only
begotten God, who is in the
bosom of the
Father, He has ex-
plained Him.

In comparison therewith, we have the following in Codex Sinaiticus (Column 2 Lines 35-40):

ℵ

35   Θ̄Ν ΟΥΔΕΙϹ ΕꞶΡΑ
     ΚΕΝ ΠꞶΠΟΤΕ Μο
     ΝΟΓΕΝΗϹ Θ̄Ϲ ΕΙϹ Το
     ΚΟΛΠΟΝ ΤΟΥ ΠΑ
     ΤΡΟϹ ΕΚΕΙΝΟϹ ΕΞΗ
40   ΓΗϹΑΤΟ

The original text was:

35   θεὸν οὐδεὶς ἐώρα-
     κεν πώποτε· μο-
     νογενὴς θεὸς εἰς τὸν

κόλπον τοῦ πα-
τρὸς ἐκεῖνος ἐξη-
40   γήσατο

35   No man has seen God
at any time; only
begotten God, in the
bosom of the
Father, He has ex-
40   plained Him.

In the space above Line 37 one corrector has supplied the obviously missing words, ὸ ὤν ("who is"), and therewith the text is in exact agreement with that of $\mathfrak{P}^{66}$ and B ("only begotten God, who is in the bosom . . ."). In the space above Line 36 another corrector has put in the article ὸ, and therewith the text is brought into agreement with the reading we have already found in $\mathfrak{P}^{75}$, "the only begotten God" (cf. § 137).

§ 159. At the point of the two specially significant passages, the evidence of Codex Sinaiticus (‭א‬) may be added, therefore, to our summary statement (§ § 138, 145) as follows:

Jn
1:3-4   οὐδὲν ὃ γέγονεν $\mathfrak{P}^{66}$
οὐδὲν ὃ γέγονεν·   ‭א‬
οὐδὲ ἐν ὃ γέγονεν $\mathfrak{P}^{75}$ B
οὐδὲ ἔν· ὃ γέγονεν $\mathfrak{P}^{75c}$ ‭א‬^{c}
ἐν αὐτῷ ζωὴ ἦν $\mathfrak{P}^{75}$ B
ἐν αὐτῷ ζωή ἐστιν   ‭א‬
1:18   μονογενὴς θεός $\mathfrak{P}^{66}$ B ‭א‬
ὁ μονογενὴς θεός $\mathfrak{P}^{75}$ ‭א‬^{c}

6. Codex Bezae (D)

§ 160. Codex Bezae or Codex Cantabrigiensis (D, 05, δ5) was given to the Cambridge University Library (where it is Ms. Nn. 2.41) in 1581 by Theodore Beza (Théodore de Bèze), the French scholar, and friend and successor of Calvin at Geneva (§ 64). In his letter of presentation to the Library, Beza explained that the manuscript had been found in the Monastery of St. Irenaeus at Lyons when this place was plundered by a Huguenot army in 1562. After earlier editions at Cambridge in 1793 by Thomas Kipling, and in 1864 by F. H. A. Scrivener, a photographic facsimile of the manuscript was published in 1899 by the Cambridge University Press, *Codex Bezae Cantabrigiensis quattuor evangelia et actus apostolorum complectens Graece et Latine, phototypice repraesentatus.*

§ 161. The manuscript presently consists of 406 leaves, each about 10 by 8 inches in size, with a single column of writing on each page. The manuscript is bilingual, with Greek text on the left-hand page, as the place of honor, Latin on the right-hand page. The contents are the four Gospels, with some gaps, in the so-called Western order (the Gospels according to Matthew and John, the apostles, first, and then those according to Luke and Mark, the companions of the apostles), plus the greater part of the Acts of the Apostles. One leaf with a Latin text from III Jn 11-15 suggests that the original manuscript contained some other books, perhaps the Catholic Letters. The text is written in κῶλα, i.e., in sense-lines (cf. above §39), so that a natural pause comes at the end of a line. There are thirty-three such colometric lines on each page. The writing is in brown ink; the first three lines of each book are in red. There are no accents or breathings, but initial Iota and Upsilon are marked with the dieresis. Punctuation is with high and middle points and colon. *Nomina sacra* are abbreviated. Sections and readings with ἀρχή and τέλος (§30) have been marked in by a later hand. The manuscript was probably copied in the sixth century, although dates in the fifth and even the fourth century have also been proposed (see Metzger pp. 49, 264 note). Some striking similarities between the text of D and the text of NT quotations by Irenaeus, suggest that the text reaches back to a relatively early date and was at home in southern France (Vogels, *Handbuch,* p. 43). Probably as many as nine correctors, dating from the end of the sixth century to the eleventh or twelfth or later, have also worked on the manuscript.

§162. Fig. 18 reproduces Folio 104[b] in Codex Bezae, with the Greek text of Jn 1:1-16. The eight leaves immediately following (f. 105-112) are lost from the codex. Of the two passages of special interest in our present investigation, Jn 1:3-4 and 1:18, we are therefore limited to the first as far as Codex Bezae is concerned. Minor points to notice first on this page are: The title is at the top, partly illegible, but no doubt reading κατὰ Ἰωάννην, "according to John." The first three lines are in red ink. In Line 3 in the first occurrence of the verb ἐγένετο ("came into being") in Jn 1:3, the scribe has accidentally transposed letters to write the impossible form ΕΝΕΓΕΤΟ. In Jn 1:6, in Line 9, the text has ἦν ("was"), and a corrector has deleted the word with two dots above it, exactly as in Codex Sinaiticus (§151). In 1:12, in Line 20, the original scribe accidentally omitted two letters in the word ἔδωκεν ("he gave"), and a corrector put them in (κε) above the line. Likewise in 1:13, in Line 22, a missing οἵ ("who") is inserted above the line, and in Line 23 an omitted ἐκ ("of"). In Line 22 αἱμάτων ("blood") is spelled ἐμάτων. In Jn 1:15, in Line 29, "bore witness" is spelled μαρτυρῖ (instead of μαρτυρεῖ), and λέγων ("saying") is omitted after κέκραγεν ("cried out"), both points exactly as in Codex Sinaiticus (§153). In Line 30, however, a corrector introduces a word not met hitherto in this place, when he writes in ὑμῖν ("to you"), so that the text reads, "This was He of whom I said to you, 'He who comes after me. . . .' "

§163. Returning now to Jn 1:3-4, we find in Lines 3-5 this text in uncial letters:

D

Jn 1:3-4

A

ΠΑΝΤΑ ΔΙ ΑΥΤΟΥ ΕΝΕΓΕΤΟ ΚΑΙ ΧΩΡΙC ΑΥΤΟΥ

Figure 18. Codex Bezae (D), f. 104[b]: John 1:1-16. *Reproduced at actual size.*

ΝΑΡΧΗΗΝΟΛΟΓΟC ΚΑΙΟΛΟΓΟCΗΝΠΡΟCΤΟΝΘΝ
ΚΑΙΘC ΗΝΟΛΟΓΟC·ΟΥΤΟCΗΝΕΝΑΡΧΗΠΡΟCΤΟΝΘΝ
ΠΑΝΤΑΔΙΑΥΤΟΥΕΝΕΓΕΤΟ ΚΑΙΧΩΡΙCΑΥΤΟΥ
ΕΓΕΝΕΤΟ ΟΥΔΕΝ ΟΓΕΓΟΝΕΝ ΕΝΑΥΤΩ
ΖΩΗΕCΤΙΝ ΚΑΙΗΖΩΗ ΗΝΤΟΦΩCΤΩΝΑΝΘΡΩΠΩ
ΚΑΙΤΟΦΩC ΕΝΤΗCΚΟΤΙΑΦΑΙΝΕΙ
ΚΑΙΗCΚΟΤΙΑΑΥΤΟ ΟΥΚΑΤΕΛΑΒΕΝ
ΕΓΕΝΕΤΟΑΝΘΡΩΠΟCΑΠΕCΤΑΛΜΕΝΟC
ΠΑΡΑΘΥ ΗΝΟΝΟΜΑΑΥΤΩΙΩΑΝΝΗC
ΟΥΤΟCΗΛΘΕΝΕΙCΜΑΡΤΥΡΙΑΝ ΙΝΑΜΑΡΤΥΡΗCΗ
ΠΕΡΙΤΟΥΦΩΤΟC· ΙΝΑΠΑΝΤΕCΠΙCΤΕΥCΟΥCΙΝ
ΔΙΑΥΤΟΥ· ΟΥΚΗΝΕΚΕΙΝΟCΤΟΦΩC
ΑΛΛΙΝΑΜΑΡΤΥΡΗCΗΠΕΡΙΤΟΥΦΩΤΟC
ΗΝΤΟΦΩCΤΟΑΛΗΘΙΝΟΝΟΦΩΤΙΖΕΙ
ΠΑΝΤΑΑΝΘΡΩΠΟΝΕΡΧΟΜΕΝΟΝ
ΕΙCΤΟΝΚΟCΜΟΝΕΝΤΩΚΟCΜΩΗΝ
ΚΑΙΟΚΟCΜΟCΔΙΑΥΤΟΥΕΓΕΝΕΤΟ ΚΑΙ
ΟΚΟCΜΟCΑΥΤΟΝΟΥΚΕΓΝΩ ΕΙCΤΑΙΔΙΑ
ΗΛΘΕΝΚΑΙΟΙΙΔΙΟΙΑΥΤΟΝΟΥΠΑΡΕΛΑΒΟΝ
ΟCΟΙΔΕΛΑΒΟΝΑΥΤΟΝ ΕΔΩΚΕΝΑΥΤΟΙC
ΕΞΟΥCΙΑΝΤΕΚΝΑΘΥΓΕΝΕCΘΑΙ ΤΟΙCΠΙCΤΕΥΟΥCΙ
ΕΙCΤΟΟΝΟΜΑΑΥΤΟΥ· ΟΙΟΥΚΕΖΑΙΜΑΤΩΝΟΥΔΕ
ΕΚΘΕΛΗΜΑΤΟC CΑΡΚΟCΟΥΔΕΘΕΛΗΜΑΤΟCΑΝΔΡΟC
ΑΛΛΕΚΘΥΕΓΕΝΝΗΘΗCΑΝ ΚΑΙΟΛΟΓΟC
CΑΡΞΕΓΕΝΕΤΟΚΑΙΕCΚΗΝΩCΕΝ
ΕΝΗΜΕΙΝΚΑΙΕΘΕΑCΑΜΕΘΑΤΗΝΔΟΞΑΝ
ΑΥΤΟΥΔΟΞΑΝΩCΜΟΝΟΓΕΝΟΥC
ΠΑΡΑΠΑΤΡΟCΠΛΗΡΗCΧΑΡΙΤΟCΚΑΙΑΛΗΘΙΑC
ΙΩΑΝΝΗCΜΑΡΤΥΡΙΠΕΡΙΑΥΤΟΥ ΚΑΙΚΕΚΡΑΓΕΝ
ΟΥΤΟCΗΝΟΝΕΙΠΟΝ ΟΟΠΙCΩΜΟΥΕΡΧΟΜΕΝΟC
ΕΜΠΡΟCΘΕΝΜΟΥΓΕΓΟΝΕΝ
ΟΤΙΠΡΩΤΟCΜΟΥΗΝ ΟΤΙΕΚΤΟΥ
ΠΛΗΡΩΜΑΤΟCΑΥΤΟΥΗΜΕΙCΠΑΝΤΕC

desiderantur omnia abhinc usq ad χc.
vид cap ij 3 4 in legalis Grae℈o.

ΕΓΕΝΕΤΟ ΟΥΔΕΝ Ο ΓΕΓΟΝΕΝ ΕΝ ΑΥΤΩ
5   ΖΩΗ ΕϹΤΙΝ˙ΚΑΙ Η ΖΩΗ ΗΝ ΤΟ ΦΩϹ ΤΩΝ ΑΝΘΡΩΠΩ̅

Above Line 3 a corrector has written in an Alpha to complete the word διά ("through"), but this is unnecessary and has not been done in Lines 12 and 17; so the word may be reproduced in our transcription below in the usual form δι'. Strangely enough, no corrector has changed ενεγετο to ἐγένετο, as obviously must be done (§162). As for the punctuation, the placement of the high points is unmistakable, at least in the crucial instance in Line 4. If this may be taken as giving the original and correct interpretation of the sentence, we have:

3 πάντα δι' αὐτοῦ ἐγένετο, καὶ χωρὶς αὐτοῦ
ἐγένετο οὐδέν. ὃ γέγονεν 4 ἐν αὐτῷ
5   ζωή ἐστιν. καὶ ἡ ζωὴ ἦν τὸ φῶς τῶν ἀνθρώπων.

3 All things came into being through Him; and apart from Him nothing came into being. What has come into being 4 is life
5   in Him. And the life was the light of men.

Codex Bezae (D) agrees, therefore, with 𝔓⁶⁶ (§128) and with Codex Sinaiticus (ℵ) (§155) in the wording οὐδὲν ὃ γέγονεν; but whereas 𝔓⁶⁶ has no punctuation (thus leaving the stopping place in doubt), and ℵ has a point after γέγονεν (thus reading, "nothing came into being that has come into being."), D has a point after οὐδέν (exactly as 𝔓⁷⁵ᶜ and ℵᶜ have it after οὐδὲ ἕν), and requires the reading, ". . . nothing came into being. What has come into being. . . ." Also in D we have the verb ἐστιν in the present tense (rather than ἦν in the imperfect), for the reading, "in Him is life," exactly as in ℵ.

§164. The evidence of Codex Bezae (D) for Jn 1:3-4 appears, therefore, as follows in our summary apparatus (§§138, 145, 159):

Jn
1:3-4   οὐδὲν ὃ γέγονεν   𝔓⁶⁶
        οὐδὲν ὃ γέγονεν·   ℵ
        οὐδέν· ὃ γέγονεν   D
        οὐδὲ ἕν ὃ γέγονεν   𝔓⁷⁵ B
        οὐδὲ ἕν· ὃ γέγονεν   𝔓⁷⁵ᶜ ℵᶜ
        ἐν αὐτῷ ζωὴ ἦν   𝔓⁷⁵ B
        ἐν αὐτῷ ζωή ἐστιν   ℵ D

7. Codex Washingtonensis (W)

§165. Codex Washingtonensis or Codex Freerianus (W, 032, ε014), most simply known as the Washington Ms. of the Gospels, was purchased by Mr. Charles L. Freer from an Arab dealer in Gizeh, near Cairo, in 1906, and was presented to the Freer Gallery of Art of the Smithsonian Institution in Washington, D.C., where it bears the registration number 06.274. The manuscript was published in facsimile by Henry A. Sanders, *Facsimile of the Washington Manuscript of the Four Gospels in the Freer Collection* (Ann Arbor: The

University of Michigan, 1912), with an accompanying study in *The New Testament Manuscripts in the Freer Collection* (New York: The Macmillan Company, 1912 and 1918). Sanders (*The New Testament Manuscripts in the Freer Collection,* pp. 1f.) thought the codex might have come from the Church of Timothy in the Monastery of the Vinedresser, which was located near the Third Pyramid. The writing is similar to that of a fifth or sixth-century fragment of the Book of Enoch found at Akhmim in 1886 (Sanders, *op. cit.,* pp. 137f.), and the present manuscript is usually ascribed to the fifth century, although Sanders (*op. cit.,* p. 139) thought it could have belonged even to the fourth.

§166. The codex now consists of 187 leaves or 374 pages, of which 372 are written, leaving two blank pages at the end of John. The contents are the Four Gospels, in the so-called Western order (Mt, Jn, Lk, Mk) as in Codex Bezae (§161). The make-up of the codex is in twenty-six quires, and the quire numbers running from Alpha (1) to Kappa Vau (26) were originally in the upper right-hand corner of the first page of each quire, where many of them can still be seen. The pages are about 8.3 by 5.5 inches in size. The writing, in somewhat sloping uncials, is in one column of thirty lines to the page, with 27 to 30 letters in a usual full line. Paragraphs are usually indicated by slightly enlarged letters, projecting into the margin, and sometimes accompanied by a paragraph mark as well, the latter sometimes being a large curving stroke. There are no accents, but a rough breathing is shown a few times, and there are dots over initial Iota and Upsilon. *Nomina sacra* are abbreviated, and OT quotations are signaled by marks in the left margin. Punctuation is not frequent, but there is some use of a middle point (sometimes almost a high point) and a colon. In lieu of punctuation, however, a small blank space is frequently left between phrases. An apostrophe is used frequently after words, especially proper nouns, ending in any consonant other than Nu or Sigma; and the same sign also marks the omission of a final vowel. As for corrections, most of the repair of mistakes was done by the scribe himself, and by a reviser (διορ-θωτής) who followed him, while a few additional changes were made by two later hands (Sanders, *op. cit.,* pp. 28-38).

§167. The situation with regard to the text of Codex Washingtonensis is relatively complex, as has already been seen in the table of text families above (§86), where W is represented in all three classifications, namely, Alexandrian, Western, and Byzantine (cf. §146). Stated in terms of the usual sequence of the Gospels (not the Western sequence, found in the manuscript itself [§166]), the text of W is analyzed as follows (Sanders, *op. cit.,* pp. 46-133; Metzger p. 57): Mt is Byzantine, Mk 1:1—5:30 is Western, Mk 5:31—16:20 is Western or Caesarean (the latter, smaller hypothetical text family is not taken account of in the table in §86, but for it see above §83), Lk 1:1—8:12 is Alexandrian, Lk 8:13—24:53 is Byzantine, Jn 1:1—5:11 is mixed, with some Alexandrian and some Western readings, and Jn 5:12—21:25 is Alexandrian. To explain these data, Sanders (*op. cit.,* p. 139) supposes that the manuscript from which W was copied (or perhaps its more distant ancestor manuscript) was one pieced together out of fragments of several different manuscripts which survived such a persecution as that by Diocletian in 303, when the sacred books were ordered destroyed. As to the first quire of John, however, which is the first sixteen pages containing Jn 1:1–5:11, there is yet more to be said. From the handwriting, it appears that one scribe wrote the balance of the codex, but that a second scribe wrote this quire, and that there were two different correctors in it too. It appears, in fact, that this quire was added at a later date to replace a quire that was lost at this point, and for this reason this portion of the manuscript is often cited as W^supp (i.e., "supplied" by a later hand where the original is missing). The contrast of this first quire of Jn with the balance of the codex includes not only the recognizably different and perhaps less practiced hand (Sanders, *op. cit.,* pp. 8f.), but also other details. In the main portion of the manuscript two dots (dieresis) are used over Iota and only one over Upsilon, but here two dots are used over Upsilon also (*ibid.,* p. 19). Punctuation is more frequent here in the first quire, regularly with a single dot in the middle position, and the divisions of the text are more numerous (*ibid.,* p. 14; *Facsimile,* pp. vi-vii). As to the date of the added quire, it is usually put in the seventh century (Metzger p. 57). Since, as stated, W^supp does contain Western readings, we have chosen to list this portion of the codex among the Western witnesses in the table above (§86), and to deal with it here along with Codex Sinaiticus and Codex Bezae.

§168. The opening portion of the Gospel according to John in the Washington Manuscript (W^supp) is shown in the next two photographs. Fig. 19 reproduces Page 113 in the codex, containing Jn 1:1-15, Fig. 20 reproduces Page 114, containing Jn 1:15-26. The section Jn 1:1-18 extends to Page 114 (Fig. 20), Line 10. The title at the top of Page 113 (Fig. 19) is εὐαγγέλιον κατὰ Ἰωάννην, Gospel according to John. Several minor points may be noted first, where W^supp agrees with ℵ and/or D. In Jn 1:6, in Line 8 on Page 113 (Fig. 19), W^supp inserts ἦν ("was"), exactly as in ℵ (§151) and D (§162). In Jn 1:15, in Line 1 on Page 114 (Fig. 20), W^supp includes ὑμῖν ("to you") as in D (§162) and ὅς ("who") as in ℵ (§153).

§169. The text of Jn 1:3-4 is found on Page 113 (Fig. 19), Lines 3-6, as follows:

W^supp

Page 113 (Jn 1:3-4)

ΠΑΝΤΑ ΔΙ ΑΥΤΟΥ ΕΓΕΝΕΤΟ ΚΑΙ ΧΩ
ΡΙC ΑΥΤΟΥ ΕΓΕΝΕΤΟ ΟΥΔΕ ΕΝ · Ο ΓΕΓΟΝΕΝ ΕΝ
5   ΑΥΤΩ ΖΩΗ · ΚΑΙ Η ΖΩΗ ΗΝ ΤΟ ΦΩC ΤΩΝ
ΑΝΩΝ ·

3 πάντα δι᾽ αὐτοῦ ἐγένετο καὶ χωρὶς αὐτοῦ ἐγένετο οὐδὲ ἕν · ὃ γέγονεν 4 ἐν
5   αὐτῷ ζωή · καὶ ἡ ζωὴ ἦν τὸ φῶς τῶν
ἀνθρώπων ·

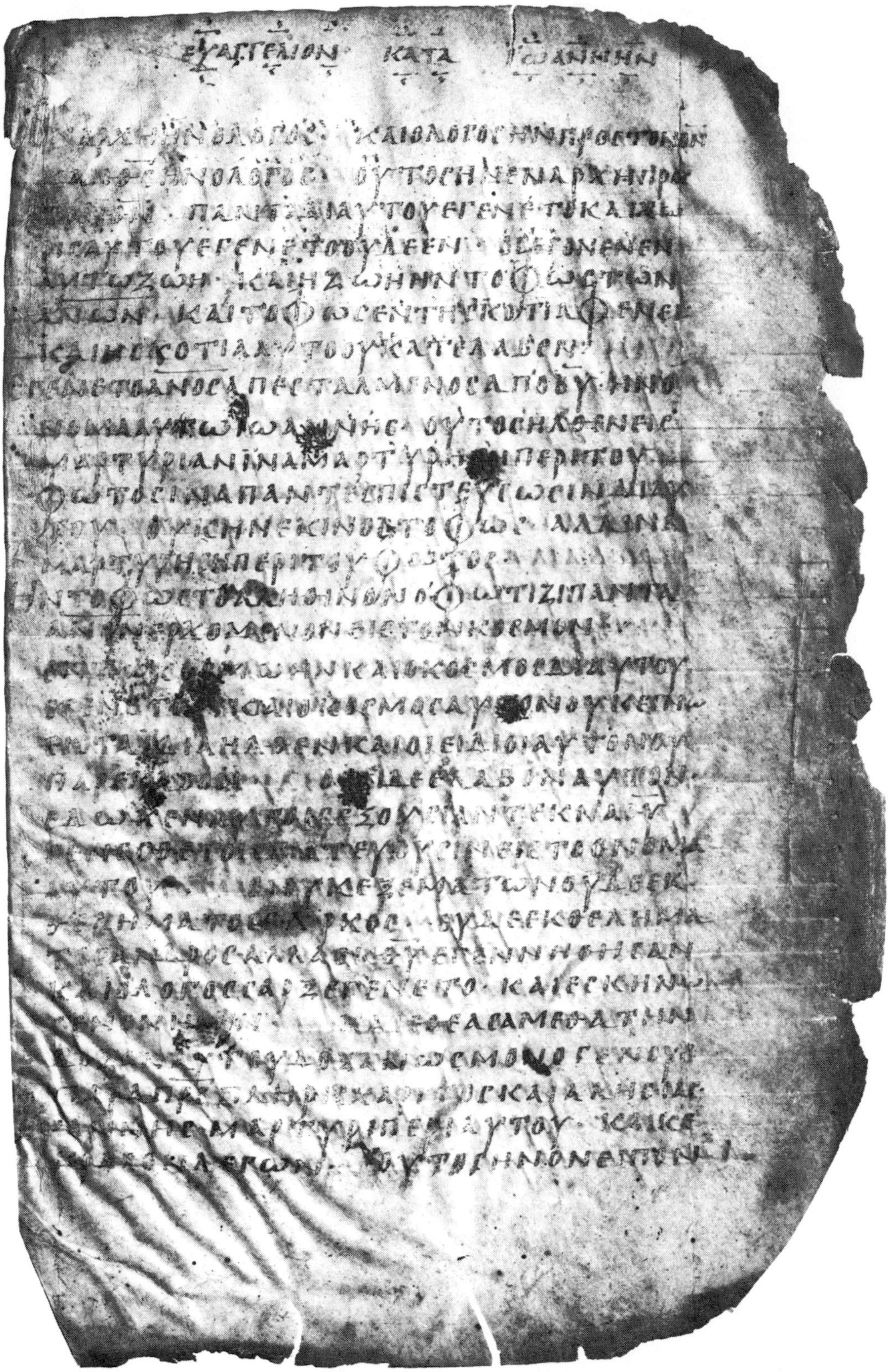

Figure 19.   Codex Washingtonensis (W), Page 113: John 1:1-15. *Reproduced at actual size.*

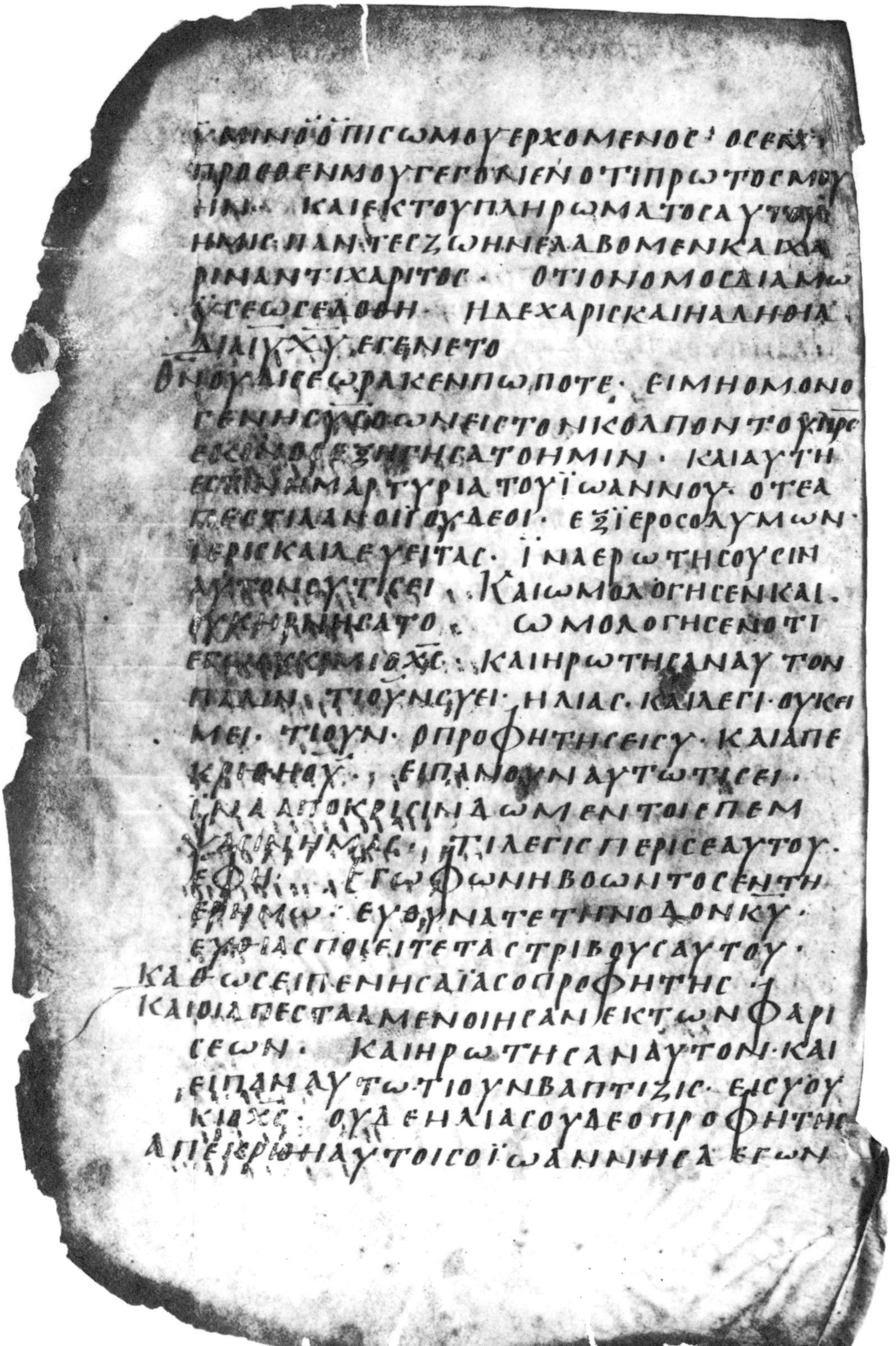

Figure 20. Codex Washingtonensis (W), Page 114: John 1:15-26. *Reproduced at actual size.*

3 All things came into being through Him; and a-
part from Him no single thing came into being. What has
come into being **4** in

5 Him (is *or* was) life. And the life was the light of
men.

The punctuation of verse **3** is unmistakable: there is a space and a
middle point after οὐδὲ ἕν ("no single thing"); here is where the stop
is to be made. The problem in verse **4** of whether to read ἦν or ἐστιν
has been solved less unambiguously: the verb has been left out
altogether; presumably the reader must decide which tense to supply.

§170. The text of Jn 1:18 is found on Page 114 (Fig. 20) Lines
8-10, where at the beginning of Line 8 a new paragraph is marked
and the first two letters are set into the left margin.

W^{supp}

Page 114 (Jn 1:18)

‾ΘN ΟΥΔΙC ΕѠΡΑΚΕΝ ΠѠΠΟΤΕ · ΕΙ ΜΗ Ο ΜΟΝΟ
ΓΕΝΗC ‾ΥC Ο ѠΝ ΕΙC ΤΟΝ ΚΟΛΠΟΝ ΤΟΥ ‾ΠΡC
10 ΕΚΙΝΟC ΕΞΗΓΗCΑΤΟ ΗΜΙΝ ·

θεὸν οὐδὶς ἑώρακεν πώποτε · εἰ μὴ ὁ μονογενὴς υἱὸς ὁ ὢν εἰς τὸν κόλπον τοῦ πατρὸς
10 ἐκῖνος ἐξηγήσατο ἡμῖν ·

No man has seen God at any time, except the only
begotten Son, who is in the bosom of the Father,
10 He has explained Him to us.

In the text, correctors' marks (a stroke in Line 8 and two dots in
Line 10) call attention to the spellings of οὐδὶς (for οὐδείς) and
ἐκῖνος (for ἐκεῖνος). The additions and changes that are found are
very important, but are almost certainly insertions and alterations as
compared with the form of the text with which we have been
familiar in the earlier manuscripts. The insertion of εἰ μή makes the
sentence say that "no man has seen God . . . *except* . . ." and the
addition of ἡμῖν at the end rounds out the statement to the effect
that "He has explained Him *to us.*" Furthermore, the difficulty that
is caused when it is stated that "the only begotten God (*or*, the only
God) . . . is in the bosom of the Father" (as in $\mathfrak{P}^{75}$, see above §137;
and in $\aleph^{c}$, see above §158), is entirely eliminated when it is said that
it is "the only begotten (*or*, the only) *Son*" who is in that position.

§171. The important evidence from the Washington Ms. of the
Gospels (W^{supp}) may, therefore, be included in our summary apparatus (§§138, 145, 159, 164) as follows:

Jn
1:3-4 οὐδὲν ὃ γέγονεν $\mathfrak{P}^{66}$
       οὐδὲν ὃ γέγονεν· $\aleph$
       οὐδέν· ὃ γέγονεν   D
       οὐδὲ ἓν ὃ γέγονεν $\mathfrak{P}^{75}$ B
       οὐδὲ ἕν· ὃ γέγονεν $\mathfrak{P}^{75c}$ $\aleph^{c}$ W^{supp}

$$\begin{aligned}
&\dot{\epsilon}\nu \ \alpha\dot{\upsilon}\tau\tilde{\omega} \ \zeta\omega\dot{\eta} \ \tilde{\eta}\nu &&\mathfrak{P}^{75} \ B \\
&\dot{\epsilon}\nu \ \alpha\dot{\upsilon}\tau\tilde{\omega} \ \zeta\omega\dot{\eta} \ \dot{\epsilon}\sigma\tau\iota\nu &&\aleph \ D \\
&\dot{\epsilon}\nu \ \alpha\dot{\upsilon}\tau\tilde{\omega} \ \zeta\omega\dot{\eta} &&W^{supp} \\
&\mu o\nu o\gamma\epsilon\nu\dot{\eta}s \ \theta\epsilon\delta s &&\mathfrak{P}^{66} \ B \ \aleph \\
&\dot{o} \ \mu o\nu o\gamma\epsilon\nu\dot{\eta}s \ \theta\epsilon\delta s &&\mathfrak{P}^{75} \ \aleph^{c} \\
&\dot{o} \ \mu o\nu o\gamma\epsilon\nu\dot{\eta}s \ \upsilon\dot{\iota}\delta s &&W^{supp}
\end{aligned}$$

(c) *Koine or Byzantine Witnesses*

(a) *Parchments*

8. Codex Alexandrinus (A)

§172. In terms of the theoretical grouping of three major text types noted above (§86), we have now studied a selected passage (Jn 1:1-18, as far as it is preserved in the respective manuscripts) in three of the Alexandrian (or, more specifically, Proto-Alexandrian) witnesses, namely, two papyri, Papyrus Bodmer II ($\mathfrak{P}^{66}$) and Papyrus Bodmer XV ($\mathfrak{P}^{75}$), and one parchment, Codex Vaticanus (B); and in three of the Western witnesses, namely, the parchments, Codex Sinaiticus ($\aleph$), Codex Bezae (D), and Codex Washingtonensis (W). All of these manuscripts are written in some form of uncial script. It remains mainly to look at the Koine or Byzantine witnesses, and here we will consider two parchments, namely, Codex Alexandrinus (A), written in uncial script, and Codex 666, written in minuscule script. The first of these, Codex Alexandrinus, is, of course, in large part considered an Alexandrian (specifically a Later Alexandrian) witness, namely, in Acts, the Pauline Letters, the Catholic Letters, and Revelation; but in the Gospels it belongs to the Koine or Byzantine family and is, indeed, our oldest example of the Byzantine text (Metzger p. 47). Therefore, for our purpose, it comes into consideration at the present point.

§173. Codex Alexandrinus (A, **02**, δ4) was presented to King Charles I of England by Cyril Lucar, Greek Patriarch of Constantinople. The manuscript reached England in 1628, and was placed in the Royal Library which, in 1757, was incorporated in the British Museum. In the British Museum the manuscript is designated as Royal I D. VIII. Cyril Lucar himself had been Patriarch of Alexandria before coming to Constantinople, and doubtless brought the manuscript with him from Egypt. In the codex a thirteenth or fourteenth-century Arabic note on the first leaf of Genesis states that the manuscript belonged to the Patriarchal Library in Cairo (in which city the Patriarchs of Alexandria then resided). A seventeenth-century Latin note on the flyleaf says that the manuscript was a gift to the Patriarchal Library in the Year 814 of the Era of the Martyrs (cf. FHBC p. 132), which was A.D. 1098. The plain uncial script of the manuscript suggests a relatively early date, yet the ornamentation, with lines in red at the beginnings of books (cf. D, §161) and panel-shaped tailpieces or colophons at the end (Milne and Skeat, *Scribes and Correctors of the Codex Sinaiticus,* Pls. 10-43), suggests a date later than B and $\aleph$, while the inclusion ahead of the Psalms of material from Eusebius (d. 339) and Athanasius (d. 373) requires a date after their time. The manuscript was written originally, it is therefore generally concluded, in the first half of the fifth century (Milne and Skeat, *The Codex Sinaiticus and the Codex Alexandrinus*, p. 31). After several partial editions, a complete full-size four-volume facsimile of the codex, edited by E. Maunde Thompson, was issued by the Trustees of the British Museum in 1879-1883. After that, *The Codex Alexandrinus (Royal MS. I D V-VIII) in Reduced Photographic Facsimile* was also issued by the Trustees in five parts, one NT part, edited by F. G. Kenyon, in 1909, and four OT parts, edited by Kenyon, J. J. M. Milne, and T. C. Skeat, in 1915-1957.

§174. As it exists today, Codex Alexandrinus consists of 773 parchment leaves, which measure about 12.6 by 10.4 inches in size. Of these, 630 leaves contain virtually the entire OT (FHRJ pp. 26f.); and 143 leaves preserve most of the NT (Mt 1:1–25:6, Jn 6:50–8:52, and II Cor 4:13–12:6 are missing), together with the First and Second Letters of Clement (FHRJ pp. 41f.). The codex is composed of quires, normally of eight leaves, numbered in Greek characters in the center of the top margin of each first page. The pages are written in two columns of text, of from 46 to 52 lines, usually 50 or 51. There are usually about 20-25 letters in a full line, and the letters at the end of the line are often of smaller size and crowded in. Sections are marked by larger letters set in the margin. It is not necessarily the first letter of the first word of the new paragraph that is thus enlarged; rather the new paragraph begins in the line wherever it may happen to fall, and then the first letter that strikes the next line is placed in larger size in the margin. The words are written continuously without separation; there are no accents and only rare breathings. High and middle points are used for punctuation, initial Iota and Upsilon have the dieresis, sacred names are abbreviated, and OT quotations are marked. The Eusebian canons are indicated, and lists of chapters are provided for some of the NT books. Two scribes are recognized as having written the OT, and the first of these probably copied the NT too. Many corrections have been made, most at an early date, some by the original copyists, others by later hands (for the scribes see *Scribes and Correctors of the Codex Sinaiticus*, pp. 91-93; *The Codex Sinaiticus and the Codex Alexandrinus*, pp. 32-34; *The Codex Alexandrinus . . . in Reduced Photographic Facsimile*, OT Part IV, pp. 1-2).

§175. The first page of the Gospel according to John in Codex Alexandrinus (A) is reproduced in Fig. 21. In the upper portion of the left-hand column is a table of the chapters in the Gospel. The numbers run to $\iota\eta$ = 18, the headings are ΠΕΡΙ ΤΟΥ ΕΓ ΚΑΝΑ ΓΑΜΟΥ, περὶ τοῦ ἐγ Κανὰ γάμου, "Concerning the Wedding in Cana," etc. The title of the Gospel stands not at the head of the work but in a panel at the end (cf. §173), εὐαγγέλιον κατὰ Ἰωάννην, Gospel according to John. In the right-hand column of the page in Fig. 21 is found the text of Jn 1:1-18. Except for the two major passages (Jn 1:3-4 and 1:18) to which we shall turn momentarily (§§176f.), there are only two points at which the text varies from that of the very earliest witnesses, namely, 𝔓⁶⁶ (§130) and 𝔓⁷⁵ (Figs. 13-14). In Jn 1:16, in Line 43, the sentence opens here with καί ("And") instead of ὅτι ("For"), as in 𝔓⁶⁶ and 𝔓⁷⁵. In Jn 1:17, in Line 47, the text reads ἡ χάρις καὶ ἡ ἀλήθεια ("grace and truth"). At this point 𝔓⁶⁶ has the slightly complex ἡ χάρις δὲ καὶ ἀλήθεια ("but grace and truth"); 𝔓⁷⁵ already has the simple phrase, exactly as found in Codex Alexandrinus.

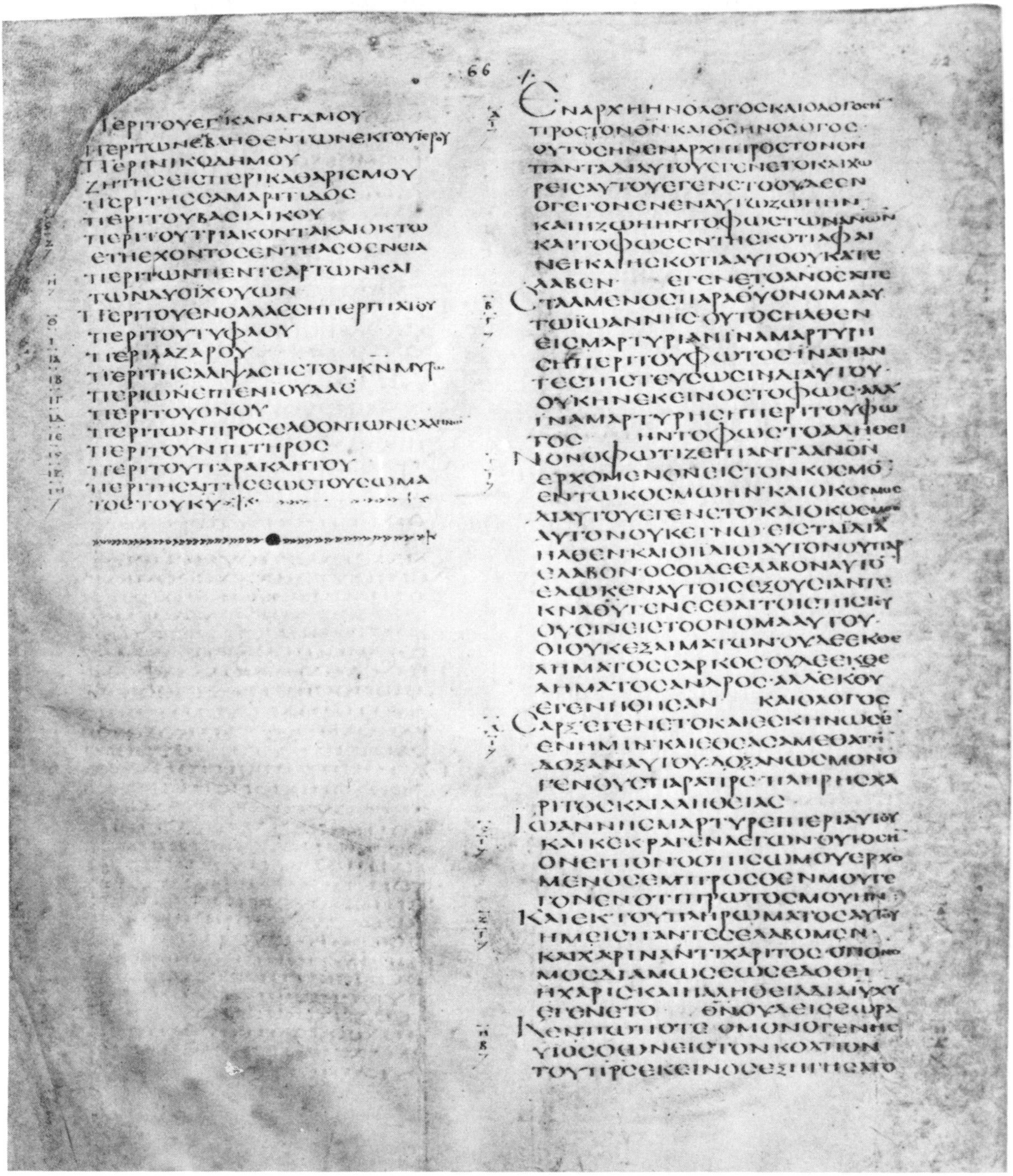

Figure 21. Codex Alexandrinus (A): John 1:1-18. *Actual size 12.6 × 10.4 in.*
Portions opposite show John 1:1-5 and 18, and are approximately actual size.

§176. Now we read Jn 1:3-4, in Lines 4-7 in the right-hand column in Fig. 21.

A

Jn 1:3-4

ΠΑΝΤΑ ΔΙ ΑΥΤΟΥ ΕΓΕΝΕΤΟ ΚΑΙ ΧΩ
5 ΡΕΙC ΑΥΤΟΥ ΕΓΕΝΕΤΟ ΟΥΔΕ ΕΝ
Ο ΓΕΓΟΝΕΝ ΕΝ ΑΥΤΩ ΖΩΗ ΗΝ
ΚΑΙ Η ΖΩΗ ΗΝ ΤΟ ΦΩC ΤΩΝ A̅N̅Ω̅N̅

3 πάντα δι᾽ αὐτοῦ ἐγένετο καὶ χω-
5 ρεὶς αὐτοῦ ἐγένετο οὐδὲ ἓν
ὃ γέγονεν4 ἐν αὐτῷ ζωὴ ἦν
καὶ ἡ ζωὴ ἦν τὸ φῶς τῶν ἀνθρώπων

The spelling χωρείς instead of the more usual χωρίς ("apart from") is noted. The words οὐδὲ ἕν ("no single thing") are found, in agreement with 𝔓⁷⁵ B ℵᶜ Wˢᵘᵖᵖ , rather than οὐδέν ("nothing") as in 𝔓⁶⁶ ℵ D. In the absence of any punctuation marks at this place, it cannot be known for sure where the stop is supposed to be made in the sentence. That οὐδὲ ἕν ends one line and ὃ γέγονεν begins another line could suggest, to that extent, that the stop should fall there (at the end of Line 5). In the next manuscript to be noticed, however, Codex 666, we have an arrangement of lines almost identical with that in Codex Alexandrinus, together with an original mark of punctuation after ὃ γέγονεν (§180), which may make it slightly more probable that this is also the better way to read Codex Alexandrinus, namely, as follows:

Jn 1:3-4

3 All things came into being through Him; and a-
5   part from Him no single thing came into being
that has come into being. 4 In Him was life;
and the life was the light of men.

§177. The text of Jn 1:18 is found in the last four lines (Lines 48-51) of the right-hand column in Fig. 21.

A

Jn 1:18

ΘN ΟΥΔΕΙϹ ΕѠΡΑ
ΚΕΝ ΠѠΠΟΤΕ Ο ΜΟΝΟΓΕΝΗϹ
50   ΤΙΟϹ Ο ѠΝ ΕΙϹ ΤΟΝ ΚΟΛΠΟΝ
ΤΟΥ ΠΡϹ ΕΚΕΙΝΟϹ ΕΞΗΓΗϹΑΤΟ

θεὸν οὐδεὶς ἑώρα-
κεν πώποτε ὁ μονογενὴς
50   υἱὸς ὁ ὢν εἰς τὸν κόλπον
τοῦ πατρὸς ἐκεῖνος ἐξηγήσατο

The arrangement of the lines illustrates the manner of paragraphing in Codex Alexandrinus (§174). The new paragraph begins, after a space, in the latter part of Line 48; it is marked by the larger size and extension into the margin of the first letter (Kappa) of the next line, even though in this case this is a letter in the middle of a word. In Line 49 the reading incorporates the article (ὁ) which was first found, among the witnesses we have surveyed (§171), in $\mathfrak{P}^{75}$ and $\aleph^c$; and in Line 50 it gives υἱός ("Son"), which we first found in W^{supp}, rather than θεός ("God"), which was in all the earlier witnesses. The translation is therefore:

Jn 1:18

No man has
seen God at any time; the only begotten
50   Son, who is in the bosom
of the Father, He has explained Him.

§178. The evidence of Codex Alexandrinus (A) is added therefore to our summary apparatus (§§138, 145, 159, 164, 171) as follows:

Jn
1:3-4   οὐδὲν ὃ γέγονεν $\mathfrak{P}^{66}$
      οὐδὲν ὃ γέγονεν· $\aleph$
      οὐδέν· ὃ γέγονεν   D
      οὐδὲ ἓν ὃ γέγονεν $\mathfrak{P}^{75}$ B A
      οὐδὲ ἕν· ὃ γέγονεν $\mathfrak{P}^{75c}$ $\aleph^c$ W^{supp}
      ἐν αὐτῷ ζωὴ ἦν $\mathfrak{P}^{75}$ B A
      ἐν αὐτῷ ζωή ἐστιν $\aleph$ D
      ἐν αὐτῷ ζωή W^{supp}
  1:18   μονογενὴς θεός $\mathfrak{P}^{66}$ B $\aleph$

ὁ μονογενὴς θεός $\mathfrak{P}^{75}$ $\aleph^c$
ὁ μονογενὴς υἱός W^{supp} A

9. Codex 666

§179. All the manuscripts studied thus far have been written in some form of uncial script; the two we will yet consider are in minuscule script (§23), one on parchment, one on paper.

The first is Ms. Gr. 1 in the Houghton Library of Harvard University, and is designated as No. 666 in Gregory's list (§52), ε1293 in von Soden's system (§55). This manuscript was received by Harvard University Library in 1899, and belonged immediately before that to Professor Gregory. The latter wrote a brief description in the front of the codex, dated May 26, 1889 at Leipzig, in which he stated that the manuscript was formerly in Albania (*olim in Albania*). Otherwise we know nothing of its place of origin. As it exists today the manuscript is a codex of thirty-seven quires, with 294 numbered leaves, containing the Four Gospels. The first quire has a list of chapter titles for the Gospel according to Matthew, and a seated portrait of that apostle; and similar lists and portraits are placed in front of the other Gospels. While this was originally a parchment codex in its entirety, a few portions were evidently lost and have been supplied by a later hand on paper (Jn 3:4-18; 5:12—6:6; 7:2—21:25). The minuscule script of the original manuscript is probably to be dated in the twelfth or thirteenth century, the later hand, found in the paper portions, in the fourteenth century. The parchment leaves are approximately 8.3 by 6.0 inches in size. Each page contains one column of text, with 23 or 24 lines of writing in the column. Words are written continuously without separation, and are provided with accents and breathings. There is punctuation with high, middle, and low points, comma, and question mark. The dieresis is sometimes used with Iota and Upsilon, and OT quotations are sometimes indicated. Initial letters are written in red, and at the beginnings of books in red, blue, and gold. The text is Byzantine, and the corrections that are found in the manuscript are only such as to bring it even more closely into conformity with what we know as the Received Text (§§65, 85, 87) (Edgar J. Goodspeed in AJT 10 [1906], pp. 687-700).

§180. In our Figs. 22-23 are reproduced the first four pages of the Gospel according to John in Codex 666. On the first page, at the left side of Fig. 22, is the portrait of John the Evangelist. John is clothed in a long, flowing robe, and has a halo behind his head. He is seated in a tall chair, beside a writing desk, the open door of which discloses writing materials including ink pots. The open pages of the book, one copy of which is on the knees of the evangelist, and another copy on a reading stand at the right, contain the opening words, somewhat abbreviated, of the Gospel: Ἐν ἀρχῇ ἦν ὁ λόγος, καὶ ὁ λόγος ἦν, "In the beginning was the Word, and the Word was." On the second page, at the right side of Fig. 22, is the title of the Gospel, surrounded by elaborate ornamentation, τὸ κατὰ Ἰωάννην

Figure 22. Codex 666: Portrait of John the Evangelist, and John 1:1-5. *Actual size of each page 8.3 × 6.0 in.*

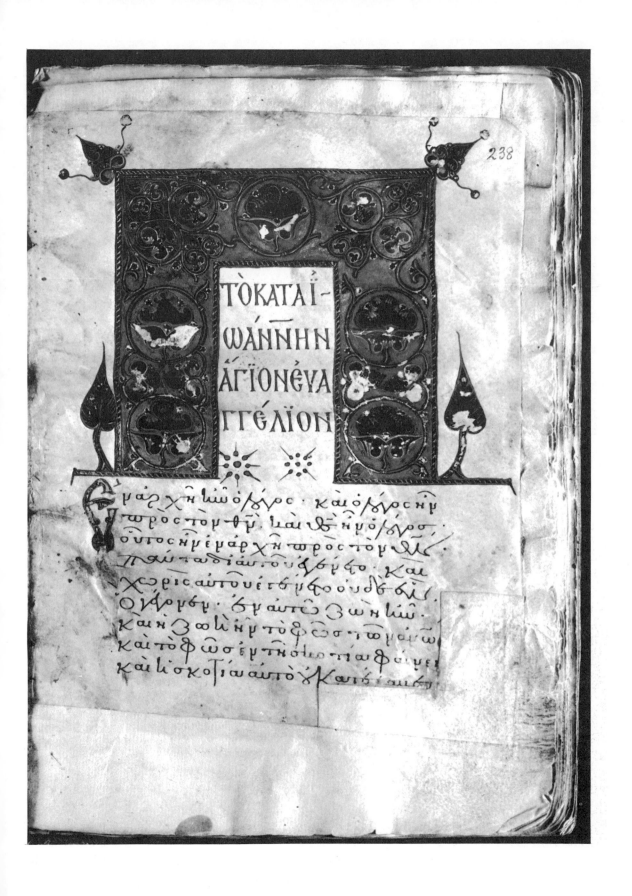

ΤῸ ΚΑΤΑ Ϊ
ΩΆΝΝΗΝ
ΆΓΙΟΝ ΕΥΑ
ΓΓΈΛΙΟΝ

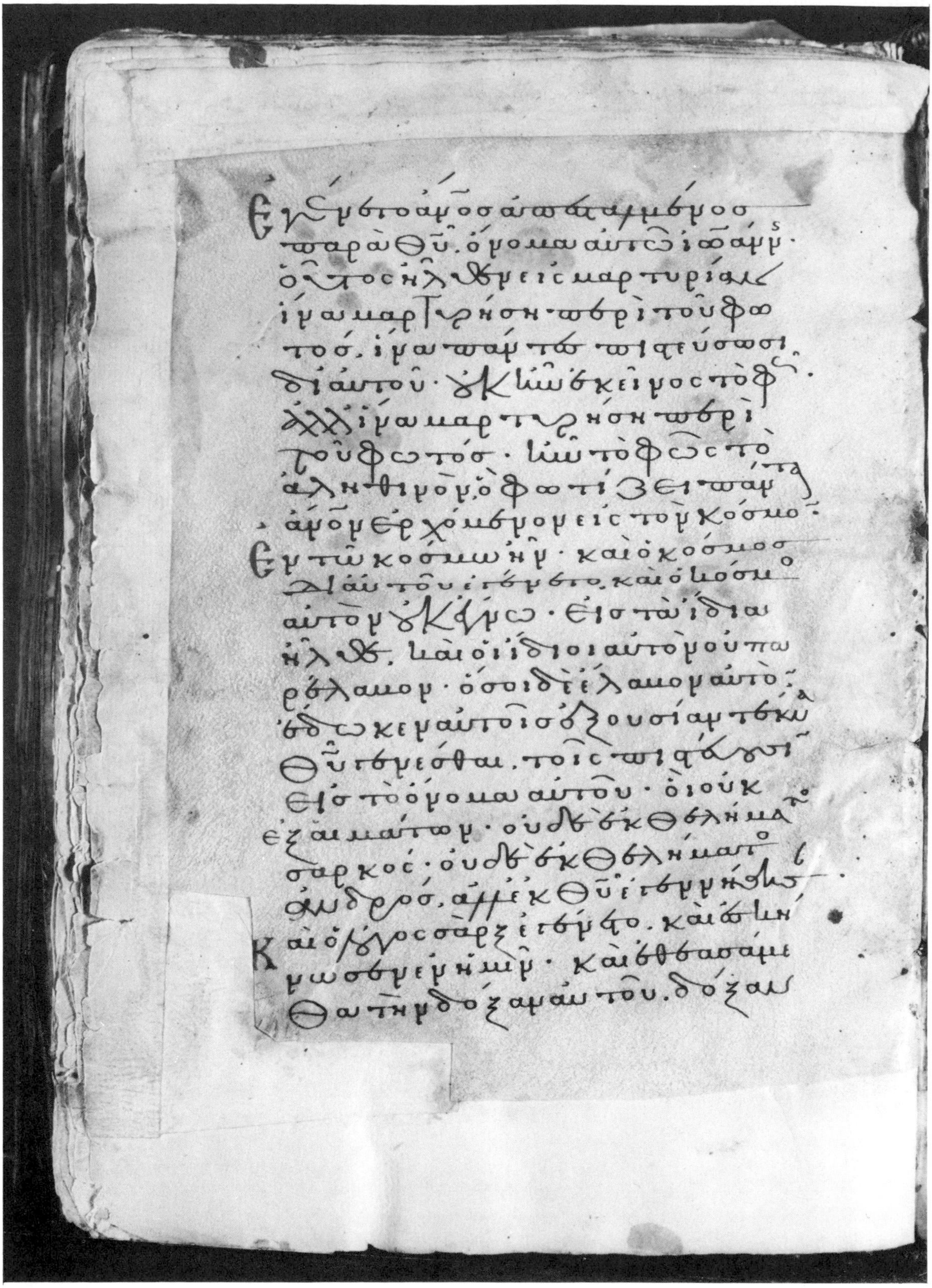

Figure 23.   Codex 666: John 1:6-14 and 1:14-21. *Actual size of each page 8.3 × 6.0 in.*

ὡς μονογενοῦς παρὰ πατρὸς
πλήρης χάριτος καὶ ἀληθείας. ωαννης μαρτυρεῖ περὶ αὐτοῦ.
καὶ κέκραγεν λέγων· οὗτος ἦν ὃν
εἶπον· ὁ ὀπίσω μου ἐρχόμενος ἔμπροσθέν μου γέγονεν ὅτι
πρῶτός μου ἦν· καὶ ἐκ τοῦ
πληρώματος αὐτοῦ ἡμεῖς
πάντες ἐλάβομεν· καὶ χάριν
ἀντὶ χάριτος· ὅτι ὁ νόμος διὰ
μωσέως ἐδόθη· ἡ χάρις
καὶ ἡ ἀλήθεια διὰ ἰυ χυ ἐγένετο·
θν οὐδεὶς ἑώρακι πώποτε·
ὁ μονογενὴς υἱός· ὁ ὢν εἰς τὸν
κόλπον τοῦ πρς· ἐκεῖνος
ἐξηγήσατο· καὶ αὕτη ἐστιν ἡ
μαρτυρία τοῦ ιωαννου ὅτε
ἀπέστειλαν οἱ ιουδαῖοι ἐξ ιε-
ροσολύμων ιερεῖς καὶ λευίτας
ἵνα ἐρωτήσωσιν αὐτόν· σὺ
τίς εἶ· καὶ ὡμολόγησεν καὶ
οὐκ ἠρνήσατο· καὶ ὡμολόγησεν
ὅτι οὐκ εἰμὶ ἐγὼ ὁ χς· καὶ ἠρώ-
τησαν αὐτόν· τί οὖν· ἠλίας

ἅγιον εὐαγγέλιον, "The holy Gospel according to John," followed by nine lines of text, containing Jn 1:1-5. Here, in Lines 4-7, Jn 1:3-4 reads as follows:

666

Jn 1:3-4

3 πάντα δι᾽ αὐτοῦ ἐγένετο· καὶ
5 χωρὶς αὐτοῦ ἐγένετο οὐδὲ ἕν.
ὃ γέγονεν· 4 ἐν αὐτῷ ζωὴ ἦν·
καὶ ἡ ζωὴ ἦν τὸ φῶς τῶν α̅ν̅ω̅ν̅

The wording of the text is identical with that in Codex Alexandrinus (A), as seen above (§176); and, although the end of Line 7 is now obscured, the abbreviation of ἀνθρώπων ("of men") appears to have been the same, α̅ν̅ω̅ν̅. As to the crucial point of punctuation, the original major stop seems clearly to have been put after ὃ γέγονεν in Line 6, for there is not only a high point at this place but there is also space left (which obviously had to be done by the original copyist) before the succeeding words, ἐν αὐτῷ ("in Him"). There appears to be also, however, a low point after οὐδὲ ἕν ("no single thing") at the end of Line 5. Because the high point in Line 6 is recognizably the original punctuation in the manuscript, the low point at the end of Line 5 must represent the change proposed by a corrector. The original reading of Codex 666 was therefore in all probability as follows:

Jn 1:3-4

3 All things came into being through Him; and
5 apart from Him no single thing came into being
that has come into being. 4 In Him was life;
and the life was the light of men.

But the punctuation of the corrector would result in the reading:

3 All things came into being through Him; and
5 apart from Him no single thing came into being.
What has come into being 4 was life in Him;
and the life was the light of men.

§181. In Fig. 23, the page of Codex 666 seen at the left begins with the beginning of Jn 1:6 and continues through the second occurrence of the word δόξαν ("glory") in 1:14. The page seen at the right begins with the balance of verse 14 and continues through the word Ἠλίας ("Elijah") in verse 21. The verse Jn 1:18 is contained in Lines 13-16 of this second page in Fig. 23. A section begins at this point, as was indicated by placing the large first letter of the passage (Theta, the initial letter of the abbreviation θ̅ν̅ = θεόν, "God") in the left margin. The verse reads as follows:

Jn 1:18

Θ̄ν̄ οὐδεὶς ἑώρακε πώποτε·
ὁ μονογενὴς υἱός · ὁ ὢν εἰς τὸν
15 κόλπον τοῦ π̄ρ̄ς̄, ἐκεῖνος
ἐξηγήσατο·

No man has seen God at any time;
the only begotten Son, who is in the
15 bosom of the Father, He
has explained Him.

This is the standard reading of Jn 1:18 in the Byzantine text, as seen already in Codex Alexandrinus (A) (§177), and as derived from the Western text (W^supp §170).

§182. The readings of Codex 666 may be added, therefore, to our summary textual apparatus (§§138, 145, 159, 164, 171, 178) as follows:

Jn
1:3-4 οὐδὲν ὃ γέγονεν 𝔭⁶⁶
       οὐδὲν ὃ γέγονεν· ℵ
       οὐδέν· ὃ γέγονεν D
       οὐδὲ ἓν ὃ γέγονεν 𝔭⁷⁵ B A
       οὐδὲ ἓν ὃ γέγονεν· 666
       οὐδὲ ἕν· ὃ γέγονεν 𝔭⁷⁵ᶜ ℵᶜ W^supp 666ᶜ
       ἐν αὐτῷ ζωὴ ἦν 𝔭⁷⁵ B A 666
       ἐν αὐτῷ ζωή ἐστιν ℵ D
       ἐν αὐτῷ ζωή W^supp
1:18   μονογενὴς θεός 𝔭⁶⁶ B ℵ
       ὁ μονογενὴς θεός 𝔭⁷⁵ ℵᶜ
       ὁ μονογενὴς υἱός W^supp A 666

(β) *Paper*

10. Codex 1345

§183. Manuscript No. 572 in the Library of St. Saba (Βιβλιοθήκη τοῦ ᾽Αγίου Σαβα) in the Greek Orthodox Patriarchate (᾽Ορθόδοξον Πατριαρχεῖον) in Jerusalem, appears as No. 1345 in Gregory's list, and as ε491 in von Soden's designation. It is a codex made of paper, and written in a minuscule hand judged to belong to the fourteenth century. The codex consists of 422 leaves, about 7.7 by 5.6 inches in size. Each page contains one column of text, with 19 or 20 lines of writing to the page. Initial letters are written in red. High and middle points, comma, and interrogation sign are used for punctuation. Dieresis, accent, and breathing marks are supplied. Contained are the four Gospels, from Mt 1:9 to Jn 21:25. While this is not a lectionary manuscript (§93), it does have the lections (§30) marked in the regular sequence of the text, with αρχ (= ἀρχή) and τελ (= τέλος) for the "beginning" and "end" of the reading, and a notation at the head of the column to give the day on which the reading was to be used, and to give a summary title of the section. There are also lists of chapters for Mark, Luke, and John, and subscriptions for the same Gospels.

§184. The available photograph of a page in Codex 1345 (W. H. P. Hatch, *The Greek Manuscripts of the New Testament in Jerusalem* [American Schools of Oriental Research, Publications of the Jerusalem School, II. Paris: Librairie Orientaliste Paul Geuthner, 1934], Pl. LV) is reproduced in our Fig. 24. The page contains the text of Jn

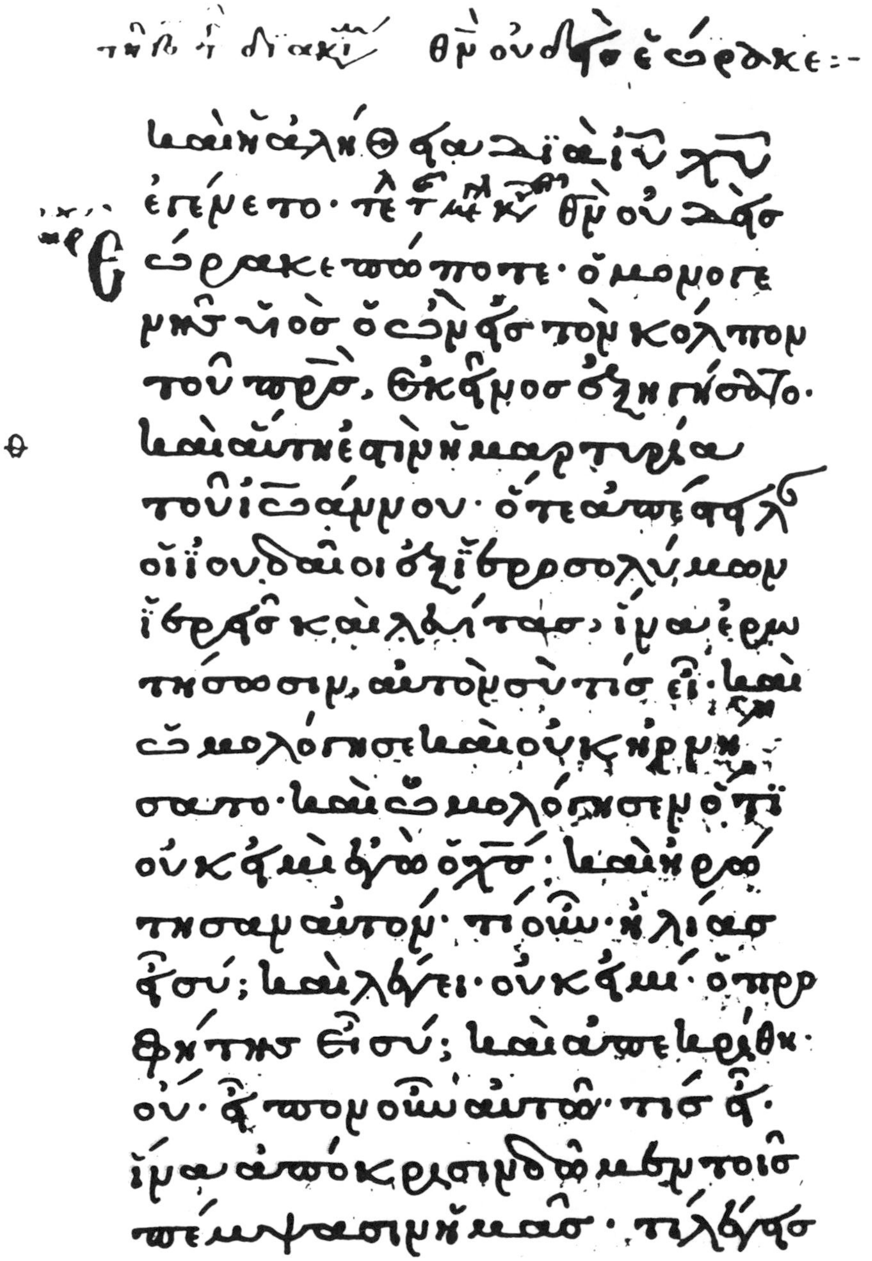

Figure 24. Codex 1345: John 1:17-22. *Reproduced at actual size.*

1:17-22. In the lections of the early church (cf. §30), Jn 1:1-17 was designated as the reading for "the holy and great Lord's Day of Easter" (τῇ ἁγίᾳ καὶ μεγάλῃ κυριακῇ τοῦ Πάσχα) (Colwell and Riddle p. 85). In the first two lines of text in the column in Fig. 24, we have the last portion of Jn 1:17, καὶ ἡ ἀλήθεια διὰ $\overline{ιυ}$ $\overline{χυ}$ ἐγένετο, ". . . and truth were realized through Jesus Christ," and thereafter, in Line 2, in abbreviated form, the indication of the τέλος or "end" of the lection. The next lection was Jn 1:18-28. This was designated to be read τῇ $\overline{β}$ τῆς διακινησίμου, i.e., on the second day of the six days of Easter week (Colwell and Riddle p. 8); and this indication appears at the top of the page on the left. On the right, at the top of the page, are the opening words of Jn 1:18, $\overline{θν}$ οὐδεὶς ἑώρακε, "No man has seen God"; and these provide the summary title for the lection. The lection itself begins, with the first two of these words, at the end of Line 2; and the initial letter (Eta) of the third word is set out in large form in the margin at the beginning of Line 3. There also the ἀρχή or "beginning" of the lection is marked.

§185. Jn 1:18 is found here, in Lines 2-5 of the page of Codex 1345 in Fig. 24, as follows:

Codex 1345

Jn 1:18

$\overline{θν}$ οὐδεὶς
Ἑώρακε πώποτε· ὁ μονογε-
νὴς υἱὸς ὁ ὢν εἰς τὸν κόλπον
5   τοῦ $\overline{πρς}$, ἐκεῖνος ἐξηγήσατο·

No man
has seen God at any time; the only
begotten Son, who is in the bosom
5   of the Father, He has explained Him.

Obviously we have here the same reading (ὁ μονογενὴς υἱός, "the only begotten Son") as in W[supp] (§170), A (§177), and 666 (§181), and indeed in the Koine text generally.

§186. The evidence of Codex 1345 on Jn 1:18 is to be added, therefore, to our summary apparatus (§§138, 145, 159, 164, 171, 178, 182), as follows:

Jn
1:18   μονογενὴς θεός   𝔓[66] B ℵ
        ὁ μονογενὴς θεός   𝔓[75] ℵ[c]
        ὁ μονογενὴς υἱός   W[supp] A 666 1345

(d) Lectionaries, Versions, and Church Fathers

11. Lectionaries

§187. In the foregoing (§§126ff.) we have grouped a number of witnesses in terms of hypothetical text types, and have considered in the Alexandrian (specifically the Proto-Alexandrian) group three manuscripts, two papyri ($\mathfrak{P}^{66}$ and $\mathfrak{P}^{75}$) and one parchment (B); in the Western group three parchments (‎א D W [specifically W^supp]); and in the Koine or Byzantine group three manuscripts, one parchment (A) written still in uncials, the script of all the foregoing manuscripts, one parchment (666) written in minuscules, and one paper manuscript (1345) also written in minuscules. Therewith we have made a representative survey of manuscripts in the three major theoretical text types, of manuscripts on the three chief writing materials, namely, papyrus, parchment, and paper, and of manuscripts in the two chief forms of writing, namely, the uncial and the minuscule script. Among the Greek witnesses all together, it would be possible also to take up the lectionary manuscripts (§93); but this will be considered not necessary, particularly inasmuch as Codex 1345, already treated (§§183-186), although not a lectionary manuscript in the sense of arrangement in terms of lections (for an example of this, see Hatch, *Minuscule Manuscripts,* Pl. XXXIII), does have the lections indicated.

12. Versions

§188. Beyond the Greek manuscripts of the NT, there are also the versions (§94) and the church fathers (§95) as witnesses to the original text. Since it has been our intention to look primarily at the Greek manuscripts, these two remaining areas will be noted only briefly and without going all the way back to the manuscripts of the versions and of the church fathers, using instead only the critical editions of these sources. The illustration of the situation with respect to the versions and the church fathers will also be limited to only a few typical witnesses (Latin manuscripts among the versions, Irenaeus and Origen among the church fathers), and to the question of text in only one passage, namely, Jn 1:18, the verse in which the most significant variations have appeared in the Greek witnesses. The versions are, of course, translations of the NT into other ancient languages than the Greek. In considering, now, the witness of the Latin version to the text of Jn 1:18, it must be remembered that the Latin language has no article, and the opening words of the Fourth Gospel, for example, which read in Greek, Ἐν ἀρχῇ ἦν ὁ λόγος, are rendered in the Vulgate, *In principio erat verbum,* and in both cases are translated into English as, "In the beginning was the Word." Hence when we find *unigenitus deus,* for example, it will not always be possible to know for sure whether this is rendering μονογενὴς θεός or ὁ μονογενὴς θεός, i.e., "only begotten God," or "the only begotten God."

§189. In a number of Itala or Old Latin manuscripts (e.g., *a* or Vercellensis of the fourth century, *b* or Veronensis of the fifth century, *aur* or Aureus of the seventh century, and others; see Adolf Jülicher, *Itala, Das Neue Testament in altlateinischer Überlieferung* [Berlin: Walter de Gruyter and Co., 4 vols. 1938-1963], IV *Johannes-Evangelium* [1963], p. 3; cf. Gregory, *Prolegomena,* pp. 952ff.), and in the standard manuscripts of the Vulgate translation (John

Wordsworth and Henry J. White, *Novum Testamentum Domini Nostri Iesu Christi Latine secundum Editionem Sancti Hieronymi* [Oxford: The Clarendon Press, 3 vols. 1889-1954], I, p. 509; cf. FHRJ pp. 32f.), Jn 1:18 reads as follows:

Jn 1:18

a b aur Vulgate

Deum nemo vidit umquam,
unigenitus filius qui est in sinu
patris ipse enarravit.

No man has seen God at any time;
the only begotten Son, who is in the bosom
of the Father, He has explained Him.

Here *unigenitus filius (unicus filius* in Itala manuscript *a)* presumably corresponds to ὁ μονογενὴς υἱός, and the Greek text presupposed is identical with that which is found in the Western text (W^supp §170), and which prevails in the Koine or Byzantine family of manuscripts (§§177, 181, 185).

§190. Two other readings also, however, are found in Latin manuscripts. In one manuscript of the Itala, namely, *q* or Monacensis of the seventh century (Jülicher, *Itala,* IV, p. 3), the phrase *unigenitus filius dei* is found. This doubtless corresponds to ὁ μονογενὴς υἱὸς θεοῦ, "the only begotten Son of God." Thus the two readings "Son" and "God" are combined. On the other hand, in one manuscript of the Vulgate (*gat* or Gatiani 8, now Suppl. Lat. 1587 in the Bibliothèque Nationale, Paris; cf. Gregory, *Prolegomena,* pp. 987f.), dating in the eighth century, the reading is simply *unigenitus.* This can correspond with either μονογενής or ὁ μονογενής, "only begotten" or "the only begotten." Here the problem of the textual reading is solved by omitting both θεός and υἱός, and simply saying "(the) only begotten," without adding either "God" or "Son."

§191. Adding this additional evidence from the Latin versions, we have this in our summary apparatus (§§138, 145, 159, 164, 171, 178, 182, 186):

Jn
1:18   μονογενὴς θεός   𝔓^66 B ℵ
      ὁ μονογενὴς θεός   𝔓^75 ℵ^c
      ὁ μονογενὴς υἱός   W^supp A 666 1345
      unigenitus filius   Itala (*b aur,* etc.) Vulgate
      unicus filius   Itala (*a*)
      unigenitus filius dei   Itala (*q*)
      unigenitus   Vulgate (*gat*)

13. Church Fathers

§192. The significance of the church fathers for the purpose with which we are concerned consists, of course, in that these post-NT writers of the early church make many quotations from the

NT text, or paraphrases thereof, or allusions thereto. The use of their evidence is complicated, however, by the need first to establish the best text of the church father himself, which usually involves comparing various manuscripts and making a critical edition. Particularly in respect to NT quotations in the text, the possibility must be considered that a copyist might bring such a quotation into line with the text with which he was familiar, even if the church father had quoted it in some other form. Also if the church father wrote in a language other than Greek, or if his work is available, in whole or in part, only in a translation into another language, then his witness is in this respect removed from the original text in much the same way as are the versions.

Irenaeus, for example, who flourished around A.D. 180, wrote in Greek, and the first book of his *Against Heresies* is available in that language (largely through extensive quotations by Hippolytus and Epiphanius); but for most of the rest of the work there is only a Latin translation, as well as portions in Armenian and Syriac. Furthermore, the church father himself, whether writing in Greek or in another language, might quote the NT passage from memory, and even give the quotation in different forms in different passages. He might also quote the text differently at different periods in his life, or in different geographical circumstances in which he found himself. For example, the *Commentary on the Gospel according to John* by Origen (A.D. 185-253) is of great interest in connection with the text of the Fourth Gospel; and it is important to note that the first four volumes of this work were probably written at Alexandria between 226 and 229, the fifth volume while Origen was on a trip in the East in 230/231, the sixth was interrupted by his exile in the next year, and the balance was composed at Caesarea, where he lived from that time onward (Johannes Quasten, *Patrology* [Westminster, Maryland: The Newman Press, 3 vols. 1950-60], II, p. 49; cf. R. V. G. Tasker in JTS 37 [1936], pp. 146-155). Given due allowance for such factors as all of these, however, the text of a NT quotation (or in some cases a paraphrase or an allusion) in a church father is an important witness to the NT text which this writer (or his scribe) knew, or which prevailed in the time and place to which the writer (or his scribe) belonged.

§193. There is a very large collection of citations of the church fathers, with respect to various textual readings, in Tischendorf's *Novum Testamentum Graece (editio octava critica maior,* 1869-1871); but the references are, of course, to the editions of the several fathers that were available and in use in the time of Tischendorf. For example, at the point of Jn 1:18 Tischendorf's first citation of the *Commentary on John* by Origen (cf. §192) is in the form of this notation: Or[4,89] . The reference is to Volume IV and Page 89 in the edition of the works of Origen by De la Rue in Paris in 1738-1759 (the first three volumes were by Charles de la Rue, the completion of the fourth volume, after his death, was by Charles Vincent de la Rue). Fortunately in the modern edition of the works of Origin by Erwin Preuschen in the GCS series, the pages of the De la Rue edition are given in the margin with the abbreviation "R." Accordingly "89R," which corresponds with Tischendorf's reference, can be found in Preuschen, *Origenes Werke* IV, *Der Johanneskommentar* (GCS 1903), on Page 93; and there in Lines 30-31, in Origen's comment on Jn 1:7, and in his own Book II, Chapter xxxv (29), and Section 212, is the quotation: θεὸν οὐδεὶς ἑώρακε πώποτε· ὁ μονογενὴς θεὸς ὁ ὢν εἰς τὸν κόλπον τοῦ πατρὸς ἐκεῖνος ἐξηγήσατο, "No man has seen God at any time; the only begotten God, who is in the bosom of the Father, He has explained Him."

§194. Turning first, now, to Irenaeus, we find that in the extant text of his *Against Heresies* (cf. §192) he cites Jn 1:18 in no less than three different forms. In a fine passage in IV 20, 11 (W. Wigan Harvey, *Sancti Irenaei Episcopi Lugdunensis libros quinque adversus Haereses* [Cambridge: University Press, 2 vols. 1857, republished Ridgewood, N.J.: Gregg Press Inc., 1965], II, p. 221; Adelin Rousseau, *Irénée de Lyon, Contre les Hérésies, Livre IV, Édition critique d'après les versions arménienne et latine* [SC 100, 2 vols. 1965], II, p. 660; ANF I, p. 491) *he writes:*

Jn 1:18

Irenaeus *Against Heresies* IV 20, 11

Igitur si neque Moyses vidit Deum neque Helias neque Ezechiel, qui multa de caelestibus viderunt, quae autem ab his videbantur erant *similitudines claritatis Domini* [Ezk 1:28] et prophetiae futurorum, manifestum est quoniam Pater quidem invisibilis, de quo et Dominus dixit: *Deum nemo vidit unquam.* Verbum autem ejus, quemadmodum volebat ipse et ad utilitatem videntium claritatem monstrabat Patris et dispositiones exponebat, quemadmodum et Dominus dixit: *Unigenitus deus, qui est in sinu patris, ipse enarravit.*

If, then, neither Moses, nor Elias, nor Ezekiel, who had many celestial visions, saw God; but if what they did see were similitudes of the splendor of the Lord [Ezk 1:28] and prophecies of things to come; it is manifest that the Father is indeed invisible, of whom the Lord also said: "No man has seen God at any time." But his Word, as He himself willed it, and for the benefit of those who beheld, showed the splendor of the Father, and explained his purposes, as also the Lord said: "(The) only begotten God, who is in the bosom of the Father, He has explained Him."

In the crucial words of his quotation in Latin the text of Irenaeus is, *unigenitus deus;* and this corresponds most probably to the μονογενὴς θεός ("only begotten God") of $\mathfrak{P}^{66}$ B ℵ, or possibly (cf. § 188) to the ὁ μονογενὴς θεός ("the only begotten God") of $\mathfrak{P}^{75}$ ℵc (§191).

§195. In *Against Heresies* IV 20, 6 (Harvey II, p. 218; SC 100, II, p. 646; ANF I, p. 489), however, Irenaeus quotes Jn 1:18 in this form:

Irenaeus *Against Heresies* IV 20, 6

*Deum nemo vidit unquam, nisi
unigenitus filius qui est in sinu
patris ipse enarravit.*

No man has seen God at any time; except
the only begotten Son, who is in the bosom
of the Father, He has explained Him.

Here the word *nisi* ("except," or "save only") corresponds with the εἰ μή ("except") found in this verse in Codex Washingtonensis (W^supp) (§170). Otherwise, as it stands the Latin text of Irenaeus is identical with the Vulgate (§189). Since in the preceding quotation (§194) Irenaeus gives the text differently, it is possible that in the present instance it is a copyist who has brought the quotation into conformity with the Vulgate (cf. above §192; Harvey II, p. 221 n. 4).

§196.   Again in *Against Heresies* III 11, 6 (Harvey II, p. 44; ANF I, p. 427) Irenaeus quotes the same verse in this form:

Jn 1:18

Irenaeus *Against Heresies* III 11, 6

Deum enim, inquit, *nemo vidit unquam, nisi
unigenitus filius dei qui est in sinu
patris ipse enarravit.*

For, he says, No man has seen God at any time, except
the only begotten Son of God, who is in the bosom
of the Father, He has explained Him.

Here again the *nisi* can correspond with the εἰ μή ("except") of W^supp (cf. §195); otherwise the text is in agreement with the Itala manuscript Monacensis (*q*) in reading *unigenitus filius dei,* "(the) only begotten Son of God" (§190).

§197.   Proceeding to Origen, we find that this church father also quotes Jn 1:18 in three different forms although, in this case, the text of the writer is still available in the Greek language. One form of the quotation has already been cited (§193) in another, introductory consideration, as follows:

Jn 1:18

Origen *Commentary on John* II xxxv 212

θεὸν οὐδεὶς ἑώρακε πώποτε·
ὁ μονογενὴς θεὸς ὁ ὢν εἰς τὸν κόλπον
τοῦ πατρὸς ἐκεῖνος ἐξηγήσατο.

The latter and crucial (as far as our textual question is concerned) part of the verse is also quoted in the same wording in Origen's Book XXXII, Chapter xx (13), Section 264 (GCS, *Origenes Werke* IV, p. 461, Lines 29-30), where he is commenting on Jn 13:23-29, as follows:

Origen *Commentary on John* XXXII xx 264

ὁ μονογενὴς θεὸς ὁ ὢν εἰς τὸν κόλπον
τοῦ πατρὸς ἐκεῖνος ἐξηγήσατο.

No man has seen God at any time;
the only begotten God, who is in the bosom
of the Father, He has explained Him.

This reading (ὁ μονογενὴς θεός, "the only begotten God"), given twice by Origen, is the same as the reading found in 𝔓⁷⁵ and ℵᶜ (§191).

§198. In another place in the *Commentary on John*, where he is commenting on Jn 13:23-29, in his Book VI, Chapter iii (2), Section 14 (GCS IV, p. 109, Lines 12-14), Origen quotes the first part of Jn 1:18, θεὸν οὐδεὶς ἑώρακεν πώποτε ("No man has seen God at any time"), and then follows this with a sort of paraphrase of the balance of the verse, in which he refers to τὸν μονογενῆ εἰς τὸν κόλπον ὄντα τοῦ πατρός, i.e., to "the one, only begotten, who is in the bosom of the Father." Since μονογενῆ ("only begotten") stands here all alone, without either the word θεός ("God") or υἱός ("Son"), this reading may be taken as reflecting the same ultimately simplified reading found in the single Vulgate manuscript (*gat*) (§190).

§199. Yet again, in his work *Against Celsus* (written when he was over sixty years old [Eusebius *Church History* VI 36, 1], therefore as late as 245, when he was living in Caesarea), Origen quotes Jn 1:18 in a third form. Here (*Against Celsus* II 71, GCS, *Origenes Werke* I, p. 193, Lines 14-16) the text reads:

Jn 1:18

Origen *Against Celsus* II 71

θεὸν οὐδεὶς ἑώρακε πώποτε·
καὶ μονογενής γε ὢν θεός, ὁ ὢν εἰς τὸν κόλπον
τοῦ πατρός, ἐκεῖνος ἐξηγήσατο.

No man has seen God at any time;
and (the) only begotten, being indeed God, who
is in the bosom
of the Father, He has explained Him.

This again is obviously a slight paraphrase of the verse, but it agrees best with the reading μονογενὴς θεός ("only begotten God") in 𝔓⁶⁶ B ℵ (§191), and supports the interpretation that reads the two words as, in effect, in apposition ("the only one, himself God" NEB margin; or "the only One, who is what God is" TEV; see above §136).

§200. The witness of the two church fathers, Irenaeus and Origen, may be added, therefore, to our summary apparatus (§§138, 145, 159, 164, 171, 178, 182, 186, 191) as follows:

Jn
1:18   μονογενὴς θεός   𝔓⁶⁶ B ℵ Orig (*Against Celsus* II 71)
        ὁ μονογενὴς θεός   𝔓⁷⁵ ℵᶜ Orig (*Comm. on Jn* II xxxv
                                212; XXXII xx 264)

ὁ μονογενὴς υἱός   W^{supp} A 666 1345

μονογενῆ   Orig (*Comm. on Jn* VI iii 14)

unigenitus deus   Iren^{lat} (*Against Heres.* IV 20, 11)

unigenitus filius   Itala (*b aur*, etc.) Vulgate Iren^{lat}
　　　　　　　　　(*Against Heres.* IV 20, 6)

unicus filius   Itala (*a*)

unigenitus filius dei   Itala (*q*) Iren^{lat} (*Against
　　　　　　　　　Heres.* III 11, 6)

unigenitus   Vulgate (*gat*)

(e) *Text Critical Conclusions*

14. Jn 1:3-4

§201. Although the textual witnesses studied in this book constitute only a small fraction of the total mass of such materials, they are representative; we have read directly from a number of the oldest and most important Greek manuscripts, and have considered along with them some typical evidence from the versions and church fathers as found in critical editions. As far as this evidence goes, therefore, it is proper to endeavor to draw conclusions from it, and in particular to try to form a judgment as to what is most probably, on the basis of this evidence, the earliest and best text available of the two passages in the Prologue of the Gospel according to John where the most significant variants have appeared, namely in Jn 1:3-4 and 1:18.

§202. For Jn 1:3-4, the summary textual apparatus built up from the Greek manuscripts which we have read directly (§§138, 145, 159, 164, 171, 178, 182) is as follows:

Jn
1:3-4　οὐδὲν ὃ γέγονεν　𝔓⁶⁶

　　　οὐδὲν ὃ γέγονεν·　ℵ

　　　οὐδέν· ὃ γέγονεν　D

　　　οὐδὲ ἕν ὃ γέγονεν　𝔓⁷⁵ B A

　　　οὐδὲ ἕν ὃ γέγονεν·　666

　　　οὐδὲ ἕν· ὃ γέγονεν　𝔓⁷⁵ᶜ ℵᶜ W^{supp} 666ᶜ

　　　ἐν αὐτῷ ζωὴ ἦν　𝔓⁷⁵ B A 666

　　　ἐν αὐτῷ ζωή ἐστιν　ℵ D

　　　ἐν αὐτῷ ζωή　W^{supp}

This means that, apart from punctuation (which is, of course, in this case, the crucial consideration, and to which we will come momentarily [§§205f.]), we have the following wordings to consider:

Jn 1:3-4

πάντα δι᾿ αὐτοῦ ἐγένετο καὶ χωρὶς αὐτοῦ ἐγένετο οὐδὲν (𝔓⁶⁶ ℵ D) or οὐδὲ ἕν (𝔓⁷⁵ 𝔓⁷⁵ᶜ B A ℵᶜ W^{supp} 666 666ᶜ) ὃ γέγονεν ἐν αὐτῷ ζωὴ ἦν (𝔓⁷⁵ B A 666) or ἐστιν (ℵ D) or om. (W^{supp}) καὶ ἡ ζωὴ ἦν τὸ φῶς τῶν ἀνθρώπων

§203. Between the two readings, οὐδέν ("nothing") and οὐδὲ ἕν ("no single thing"), it is probable that οὐδέν was the original reading. This is the reading in 𝔓⁶⁶, which, at this point, is the oldest available manuscript. In 𝔓⁶⁶ the preference, if any, is for οὐδὲ ἕν as a manner of expression. In Jn 3:27; 5:19; 5:30; and 8:28, 𝔓⁶⁶ stands alone or with a very few other witnesses (see Nestle-Aland, 25th ed., *ad loc.*) in reading οὐδέ ἕν where most other manuscripts have οὐδέν. But here, in spite of that apparent preference elsewhere, 𝔓⁶⁶ reads οὐδέν, which makes it a weighty reading. A change from the less strong ("nothing") to the strongest possible ("no single thing") statement is more likely than the reverse. The change was made early, for it appears already in 𝔓⁷⁵; but it could well have been made, even early, over against the Gnostics, who taught that some things, and indeed the material world itself, were made by a lower principle, the Demiurge (Origen *Comm. on Jn* II xiv (8) [GCS, *Origenes Werke* IV, pp. 70f.] attributes such doctrine, e.g., to Heracleon, whom he calls a personal acquaintance [γνώριμος] of Valentinus, the famous Gnostic teacher of the middle of the second century [FHRJ p. 98]; cf. Rudolf Schnackenburg, *Das Johannesevangelium* [Herders Theologischer Kommentar zum Neuen Testament], I [1965], pp. 215-217).

§204. As for the choice among ἦν ("was"), ἐστιν ("is"), and the omission of the verb altogether, ἦν is the best-attested in the manuscripts. As the imperfect tense, it is the appropriate form of the verb for reference to the whole long past, stretching back into the beginning. As such, the same verb form (ἦν) occurs six times in the first four verses of the Gospel; only in the fifth verse is the transition made to the present, where the verb (φαίνει, "shines") is written in the present tense (cf. Kurt Aland in ZNW 59 [1968], pp. 206f.). A reason, furthermore, for a change from ἦν to ἐστιν appears in connection with the problem of the punctuation of the sentence, and will be noted momentarily (§209). As for the omission of any verb at this point by Wˢᵘᵖᵖ, it may have been a simple solution to the harder problem of having to choose between the two alternate verb forms (cf. above §169).

§205. Taking the judgments worked out in §§203-204 (preferring as more probably original οὐδέν rather than οὐδὲ ἕν, and ἦν rather than ἐστιν), we will write the text, still without punctuation, as follows, in a wording that in fact corresponds exactly with our restored text of 𝔓⁶⁶ (§130), our oldest witness.

Jn 1:3-4

πάντα δι' αὐτοῦ ἐγένετο
καὶ χωρὶς αὐτοῦ ἐγένετο οὐδὲν
ὃ γέγονεν ἐν αὐτῷ ζωὴ ἦν
καὶ ἡ ζωὴ ἦν τὸ φῶς τῶν ἀνθρώπων

In 𝔓⁶⁶ and also in 𝔓⁷⁵, B, and A, there is no punctuation in the passage; but it is evident that, in order to read the statement at all intelligibly, a major break must be introduced, and this must come either after οὐδέν so that ὃ γέγονεν goes with what follows, or after ὃ γέγονεν so that these two words go with what precedes. Such punctuation is, in fact, provided in later manuscripts, namely, a stop after ὃ γέγονεν in ℵ (§155) and in 666 (§180), and a stop after οὐδέν in D (§163) as well as after the corresponding οὐδὲ ἕν in 𝔓⁷⁵ᶜ (§135), ℵᶜ (§156), Wˢᵘᵖᵖ (§169), and 666ᶜ (§180).

§206. In terms of the two major possibilities of interpretation of the passage, and of the actual punctuation corresponding thereto in the later manuscripts (§205), we have then two major possible readings, as follows:

Jn 1:3-4

First Reading (major punctuation mark after ὃ γέγονεν — ℵ and 666)

> All things came into being through Him;
> and apart from Him nothing came into being
> that has come into being. In Him was life;
> and the life was the light of men.

Second Reading (major punctuation mark after οὐδέν — D, etc.)

> All things came into being through Him;
> and apart from Him nothing came into being.
> What has come into being was life in Him;
> and the life was the light of men.

§207. With respect to a decision between these two readings (§206), the proper punctuation cannot be determined with certainty from the manuscripts alone, inasmuch as punctuation is nonexistent at this point in the oldest witnesses (𝔓⁶⁶ 𝔓⁷⁵ B A). In the witnesses of which we have taken account, the punctuation in ℵ and 666, and in D, appears to come from the original writers of the manuscripts respectively, although this can be questioned in ℵ (§157). Certainly it is correctors of ℵ and of 666 who have introduced in these manuscripts the punctuation mark at the earlier point. Therewith, the original punctuation mark in ℵ and 666 (a stop after ὃ γέγονεν) probably has priority over the mark (after οὐδέν) in D and (after οὐδὲ ἕν) in ℵᶜ and 666ᶜ. How early the corresponding mark is, which was introduced by the corrector of 𝔓⁷⁵, is difficult to say; but at any rate it was put in after the words οὐδὲ ἕν which are, we think, themselves later than οὐδέν (§203). Wˢᵘᵖᵖ is, of course, also relatively late (§167). Accordingly, the evidence of the punctuation, such as there is, in the manuscripts surveyed, looks to some extent as if the earlier understanding called for a break after ὃ γέγονεν, while the later understanding and particularly the work of correctors tended to put it after οὐδέν, and even more to put it after οὐδὲ ἕν when this wording came to prevail. This evidence, then, tends to support our First Reading (§206).

§208. Since there was, however, no punctuation whatsoever at the critical point in the earliest available manuscripts, it may be supposed that the earliest readers had to read the passage according to their own understanding and without the help of any punctuation. They must, therefore, have been under the necessity of simply trying to discern the original meaning and intent of the author of the passage, and that is in fact precisely the heart of the problem, in this case, for ourselves as well. Here it can only be said that the First Reading (§206) is more straightforward grammatically, and provides better sense in the context, than the Second Reading. As Theodor Zahn (*Das Evangelium des Johannes* [Kommentar zum Neuen Testament, 4, 5th-6th ed. Leipzig, 1921], pp. 52f.) has put it, to make ὃ γέγονεν ἐν αὐτῷ ζωὴ ἦν into a new and self-contained sentence is justifiable neither linguistically nor exegetically (*ist weder sprachlich noch sachlich zu rechtfertigen*). A rule that is often useful in textual criticism is that the more difficult reading is to be preferred (§69), and on this ground it could be argued that what we have called our Second Reading (§206) should be preferred (Kurt Aland does in fact argue for this reading on this ground in his exhaustive articles in Boyd L. Daniels and M. Jack Suggs, *Studies in the History and Text of the New Testament,* SD pp. 161-187; and in ZNW 59 [1968], pp. 174-209). But in this case the original text which we assume (and in fact find in our oldest witness, 𝔓⁶⁶) back of our two possible readings is one and the same text as far as the wording is concerned. It is not a question of choosing between a more difficult and a less difficult word or words. The words are identical, and it is only a question of choosing in which way to read them. As to this, those who eventually supplied punctuation in the manuscripts, expressed opinions by the punctuation they supplied. But it is not in this case incumbent upon us to prefer that punctuation, supplied later, which makes it more difficult to understand the text.

§209. Another rule, also often useful in textual criticism, is that that reading is to be preferred which best accounts for the rise of other forms of the text (cf. §80). Here, such evidence as we have points to the conclusion that the Second Reading (§206) arose out of the First. The possible evolution could have run like this: The word οὐδέν ("nothing") was changed to οὐδὲ ἕν ("no single thing") to make the statement more emphatic, perhaps against the Gnostics (§203). These words (οὐδὲ ἕν), however, would normally appeal to a person thinking in Greek as the end of a clause or a sentence (cf. Rom. 3:10, οὐδὲ εἷς, "not even one"; TEV, "not a single man"; Schnackenburg, *Das Johannesevangelium,* I, p. 217; and cf. above §135), therefore it would be natural to put a stop immediately after them, and from that the usage would spread also into some manuscripts that preserved οὐδέν. But this made ὃ γέγονεν no longer the end of the preceding sentence (". . . nothing came into being that has come into being"), but rather the beginning of the next sentence. Therewith a grammatical difficulty was produced, in that a perfect tense (γέγονεν), telling about what has come into its presently existing state, was used with an imperfect tense (ἦν), telling about a situation in existence in the past (cf. §157). This may be brought out by italicizing the verb forms in the translation: "What *has come* into being *was* life in Him." This, therefore, led to the change of ἦν (imperfect) into ἐστιν (present) (§204), with the consequent reading: "What *has come* into being *is* life in Him." This substantiates the conclusion that the probable original wording of Jn 1:3-4 was that most nearly preserved and most probably to be restored in our oldest available witness, Papyrus Bodmer II ($\mathfrak{P}^{66}$), and that the meaning of the words is most probably that brought out by the punctuation first found in Codex Sinaiticus ($\aleph$), and preserved in 666, resulting all together in our First Reading (§206):

Jn 1:3-4

> All things came into being through Him;
> and apart from Him nothing came into being
> that has come into being. In Him was life;
> and the life was the light of men.

15. Jn 1:18

§210. In the case of Jn 1:18 our summary critical apparatus includes the evidence of the Greek manuscripts which we have read directly (§§138, 145, 159, 164, 171, 178, 182, 186), and also of the Latin versions (Itala and Vulgate) (§191) and the church fathers (Irenaeus and Origen) (§200) which we have read in critical editions. This apparatus (§200) is as follows:

Jn
1:18 | μονογενὴς θεός | $\mathfrak{P}^{66}$ B $\aleph$ Orig (*Against Celsus* II 71)
ὁ μονογενὴς θεός $\mathfrak{P}^{75}$ $\aleph^c$ Orig (*Comm. on Jn* II xxxv 212; XXXII xx 264)
ὁ μονογενὴς υἱός W^{supp} A 666 1345
μονογενῆ Orig (*Comm. on Jn* VI iii 14)
unigenitus deus Iren^{lat} (*Against Heres.* IV 20, 11)
unigenitus filius Itala (*b aur,* etc.) Vulgate Iren^{lat} (*Against Heres.* IV 20, 6)
unicus filius Itala (*a*)
unigenitus filius dei Itala (*q*) Iren^{lat} (*Against Heres.* III 11, 6)
unigenitus Vulgate (*gat*)

§211. Here μονογενὴς θεός is the reading of the Proto-Alexandrian text family (§86) as represented by $\mathfrak{P}^{66}$ and B, is preserved in $\aleph$ although this manuscript has otherwise many Western readings (§146), is probably the reading of Irenaeus in *Against Heres.* IV 20, 11 (where *unigenitus deus* is probably the equivalent, although the Latin could also represent ὁ μονογενὴς θεός), and is still reflected in Origen *Against Celsus* II 71 (μονογενὴς γε ὢν θεός), even though this work was not written until he was living in Caesarea (§199). It is, therefore, the oldest attested reading. It is at the same time the most difficult. The words are literally, "only begotten God." As the form in which they are given by Origen, *Against Celsus* II 71, helps to suggest, they are probably to be thought of as in apposition and to be translated in some such fashion as was noted above (§136):

NEB margin

No man has ever seen God; but the
only one, himself God, the nearest to the
Father's heart, has made him known.

TEV

No one has ever seen God. The
only One, who is what God is, and who is near the
Father's side, has made him known.

§212. As such a subtly phrased and not altogether easy to
understand wording, this reading also explains the other readings that
were derived from it. The evolution of the several forms appears to
have been as follows: In the absence of full appreciation of the subtle
meaning of the two words in their original apposition, the article was
supplied, resulting in the reading, ὁ μονογενὴς θεός, "the only
begotten God." This change appears already as early as in 𝔓75, and is
found also in a correction of ℵ, and in Origen's *Commentary on
John* in two passages (II xxxv 212; XXXII xx 264).

§213. The change made by the insertion of the article provided a
new difficulty, however, for now the text stated that "the only
begotten God" was "in the bosom of the Father" (so NASB), an
assertion that could appear almost self-contradictory. Accordingly
the further change was made to ὁ μονογενὴς υἱός, "the only begotten
Son" (NASB margin). This change would be readily supported by
other occurrences of the designation, "the only begotten Son" (in
varying arrangements of the Greek words) in Jn 3:16, 18, and I Jn
4:9. The change is found in Wsupp and also in the Itala, the Vulgate,
and Irenaeus (*Against Heres.* IV 20, 6), and is accordingly characteristic of the Western text. There also, in Wsupp, we find yet other
interesting additions (§170), to which attention is called with italics
in the following translation:

Jn 1:18

Wsupp

No man has seen God at any time; *except* the
only begotten Son, who is in the bosom
of the Father, He has explained Him *to us.*

§214. Other variations of the basic words occur sporadically in a
few other manuscripts. In one manuscript of the Itala (*q*) and in one
passage in Irenaeus (*Against Heres.* III 11, 6) the problem of whether
to read "God" or "Son" is solved by reading both: *unigenitus filius
dei,* "(the) only begotten Son of God." Contrariwise, in one manuscript of the Vulgate (*gat*) and in one passage in Origen (*Comm. on
Jn* VI iii 14) the problem is solved by omitting both words and
retaining only *unigenitus/μονογενῆ,* "only begotten."

§215. Finally, according to our retracing of the probable evolution of the textual tradition, the aberrant Western additions ("except" and "to us" §§170, 213), and the miscellaneous variations in

the versions and fathers (§214), were dropped, but the basic simplification and change to ὁ μονογενὴς υἱός was retained and made the essential feature of the Koine or Byzantine text. This is seen already, in our witnesses, in A, 666, and 1345. Here the text reads:

Jn 1:18

A 666 1345

θεὸν οὐδεὶς ἑώρακεν πώποτε·
ὁ μονογενὴς υἱὸς ὁ ὢν εἰς τὸν κόλπον
τοῦ πατρὸς ἐκεῖνος ἐξηγήσατο

KJV

No man hath seen God at any time;
the only begotten Son, which is in the bosom
of the Father, he hath declared him.

§216. In precise opposition to the foregoing (§§211ff.) reconstruction of the probable textual evolution, the translators of the New English Bible (§80) consider that the reading μονογενὴς θεός in B, ℵ, etc., "does not yield a tolerable sense," hold that the reading ὁ μονογενὴς υἱός in W^supp, A, most of the late Greek manuscripts, etc., is "intrinsically more probable," and think it is possible that the reading ὁ μονογενής, although found only (in the form *unigenitus*) in the single manuscript (*gat*) of the Latin Vulgate, "might have given rise to the other two" (Tasker, *The Greek New Testament,* 1964, pp. 424f.). Surely so poorly attested a reading (ὁ μονογενής), and one so readily explainable in other ways (§214), is a slight foundation for this theory; and it is not, in fact, adopted in the Greek text (Tasker, *op. cit.,* p. 140) from which the translators of the NEB worked. Rather, their chosen Greek text contained the reading ὁ μονογενὴς υἱός, and was identical with the Koine text (§215), surely, in our judgment, the latest major form in which the passage is found. Their translation was, accordingly:

Jn 1:18

NEB

No one has ever seen God;
but God's only Son, he who is nearest to
the Father's heart, he has made him known.

§217. Contrariwise, and in agreement with our text-critical conclusion, the reading μονογενὴς θεός, found in 𝔓^66 B ℵ Iren^lat (*Against Heres.* IV 20, 11), Orig (*Against Celsus* II 71), etc., is accepted in the Greek text printed by the Bible Societies (§81), which reads as follows:

Jn 1:18

The Greek New Testament (Bible Societies)

θεὸν οὐδεὶς ἑώρακεν πώποτε·
μονογενὴς θεὸς ὁ ὢν εἰς τὸν κόλπον
τοῦ πατρὸς ἐκεῖνος ἐξηγήσατο.

This may be translated literally, in the style of the NASB:

> No man has seen God at any time;
> only begotten God, who is in the bosom
> of the Father, He has explained Him.

It may be translated less literally, but in a way designed better to bring out the probably appositional meaning (cf. §199) of μονογενὴς θεός, as is done in the TEV (cf. also NEB margin), a rendering cited already above (§136) at the point where this Greek text was first encountered in its earliest known witness, Papyrus Bodmer II ($\mathfrak{P}^{66}$). This rendering, then, is the best translation known of the oldest known text (according to our judgment) of this passage:

Jn 1:18

TEV

> No one has ever seen God.
> The only One, who is the same as God and is at
> the Father's side, has made him known.

IV. THE FUTURE TASK

§218. In earlier sections of this book the Greek texts have been identified that underlie such recent translations of the New Testament as those of the RSV and NASB (§79), the NEB (§80), and TEV (§81), several of the projects have been described that are currently underway to produce new critical editions of the Greek text (§81), and it has been said that the work of the textual criticism of the NT is an unending task (§82). In looking toward the future, it is at the present time the question of proper methodology that is being most prominently raised.

§219. The question of method is so strongly brought to attention because of the coming into our view in recent time of so many previously unknown manuscripts, and particularly of so many so early papyri. Above (§81), we noted the contrast in quantity and in antiquity of what was available to Tischendorf with what is now available. A similar contrast is equally striking in the case of Westcott and Hort. In the Introduction to their great work those scholars do not even mention the word "papyrus"; now eighty-one Greek NT papyri are listed. Altogether they may have had nominal acquaintance with 1500 Greek NT manuscripts; now the total number known is over five thousand (§§53f.; Kurt Aland, "Der gegenwärtige Stand der Arbeit an den Handschriften wie am Text des griechischen Neuen Testaments...," in *Studien zur Überlieferung des Neuen Testaments und seines Textes*, ANT 2, 1967, pp. 206f.). Of the parchment majuscules, which were their earliest available witnesses, Westcott and Hort said that "few of this number belong to the first five or six centuries, none being earlier than the age of Constantine"; and from the fourth century they had, in fact, only two witnesses, namely, Codex Vaticanus and Codex Sinaiticus from the middle of the century; now, as we have seen (§90), we have a papyrus fragment from the early second century ($\mathfrak{P}^{52}$), and relatively extensive papyrus manuscripts from about A.D. 200 ($\mathfrak{P}^{46}$, $\mathfrak{P}^{66}$) and the early third century ($\mathfrak{P}^{75}$), which, of course presuppose even earlier exemplars from which they were copied. Because of such facts as these, the situation of the present is radically different from that of the earlier researchers, and it is appropriate to try to look at the problems afresh in the light of what is now known (Aland, "Die Konsequenzen der neueren Handschriftenfunde für die neutestamentliche Textkritik," in *Studien zur Überlieferung des Neuen Testaments und seines Textes,* pp. 180-201).

§220.   As the earlier manuscripts have become known it has been almost inevitable that they should have been looked at first in the light of the already known but later witnesses, and that their text should have been described as like this or that text type, already defined in terms of the later manuscripts, or described as a "mixture" of some of those text types. Even Aland (in *Studien zur Überlieferung des Neuen Testaments und seines Textes,* p. 188) has spoken, in respect to the papyri, of "mixed texts," but has also pointed out that, strictly speaking, one may speak of a mixed text only after "recensions" have been established, and here we are dealing with manuscripts that existed before the hypothetical recensions were made; therefore it would be preferable to use some other designation, although the proper one is not easy to find, perhaps "fluid text," "free text," or, perhaps best of all, simply "early text." In general, therefore, as far as method is concerned, it would appear that we should now endeavor to look first of all at the very earliest available manuscripts, especially the papyri, to discern what was happening in the copying of each document in and of itself, and to build up from there an understanding of the history of the manuscript tradition, and so come, finally, to conclusions as to the earliest accessible form of the text. This is, in fact, the procedure we have suggested already (§88) and have in a small way, we hope, illustrated in our encounter with the manuscripts. This method, in general, has been pointed to by Ernest C. Colwell with the injunction to "begin at the beginning." As he puts it (in "Method in Grouping New Testament Manuscripts," SMTC p. 24):

> The nineteenth century's battle with the Textus Receptus fastened attention upon that text, and the study of variation from it was a natural development. The wide acceptance of the theory of genealogical method after A.D. 1880 supported this trend; as good genealogists always do, textual critics started with the lowest, the most recent generations, and worked back. But current theory and currently available sources from the early centuries demand a reversal. We should start with the earliest sources and work our way down to the late medieval copies, refashioning our concepts as we go. . . . If the history were written from the beginning instead of from the end, more appropriate terms would suggest themselves to us. As a result we would work with more clarity in the reconstruction of the history of the text.

§221.   In particulars, the method of work recommended by Colwell (in "Hort Redivivus: A Plea and a Program," SMTC pp. 160-171) is outlined in five steps, namely: (1) begin with readings; (2) characterize individual scribes and manuscripts; (3) group the manuscripts; (4) construct a historical framework; and (5) make a final judgment on readings. That text-critical work must (1) **start with the observation and investigation of what are called "variant readings" in the available manuscripts** seems obvious. Less obvious, however, is the proper definition of a "variant reading." In this phrase the word "variant" seems to imply divergence from some other reading, and thereby the other reading may seem to be implicitly accorded, in some sense or other, the standing of a norm. This, however, can be misleading. If a given reading is established as divergent from the Textus Receptus, for example, it is of course not to be assumed that the reading in the Textus Receptus is correct but, on the other hand, it is not to be assumed either that by the determination of a variant from the Textus Receptus a preferable reading has automatically been obtained. To state the actual situation with respect to variant readings with greater clarity and precision, and to avoid possibly misleading implications, Colwell, with Ernest W. Tune (in "Method in Classifying and Evaluating Variant Readings," SMTC pp. 97-100), has suggested the use of what may be called a unit-of-variation or a variation-unit. In John 11:29, for example, where Tischendorf indicates that the manuscripts diverge at three points, the situation may be pictured in such a diagram as this:

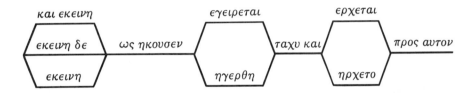

The words in which all the manuscripts involved agree exactly, appear on the single center lines; the words that are different in different manuscripts are placed on the lines of the expanded sections, and the latter represent variation-units. With a diagram of this sort in view, it is then possible to define a "variant reading" quite simply as one of the alternative readings that occur in a unit of variation. Thus the elements of the problem are at least set forth without the latent ambiguity that may otherwise obtain.

§222. Insofar as it is possible to (2) **recognize the characteristics of individual scribes and manuscripts**, it becomes possible at the same time to **set aside from consideration in the search for earlier and better forms of the text those variant readings which recognizably correspond with individual idiosyncrasies.** Here study naturally focuses in particular upon "singular" readings, i.e., upon readings that are altogether peculiar to a given document and are not found anywhere else in the whole range of available manuscripts. Here it is at least likely that what appears is due to the individual scribe from whom the text comes, and this likelihood is made greater if what appears can be shown to be of the same sort as also appears elsewhere in the work of the same scribe. From this point of view a preliminary survey has been made by Colwell (in "Method in Evaluating Scribal Habits," SMTC pp. 106-124) of 𝔓⁶⁶ (the Bodmer Papyrus II, containing much of the Gospel according to John and dating c. A.D. 200, with which we have dealt above), 𝔓⁷⁵ (the Bodmer Papyri XIV-XV, containing portions of the Gospel according to Luke and of the Gospel according to John and dating in the early third century, some of the Johannine parts of which we have also considered above), and $\mathfrak{P}^{45}$ (the third-century Chester Beatty Papyrus of the Gospels and the book of Acts). In this study singular readings were defined, in a slightly more limited but more precisely controllable way, as those for which there is no support in the critical apparatus of the 8th edition of Tischendorf. By this definition, and according to the survey being cited, there are 1649 singular readings in the three papyri, or 1014 if an approximate number of 635 itacisms (i.e., differences in spelling, mostly due to the interchange of similar vowel sounds) are considered relatively insignificant and therefore excluded from the count. Broken down among the three documents, $\mathfrak{P}^{66}$ has 482 singular readings (plus about 400 itacisms), $\mathfrak{P}^{75}$ has 257 singular readings (plus about 145 itacisms), and $\mathfrak{P}^{45}$ has 275 singular readings (plus approximately 90 itacisms).

§223. In the attempt to analyze the singular readings of these and other manuscripts with a view to recognizing the characteristics of the scribes, two kinds of error are in particular quite unmistakably recognizable. One of these is homoioteleuton, where the eye of the copyist obviously skips either forward or back from one word to another with a similar ending and, in consequence, either omits or repeats a passage. On this score, $\mathfrak{P}^{66}$ has 76 examples of homoioteleuton, $\mathfrak{P}^{75}$ has 37, and $\mathfrak{P}^{45}$ exhibits 18 such cases. The other type of error spoken of here is that which results in a reading that simply and plainly does not make sense either grammatically or contextually or both. In $\mathfrak{P}^{66}$ two out of five singular readings are such "nonsense" readings, in $\mathfrak{P}^{75}$ the ratio is one out of four, and in $\mathfrak{P}^{45}$ less than one out of ten singular readings fails to make sense. By close scrutiny of the singular readings it is also possible to discern the basic method the respective scribes employed in their copying. Since $\mathfrak{P}^{66}$ omits 61 syllables as well as a dozen articles and 30 short words, it is probable that this scribe copies by syllables. Since $\mathfrak{P}^{75}$ has more than 60 singular readings that involve a single letter, and not more than ten that involve a syllable, it is probable that this scribe copies by individual letters. In the case of $\mathfrak{P}^{45}$ however, whole words are often different, or omitted, or words are rearranged as to order; and in changes in word order, out of 37 such transpositions 20 involve more than three words. Therefore, it is concluded, $\mathfrak{P}^{45}$ really copies according to the idea-content of what is before him, and feels free to rearrange, to shorten, and to change, in order to bring out the idea and to produce a concise and readable text. The corrections found in a manuscript are also relevant to the attempt to assess the situation of the writer. On this score it may be noted that the manuscript of $\mathfrak{P}^{66}$ has been extensively corrected, with corrections appearing at the point of two out of three of all the singular readings, and nine out of ten of the readings that make no sense. Whether the original scribe went back and corrected his own manuscript, or whether the corrections were made by another, is not easy to determine with certainty. Some would like to picture the scribe as having worked in what we would call a publishing house, i.e., a scriptorium, under supervision, with another to go over his work and bring it up to standard. At any rate his work was under a large measure of control, whether by himself or by someone else. In the case of $\mathfrak{P}^{75}$, however, only one out of five of the singular readings (including the "nonsense" readings) has been corrected, and there is no evidence of revision of the work of the scribe by anyone else; the relatively high degree of accuracy of the entire manuscript is evidently due to the care and precision of the original writer as he wrote for the first time. Again in $\mathfrak{P}^{45}$ there is no evidence of external controls of any kind, and fewer than three singular readings per hundred are corrected. The manuscript we have is evidently the result of the free but careful work of the original scribe. Thus, in summary, $\mathfrak{P}^{66}$ is the work of a relatively careless copyist, but his product has been carefully corrected; $\mathfrak{P}^{75}$ is the uncorrected product of a disciplined writer; and $\mathfrak{P}^{45}$ was produced by a careful workman who aimed at concise expression, clarity, and good style, and felt free to make changes that, he thought, would accomplish those ends. This type of investigation, focusing on the characteristics of individual scribes, is now being carried further and applied to more manuscripts by James R. Royse, a graduate student in Pacific School of Religion and the Graduate Theological Union, in a doctoral thesis tentatively entitled, "Scribal Habits in Early Greek Papyri of the New Testament."

§224. On the matter of (3) **grouping the manuscripts**, a sharpening of terminology is proposed (Colwell, "Method in Grouping New Testament Manuscripts," SMTC pp. 1-25, and "Genealogical Method: Its Achievements and Its Limitations," SMTC pp. 63-83), as follows: (a) A "family" is the smallest identifiable group, and is relatively homogeneous. The manuscripts that make up a family are usually close together in time and place, and they agree to such a large extent in their readings that it is possible to proceed genealogically and work back toward or to the hypothetical archetype from which they are descended. An example in this category is a small group of minuscule manuscripts headed by Codex 1 and known as Family 1 (Kirsopp Lake, *Codex 1 of the Gospels and Its Allies,* in J. Armitage Robinson, ed., *Texts and Studies,* VII, 3, 1902). (b) A "tribe" (sometimes also called a "clan") is a medium-sized group, larger than a "family" and smaller than a "text type." The manuscripts constituting a tribe exhibit unmistakable interrelationships, yet their pattern of readings is complex enough to make it doubtful whether the genealogical method is any longer applicable in as wide an area as they represent. An example in this category is provided by the so-called Caesarean witnesses (Kirsopp Lake, Robert P. Blake, and Silva New, *The Caesarean Text of the Gospel of Mark,* reprinted from HTR 21 [1928], pp. 207-404). "Caesarean" alludes to agreements with the text Origen used at Caesarea; manuscripts include those of Family 1, Family 13, Θ (Codex Koridethi of the Gospels), and others. Upon occasion all have been grouped together under the designation of Family Θ. Now, however, they appear to divide into at least two groups (Colwell, SMTC p. 49), thus the name of family is too narrow and that of tribe is proposed as better applicable. (c) A "text type" is the largest group of related manuscripts. This designation applies properly to the three large groups of the Alexandrian witnesses, the Western witnesses, and the Koine or Byzantine witnesses, which we have listed above (§86). It is also suggested that it would be preferable to call these text types by names that are purely objective and do not in any way prejudge the character or origin of the groups. Accordingly, following Frederic G. Kenyon (*The Text of the Greek Bible,* new ed. 1949, pp. 197ff.), these names may be used: The Alpha (*a*) text type corresponds to what we have called Koine or Byzantine, and is the text type to which Codex Alexandrinus (A) is most closely related (in the Gospels). The Beta (β) text type is that which we have called Alexandrian, and is the text type to which Codex Vaticanus (B) is most closely related. The Delta (δ) text type designates what we have called Western, and is the text type to which Codex Bezae (D) is most closely related. Kenyon also suggested Gamma (γ), the third letter of the Greek alphabet, for the Caesarean text, to which the Codex Koridethi is most closely related; but this and the related manuscripts have been treated in our immediately foregoing discussion as constituting a tribe rather than a text type. He also proposed that Epsilon (ε) might stand for the Syriac text, treated separately from the Western or Delta text type; and Vau (ς), the sixth letter of the Greek alphabet in its earlier form, for the considerable residue of readings not otherwise classified. For our present purposes it suffices to have cited as examples of text types those designated as Alpha, Beta, and Delta.

§225. As to how manuscripts are to be recognized as belonging together in a family, tribe, or text type, three steps are proposed (Colwell, "Method in Locating a Newly-Discovered Manuscript," "Method in Establishing the Nature of Text-Types of New Testament Manuscripts," and "Method in Establishing Quantitative Relationships between Text-Types of New Testament Manuscripts" [with Ernest W. Tune], SMTC pp. 26-62). The first step is regarded as preliminary, and is based upon reference to "multiple readings." A list of readings is prepared in which at least three variant forms of the text are known, e.g., the Alexandrian (Beta text type), the Western (Delta text type), and the Byzantine (Alpha text type); and a given manuscript is analyzed provisionally by determining the number of agreements it shows with each of these text types. Beyond that, the second and third steps are considered to constitute the essential procedures. The second step is to establish the agreement of the manuscript being studied at the point of readings that are peculiar to the text type to which its adherence is being demonstrated, and which are not found in other groups. The third step is to establish the agreement of the manuscript in question with the same text type in a large majority (say, approximately 70 percent) of all the cases where variation occurs among Greek manuscripts. To this it should be added that, as far as the grouping of manuscripts is concerned, it does not matter whether the readings involved are good readings or bad readings; what does matter is the sharing in readings of the members of the group, whether the readings are ultimately judged to be original or to be corrupt.

§226. From the earlier description (§224) of the comprehensive character of a "text type," it is evident that the different manuscripts in such a large group, separated as some of them may be by centuries and continents, will not be apt all to contain the same text as a homogeneous unit, but will more likely be witnesses to various stages in a process in which the text type was emerging. In other words, text types developed and grew as a selection was made from available readings, and as various standards were applied in various places in the course of the copying. It is therefore both possible and necessary to try (4) to **reconstruct the history of the manuscript tradition.** It is in this respect that the papyri are so especially interesting, because they allow us glimpses of remarkably early stages in the process, as when, e.g., $\mathfrak{P}^{46}$ appears as "proto-Alexandrian," but also contains readings that are preserved in the Byzantine text type (G. Zuntz, *The Text of the Epistles* [1953], pp. 49-56, 155f., 267, 271f.).

Finally (5) a **judgment** has to be arrived at **on individual readings.** Obviously, in the proposed program of work which has here been reviewed, this fifth step is predicated upon the first four, but, as is equally obvious, it is the goal toward which the preceding endeavors were directed. Examples of some of our own judgments of this sort, provisional as all judgments in historical questions must be, but illustrative, we hope, of sound procedures, have been given in earlier portions of the present book; indeed the entire book is intended to provide background for reading with understanding the texts that lie before us and for finding our way in them as far as possible toward the original word.

Appendix

A Table of the Letters of the Greek Alphabet as Written in Several of the Oldest New Testament Papyri

	𝔓52	𝔓66	𝔓75	𝔓28	𝔓60
Α					
Β					
Γ					
Δ					
Ε					
F, Ϛ					
Ζ					
Η					
Θ					
Ι					
Κ					
Λ					
Μ					
Ν					
Ξ					
Ο					
Π					
Ϙ, Ϥ					
Ρ					
Σ, C					
Τ					
Υ					
Φ					
Χ					
Ψ					
Ω					

Index of Scriptural References

All references are to Sections (§ §) of this book.

Index of Greek Words

All references are to Sections (§ §) of this book.

General Index

All references are to Sections (§ §) of this book.